Shifting Centres

Shifting Centres
Women and Migration in New Zealand History

Lyndon Fraser & Katie Pickles

Published by University of Otago Press
56 Union Street West/PO Box 56, Dunedin, New Zealand
Fax: 64 3 479 8385
email: university.press@stonebow.otago.ac.nz

First published 2002
Introduction © Lyndon Fraser and Katie Pickles 2002
Individual essays © Individual authors as listed in the Contents 2002
ISBN 1 877276 32 4

Printed by PrintLink Ltd, Wellington, New Zealand

Contents

Shifting Centres: An Introduction 9

1 **Angela Wanhalla**
  Maori Women in Waka Traditions 15

2 **David Hastings**
  Women at Sea, 1870–1885 29

3 **Lyndon Fraser**
  'No one but black strangers to spake to god help me':
  Irish Women's Migration to the West Coast, 1864–1915 45

4 **Katie Pickles**
  Pink Cheeked and Surplus: Single British Women's
  Inter-War Migration to New Zealand 63

5 **Ann Beaglehole**
  Refugees from Nazism, 1936–1946: The Experiences of Women 81

6 **Aroha Harris**
  Letty Brown, Wahine Toa 103

7 **Megan Woods**
  Dissolving the Frontiers: Single Maori Women's Migrations,
  1942–1969 117

8 **Peggy Fairbairn-Dunlop**
  Emele-Moa Teo Fairbairn 135

9 **Manying Ip**
  Redefining Chinese Female Migration: From Exclusion
  to Transnationalism 149

10 **Brigitte Bönisch-Brednich**
  Gendering German Migration Experiences in the
  1980s and 1990s 167

About the Authors 177
Notes 179
Index 207

List of Tables

Table 3.1 Birthplaces of West Coast's female population, 1867–1916 *48*

Table 3.2 Demographic characteristics of West Coast Irish at date of arrival in New Zealand, 1864–1915 *50*

Table 3.3 Age distribution of Irish female migrants to the West Coast at date of arrival in New Zealand, 1864–1915 *51*

Table 3.4 Regional proportions of West Coast Irish female migrants by date of arrival in New Zealand, 1864–1915 *54*

Table 4.1 Domestics who arrived in New Zealand, 1920–32 *64*

Table 4.2 Regional destinations of domestics after they disembarked in Auckland and Wellington, 1923–32 *71*

Table 7.1 Occupations of residents of Maori hostels in 1948 *122*

Figure 7.1 Total and relative number of hostel places provided for Maori boys and girls, 1948–68 *132*

Acknowledgements

Colleagues at the University of Canterbury and around the country have offered valuable advice and ideas. In particular we thank Tom Brooking, Malcolm Campbell, Chris Connolly, John Cookson, Graeme Dunstall, Miles Fairburn, Bob Hall, Peter Hempenstall, Wendy Larner, Charlotte Macdonald, Philippa Mein Smith, and Ann Parsonson.

We would like to thank Wendy Harrex, Fiona Moffat and Amanda Smith at the University of Otago Press for guiding the manuscript through from proposal to book with skill and efficiency. Anna Rogers deftly copy-edited the manuscript. Angela Wanhalla provided research assistance and Pauline Wedlake word-processed chapter eight.

Permission to publish chapter eight, an earlier version of which appeared in Peggy Fairbairn-Dunlop (*et al.*), *Tamaitai Samoa: their stories*, 1996, is kindly granted by the Institute of Pacific Studies, University of the South Pacific, Suva and KIN Publications, Carson City, California.

All royalties from this book are being donated to the Refugee and Migrant Service to go towards women's programmes.

LYNDON FRASER AND KATIE PICKLES
University of Canterbury

Abbreviations

AIML	Auckland Institute and Museum
AJCP	Australian Joint Copying Project
AJHR	*Appendices to the Journals of the House of Representatives*
ANL	Australian National Library
ANZ-W	Archives New Zealand, Wellington
APL	Auckland Public Library
ATL	Alexander Turnbull Library
NA-A	National Archives, Auckland
NA-C	National Archives, Christchurch
NA-W	National Archives, Wellington
NZJH	*New Zealand Journal of History*
NZPD	*New Zealand Parliamentary Debates*

Shifting Centres:
An Introduction

༄༅

Lyndon Fraser and Katie Pickles

A generation of New Zealanders has now grown up with the benefit of an ever-expanding knowledge of women's part in the past. We have learnt how New Zealand was the first country in the world to grant the suffrage to all women, both Maori and Pakeha.[1] Through oral history and documentary sources we hear women's voices telling us diverse stories of nineteenth-century home-makers, Maori women's struggles with colonialism and women's role in the twentieth century's world wars.[2] We are constantly expanding our knowledge of women's work, social conditions, health, education and welfare.[3] We have recovered valuable hidden political aspects of women's lives, including voluntary work and the quest for women's rights.[4] Through sources such as *The Book of New Zealand Women*, entries in *The Dictionary of New Zealand Biography* and a whole range of biographies, we know about individual women's hopes, fears, achievements and struggles.[5]

This collection continues to recover women's experiences through one historical process in which women have been present but all too often silent – migration. Bringing together women's history and migration history, we examine the diverse experiences of migrant women in New Zealand since the beginnings of human settlement on these shores. We span outwards from pages on women contained in books by Megan Hutching and by Tony Simpson on migration from Britain to New Zealand, by Lyndon Fraser and Anna Rogers on the Irish, and by Maureen Molloy and Tom Brooking on the Scottish.[6] Specifically, we continue the project begun by Charlotte Macdonald's path-finding work on assisted single women's migration to New Zealand, and other work on women from a variety of New Zealand's major immigrant groups by Ann Beaglehole, Manying Ip, Angela McCarthy, Rosalind McClean and Val Wood.[7]

Internationally, the field of migration history has been newly invigorated in recent years, and the contributions to this book are influenced by the vast literature on women and migration.[8] Focusing solely on women migrants, however, is still rare, and there is much that we do not know. Building on the work that has gone before it, *Shifting Centres* aims to remedy this neglect and stimulate further research into the processes that shaped the movement of women from one place to another, as well as their adaptation to new environments. The essays presented here offer a wide-ranging coverage of women's movement to, and settlement within, this country. Each contributor has sought to recover the hidden stories of migrant women by pulling together scattered evidence and reading source materials in a new light. Life stories and oral testimony have an important part to play,[9] and here history, geography, sociology and anthropology overlap.

This collection is also driven by the latest developments in gender relations and cultural history.[10] During the past decade women's and gender history have noted the criticism that, all too often, white and middle-class women's narratives have received the most attention from historians. We are now acutely aware, too, of white women's frequent complicity in racism and their demands that 'other' women assimilate into the dominant culture.[11] In an attempt to redress such imbalances, some of the life stories contained within these pages are from women often not given prominence in mainstream history, or even women's history. Aroha Harris's and Megan Woods's chapters on Maori women's postwar migration to New Zealand cities offer an example of migration that challenges national boundaries, and our view of New Zealand as a nation. They also reveal women's strength and ability to cope with new circumstances. Meanwhile, the Chinese, Samoan, Jewish and German women who arrived in New Zealand as cultural outsiders were expected to adapt and assimilate. This was a very different situation from the English, Scottish and even Irish women whose migrant experiences have become insider stories and a part of dominant Pakeha settler narratives. And even within these better-known narratives there are further inequities and biases, most notably the predominance of Protestant over Catholic stories.[12]

In recent theoretical turns, 'space' and 'shiftiness' have become preoccupations, making migration hot academic currency. Bolstered by new understandings of diaspora, transnationalism and colonialism, we reinvigorate and advance the history of women and migration in New Zealand. In so doing, we keep women's experiences at our heart, ever mindful that the raw experiences of people – their everyday lives and the traumas so often involved with migration – demand that this important topic not lose track of the emotions of the past. And so too should the often compulsory nature of migration be remembered. We grapple with the tensions between women's agency and choice in migration, versus a time of pragmatic forced out-migration, and a strongly patriarchal age where societies deemed that women followed their fathers and husbands, and obey the dictates of church and state.

In our title, 'shifting', a term used colloquially in New Zealand for moving house, draws attention to the way in which notions of home are reshaped during the migration process. On another level, it indicates our intention to place women at the centre of migration history. Katie Pickles's chapter, for example, tells the story of single British women who came to this country as domestic servants under the 1922 Empire Settlement Act. Considered 'surplus' women by contemporaries, these newcomers gained some degree of control over grandiose imperial and national migration plans based on the view that 'it was somehow wrong and unnatural, and definitely wasteful, to have an uneven distribution of the sexes'. David Hastings uses shipboard diaries to illuminate the experiences of migrant women who made the long and arduous voyage from Britain to New Zealand between 1870 and 1885. In his meticulous exploration of shipboard life, he finds that an individual woman's experience was shaped largely by her social standing: 'it influenced how much room she had, what she ate, what work she did, how she was entertained and how much freedom she had'. David's work demonstrates the validity of historical research into gender-specific migration, provided adequate recognition is also given to class, ethnicity, sexuality, generation, marital status and parenthood.

Shifting Centres questions the depiction of migration as a linear journey from particular homelands to permanent settlement and assimilation in New Zealand. Lyndon Fraser's chapter examines the transnational existence of Irish women on the West Coast of the South Island, a movement that involved the re-creation of kin-based networks across national borders. This inflow reflected the distinctive pattern of Irish women's migration to Victoria during the 1850s and the complex linkages of kinship and mobility that tied goldfields communities to the eastern Australian colonies. Lyndon uses a combination of sources to show that migrants 'constructed complex webs of association, stretching from Nelson Creek to Ballarat, and from south Westland to distant parishes in County Clare'.

As for their Irish counterparts a century earlier, transnationalism has become a long-term strategy for the new Chinese migrants who have established extended family networks in a number of cities scattered around the Pacific Rim. Manying Ip's extensively researched essay documents the transnational lives of Chinese women in New Zealand 'at the dawn of the new millennium' and contrasts their experiences with the 'live-widowhood' endured by the wives of 'Gold Mountain men' during the nineteenth century. Whereas the latter waited patiently for their men's return visits home and dutifully served their husbands' parents, recent Chinese female migrants have become active participants in migration, 'bravely and innovatively building their futures, at once coping with the challenges of frequent commuting and looking after the changing needs of their families as opportunities unfold'. The outcomes of this process are by no means certain and may involve further mobility, the maintenance of homes in different countries and the acquisition of dual citizenship. An historical perspective on shifting populations enables us to see that transnational lives are not a new phenomenon bound up with the most recent phase of globalisation. The notion of diaspora, now widely used in political and academic discourse, seems an appropriate lens through which to view the identities and experiences of Irish, Chinese and indeed other groups of women migrants.

If concepts such as diaspora and transnationalism raise questions about the salience of national boundaries and point towards the entanglement of migrants in 'powerful global histories'[13] such as colonialism, then, alongside international population movements, it is also time to consider migration within nation states. Past accounts of New Zealand's nationhood have focused on imperialism and colonisation – largely British – in which the efforts of pioneering women often played a glorified part. This collection moves beyond these celebratory narratives to challenge the view that the history of women and migration is solely the domain of the colonisers. Angela Wanhalla's ambitious chapter on women and waka traditions considers the importance of the great Polynesian migrations, juxtaposing pre- and post-European contact traditions. And if we consider population movements within the space of Aotearoa New Zealand, in the mid nineteenth century, and again in the years after the Second World War, the most visible migrants to New Zealand urban areas have been Maori. Aroha Harris and Megan Woods take up the two-fold challenge of recasting New Zealand history to consider the importance of Maori migrations, and then shifting the focus to Maori women. Aroha's chapter offers a moving account of a single Maori woman: 'Letty Brown, he wahine toa'. Aroha found that many of the common, often negative, themes associated with the adjustment of Maori to urban society did not match Letty's experiences. Here is a positive story that involves transplanting traditional values from the East Coast and the continuing struggle to shape 'a future for generations to come'. Aroha's life-story approach is neatly complemented by Megan Woods's close analysis of the rural-urban migration of young single Maori women. Megan reveals the gender contrasts involved in these population movements and examines the ways in which they were connected to particular western notions of domesticity.

In removing the story of pioneering women from its pedestal in migration folklore, *Shifting Centres* recognises tangata whenua in a new way. Maori women are given status that recognises both waka traditions and the importance of population movement within Aotearoa New Zealand. This does not mean submerging or denigrating the experiences of Pakeha women migrants; rather it allows both groups to share the centre stage. This collection also broadens the canvas to include major migrant groups other than Maori and Anglo-Celts. But size of population does not necessarily equate with influence: a number of migrant groups featured in the book have had an impact disproportionate to their numbers. This is particularly true of the Jewish refugees from Nazism who arrived in New Zealand during the 1930s and 1940s. Ann Beaglehole lucidly portrays the lives of Jewish women as they escaped the European communities that had been their homes for generations and made their way to this country. Most were 'middle-class, well-educated city people' accustomed to a much richer material and social existence than they encountered in New Zealand. Although their destination initially seemed poor, backward and dilapidated in comparison with Central Europe, it 'offered what was most important for these women and their families: a home at last, somewhere in the world'. By contrast, in the 1980s and 1990s German migrants came to New Zealand as a lifestyle choice. Brigitte Bönisch-Brednich uses a combination of ethnographic fieldwork and oral histories to explore the rich textures of German women's lives. She quotes generously from her interviews with recent migrants to show that women and men used very different language to describe their experiences of migration. Whereas German women spoke about homesickness, personal development and family relationships, men's accounts of their move to New Zealand emphasised personal success. Brigitte's essay reminds us that the historical study of gender-specific migration needs to illuminate the different ways in which men and women experience social change.

Most of the contributors to this book have chosen to look at the movement of women to New Zealand since the 1930s, and this movement away from a nineteenth-century focus is quite appropriate, given the increasing ethnic diversity that has accompanied the gradual liberalisation of this country's immigration policies. Most of these changes span the portion of Emele-Moa Teo Fairbairn's life spent in New Zealand. When she arrived in 1943, her family were 'the only Samoans in Kilbirnie, and for many years it seemed like we knew every Samoan in Wellington, and New Zealand. Not like today'. Emele's story, retold here by her daughter, Peggy Fairbairn-Dunlop, documents the difficulties faced by some aiga in their new country: 'the cold, the homesickness, parties and drink', as well as racism. Yet the many hardships encountered by migrants need to be balanced against the fulfilment of their aspirations. Emele's children all did well educationally, the Sa Petaia family lotu started in Wellington and her son Ian was chosen to be the teo after the death of her brother in 1981. She vividly recalls church meetings, the kindness of New Zealand women, the hard work and the joy felt when Peggy's family went back to live in Tanugamanono. After reading an *Evening Post* article on her life, Emele wondered whether she had ever been as lonely as the reporter described. Whether women view their migration as 'successful' is a personal matter, but one also affected by complex group circumstances. Whatever the migrant group, however, the women in this book share family, friendship, marriage and domestic labour as key influences in their lives.

Perhaps the most important theme to emerge from these essays is the relationship between the individual women migrants and their wider historical contexts. One thinks here of Letty Brown, working with others to create a space for urban Maori in West Auckland 'that simultaneously drew on the cultural imperatives of the tribe *and* transcended tribal boundaries'. One thinks also of the strong commitment shown by Catholic women such as Ellen Piezzi to their children's education in a new land or Emele Fairbairn's determination to raise her family 'very strictly according to the faaSamoa.' The historical analysis of migrant women's lives requires careful attention to their cultural, biographical and familial circumstances. Yet it must also be linked to much larger global forces such as colonialism and industrial capitalism. How, for example, can we approach the migration of single women to New Zealand during the 1920s without considering the imperial context, the problem of 'surplus' women or the rise of 'the cult of domesticity'? In examining women's historical experiences of migration the essays in this book move towards an integration of the global and the local. It is significant that several disciplines are represented here: recovering the voices of migrant women is a collaborative venture involving historians, social scientists and genealogists, along with migrants and their descendants.

Vastly different women are represented within these pages, yet they are united through the experience of migration. We have resisted the temptation to arrange the book thematically, under key topic headings such as life stories, transnational lives, work, domesticity and single women. Although this framework may have provided useful guidance to academic specialists, it would have been less accessible to teachers, students and general readers. The book therefore has a broadly chronological structure. We hope that this will make it easier to make cross-cultural comparisons between different migrant groups and also reveal new areas for investigation in the historical study of women's migration. We hope that in the future, while recognising our differences, we can transcend ethnic solitude and comfort zones. These essays are about our own people – some of us ourselves migrants, others the children of migrants. We trust this approach to women's migration will promote more tolerance and acceptance of difference, reverse the concept of insiders and outsiders, rethink boundaries and shift centres.

1
Maori Women in Waka Traditions

Angela Wanhalla

Like many other children in Aotearoa New Zealand, I grew up with some knowledge of the 'legends' of the Maori migration to this country from Hawaiki on the waka of the Great Fleet. But such primary school accounts, told through children's literature and the *New Zealand School Journal,* were romantic and heroic. This chapter takes a gendered lens to these waka traditions to reveal the significant roles of Maori women. Waka traditions are central to self-definitions of Maori and iwi identity. As migration narratives, they act as testimony to iwi land and occupation rights. This chapter will summarise the extensive historiography on waka traditions and its intersection with the question of Maori migration to, and within, Aotearoa New Zealand. Most of the chapter will analyse the various popularisations of these traditions in Aotearoa New Zealand, looking particularly at children's literature and artistic representations, in order to convey the ways in which waka traditions have been, and are, continually constructed, remade and contested. Most importantly, the chapter brings these sources together in order to centre Maori women within the traditions of Maori migration to Aotearoa New Zealand.

WAKA TRADITIONS

Waka traditions generally refer to the migration, by canoe, of Maori ancestors from the original homeland of Hawaiki, to Aotearoa New Zealand. Rawiri Taonui provides the most succinct definition of what waka traditions are and how they function today: '[w]aka traditions are accounts of arrivals, dispersal and settlement. They tell of how tribes came into being and occupied their tribal lands. They not only explain origins but are also expressions of mana and identity. They define territorial boundaries and intertribal relationships. They merge poetry and politics, history and myth, fact and legend.'[1] In short, waka traditions are more than accounts of migration: they also act as markers of identity. In the process of defining boundaries, traditions provide iwi, hapu and whanau with mana or status. This boundary marking was particularly important in the nineteenth century, when waka traditions functioned as claims to mana and occupation rights before the Maori Land Court.[2] Margaret Orbell also signals the significance and continued importance of waka traditions to iwi. Waka, she states, serve to explain and justify tribal and subtribal origins, to establish and name landmarks, and to provide precedents for individuals to follow, and ritual chants to ensure success.[3]

Because waka traditions vary from region to region, they reflect different understandings of identity at the iwi, hapu and whanau level. There are over two hundred migrating waka known in a multitude of traditions, with thirteen in Taranaki, nine in the Bay of Plenty and twenty in Northland.[4] Some traditions are more detailed than others, ranging from those that remember only names to those that provide details about the crew, their kin and the cargo. In general, distance is not a concern of many waka traditions and places of origin are vague, with the emphasis being on 'arrival, exploration and dispersal, and settlement'.[5] The numerous tribal histories, or iwi biographies, that have been published over the past century reflect the central importance of waka traditions in demarcating iwi identity and the exercise of mana. Collections such as Elsdon Best's *Tuhoe*, John Grace's *Tuwharetoa*, John H. Mitchell's *Takitimu* and Don Stafford's *Landmarks of Te Arawa* recognise that the question of place is essential and that an all-encompassing Great Fleet cannot adequately account for tribal differences in waka tradition.[6]

Much of the scholarly debate about Maori origins over the last forty years has been concerned with the issue of myth versus tradition. In particular, Margaret Orbell has argued that migration traditions, which she describes as 'stories which tell how their ancestors first came to this country from Hawaiki', are centred in myth rather than history.[7] Arguments follow Andrew Sharp's 1957 theory of accidental voyages.[8] In the same vein as Orbell are the theories of D.R. Simmons and M.P.K. Sorrenson. For Simmons, waka traditions refer not to voyages from Hawaiki to Aotearoa New Zealand but to internal migrations from Northland to the more sparsely populated south. He proposes that the pressure of overpopulation, among other things, drove internal migrations between 900 and 1350, the dates that correspond with many of the collected waka traditions.[9] Sorrenson concludes that theories about Maori origins and migrations are Pakeha myths. In particular, he suggests that the Great Fleet, the belief that Maori migrated to Aotearoa New Zealand in one wave of seven great waka, is a construct of Pakeha collectors and editors of Maori tradition, and not of Maori themselves.[10] The implication that Maori origins and migrations were 'invented' by Pakeha collectors, such as Ernst Dieffenbach, Sir George Grey, Elsdon Best, John White and Stephenson Percy Smith, suggests that a romantic past was, and can be, constructed for Maori.

In 1998, Jeff Evans described the Maori colonisation of Aotearoa New Zealand as, 'one of the world's great migrations'.[11] Such a statement still tends to romanticise the migrations and cast the crew, especially the captains, as 'great adventurers'. The collecting and writing of waka traditions allowed for editing and reconstruction. In children's literature, especially, '[t]he book of mythological narratives – of the gods and ancestors in the Polynesian homeland 'Hawaiki', of the canoe voyages to Aotearoa, of encounters with the supernatural, especially in the 19th century – emphasised the romantic and picturesque over the explanatory or educative'.[12] It is not difficult to understand why Maori migrations became, and still are, essential components of the *New Zealand School Journal* reading material.

Maori waka migrations to Aotearoa New Zealand have long been a popular subject for children's literature. The earliest *School Journal*, published in 1907, includes a story entitled 'The Maori Canoe'.[13] Generally, however, the journal has focused on the legendary figures of Kupe and Toi, and the traditions of the great waka builder Rata.[14] Elsewhere, the publisher Reed has been the champion of New Zealand children's literature about Maori myths and legends, with the emphasis on Maori migrations as adventures and the waka crew as romantic heroes. Such a characterisation is revealed by A.W. Reed's 1977 statement that the traditions of 'voyagers present the spirit of high adventure in which rivers, mountains, lakes, and plains were discovered by the true pioneer explorers of New Zealand'.[15]

Romanticism also colours this country's written maritime history. Those who have written about Aotearoa New Zealand's relationship with the sea have frequently pointed to a long heritage of ocean voyaging, starting with a brief outline of waka traditions and the Great Fleet. For instance, Gavin McLean's *Captain's Log: New Zealand's Maritime History*, published recently in association with the Television New Zealand series,[16] continues the practice of beginning its narrative with a brief survey of Maori waka traditions and voyages, before quickly moving on to the early European explorers of this country. In short, there has been a dearth of quality scholarship on waka traditions in general New Zealand maritime histories.

Many historians have debated the maritime achievements of the Maori migrations, and underlying such discussion is the question of whether these voyages are fact or fiction. Since the nineteenth century, Pakeha scholars and government officials have concerned themselves with the question of Maori origins, often conflating oral traditions with history in their approach. Moreover, they have often imposed western understandings of history upon oral tradition. Although the boundaries between myth and history in Maori tradition are difficult to distinguish, nevertheless iwi use oral traditions to understand their past and present.[17] In the nineteenth century Grey, Edward Tregear and White and, in the twentieth century, Best, Smith and the Maori scholar Sir Peter Buck (Te Rangi

Hiroa) were associated with theories on Maori origins and migrations. It is a topic that has attracted not only a large scholarship but also one that, into the twenty-first century, remains controversial.

There have been numerous theories about Maori origins. The missionary Richard Taylor claimed Maori as one of the lost tribes of Israel; Tregear found in Maori language a direct link to the Aryan peoples of India and the Iranian plateau, and Best saw in the Maori migrations a parallel with the Vikings of Scandinavia, going so far as to label Maori as the 'Vikings of the Sunrise'.[18] A great many of these early theories and scholarship conflate history with tradition, and are overlaid by, and combined with, theories from physical anthropology. James Cowan, in *Legends of the Maori*, postulated the theory that Maori had Arabian origins and argued that it was this Arab heritage that 'gave the composite race its sea-roving bent and shaped its inclination for far travel'.[19] Furthermore, Cowan theorised that a mixture of Indian, Arabic and Egyptian heritage created a blend of Polynesian that 'was of the most enterprising and intelligent of all ancient races, [and] developed into the most skilful long-distance sailing seaman in the primitive world'.[20] Cowan projected a Pakeha heritage for Maori, arguing that this 'racial' heritage explained their ability to migrate by waka to Aotearoa New Zealand. His approach also placed the Maori voyagers in a history of adventure.

Although much of the academic and non-academic scholarship and literature on Maori origins has been concerned with the traditions recounting the migration there is also a literature, mostly anthropological, centred on the mechanics of getting here. This scholarship focuses not only on the traditions but also on the migrants' navigational skills and their knowledge of the ocean, the stars and the wind. In short, these writers are interested in what it took to achieve the migrations across vast oceans, in double-hulled canoes, carrying men, women, children, animals, plants and food bound for new places to settle. Tipene O'Regan states: 'Our people came out of Te Moana Nui a Kiwa, the warm tropical world of small Pacific islands. Successive generations found their way over vast expanses of ocean, sailing in great double-hulled canoes, navigating down the long corridors of the stars, tacking westwards and southwards, seeking and settling new lands, new reefs, new lagoons.'[21]

According to Janet Davidson, '[n]o aspect of Polynesian prehistory has caught the imagination more than the voyaging ability of these people and the extent to which their voyages were accidental or deliberate'. She suggests that the carrying of women, pigs, dogs and chickens as well as plants implicates Maori in deliberate voyages of colonisation rather than accidental migrations.[22] The implication, of course, is that women were migrants not only because they were kin or wives but also because of their ability to reproduce.

Statistics suggest that women *were* on the waka that sailed to Aotearoa New Zealand. In 1999, Rosalind Murray McIntosh of Massey University released the findings of her research that traced DNA down the female line of waka descendants.[23] McIntosh concluded that about seventy women formed the founding female population, a figure, Lloyd Ashton suggests, ties in with the tradition that eight to ten waka arrived from Polynesia, with five to ten women in each vessel.[24]

Nevertheless, an entrenched gendered mythology has surrounded the waka traditions, emphasising the male captains and crews as heroic adventurers, as Aotearoa New Zealand's first pioneers. For over a century, Maori migrations have been a popular topic for Pakeha artists. For instance, a romantic view of the voyage is represented in *The Legend of the Voyage to New Zealand*, painted in 1912 by Kennett Watkins. In contrast, Charles F. Goldie and L.J. Steele's, *The Arrival of the Maoris in New Zealand*, 1898, depicts an epic voyage. Although very different from the calm sea and healthy crew depicted in Watkins's painting, Goldie and Steele's view of the arrival is, nonetheless, still romantic. It depicts starvation, desperation and danger as heroic male adventurers survive stormy seas. Neither painting is at all similar to the images conjured up by the oral traditions. Both, too, are born of the late-nineteenth/early twentieth-century belief in Maori as a 'dying race'. This theory promoted the importance of 'saving' indigenous knowledge and also allowed for the 'invention' of a romantic past for Maori, casting them in the role of a once 'noble race'.[25] In response, artists such as Gottfried Lindauer, Watkins, Steele and Goldie captured Maori history, tradition, custom and mythology through art, in an effort to contribute to the so-called preservation of Maori tradition.[26]

Some visual images of the Maori migration to Aotearoa New Zealand present Maori women as sexualised figures. Notably, Wilhelm Dittmer's *The Journey* has as its focal point a woman with flowing hair, outstretched arms and bared breasts.[27] Dittmer's representation of the first sighting of Aotearoa New Zealand by Maori is yet again a stylised and romanticised image that bears little similarity to traditional accounts of the migrations. Ngai Tahu artist Cliff Whiting's *Farewelling Uruao*, an illustration for the New Zealand Geographic Board's *Maori Oral History Atlas*, shows the waka on which Waitaha, who form the first of the three strands of modern Ngai Tahu, migrated to Aotearoa New Zealand, but depicts only one woman on board.[28]

It is not only the ocean that has traditionally been cast as a male preserve in western culture: so too, have been the vessels that cross the sea. In Aotearoa New Zealand scholarship, both James Belich and Jock Phillips have picked up on this theme, with particular reference to whaling.[29] Phillips portrays frontier life as rugged and essentially the sphere of men, with whalers making up one of the male groups of pioneers who exploited the resources of the land and sea. Similarly, Belich, in writing about 'crew culture', an international and ocean-based set of behaviours and characteristics, depicts whalers and crews as inhabiting a male domain centred on violence and drinking. Waka, too, have been regarded in terms of male activity. In popular imagination, the waka are great war canoes, with large crews of male warriors,[30] and many visual depictions of the Maori migrations represent the voyagers as overwhelmingly male.

CENTRING MAORI WOMEN

When I began to research this chapter, I was continually frustrated by what seemed to be a conspicuous absence of Maori women in waka traditions. Kuini Jenkins, writing about the histories of Maori women in 1992, states that there is 'a general paucity of literature relating directly to their activities so collecting and piecing together of evidence is quite a challenge'.[31] She suggests that, despite this lack of scholarly information, Maori women occupied important roles in Maori mythology. In particular, women had the power to control the forces of the universe and to forbid male entrance to the heavens or the underworld.[32] Moreover, there are, within every tribal area, a number of notable female figures who existed around the migration period of Maori tradition.[33] Jenkins mentions, for instance, Wairaka, who is remembered by descendants of the Mataatua canoe for having saved the waka from floating out to sea when the men had gone inland to explore the interior. The town of Whakatane is named in honour of Wairaka, who acquitted herself like a man to drag the canoe ashore.[34] This waka tradition illustrates the way in which Maori women, although not always central in the traditions – they are never the captains – did play significant parts in the migrations and, once in Aotearoa New Zealand, proved to be essential to colonisation. An analysis of waka traditions reveals, however, that Maori women have been cast in particular roles, often as helpers and/or protectors.

Margaret Orbell is one of the few scholars who has discussed the place of Maori women in mythology and tradition. She concludes that, although a broad analysis of Maori mythology and tradition suggests that Maori women did not occupy a central place as characters or actors, they were there. Their presence, Orbell argues, is felt in terms of the roles they fulfilled: they are cast as 'female helpers', 'through whose knowledge and powers the man can employ this presence'.[35] Their assistance enabled the male protagonists to carry out their activities and heroic deeds.

The presence or non-presence of women in waka traditions does not merely illustrate the position of women in Maori society: such an argument is far too simplistic. A more complex picture is revealed when we take into account that the narrators and collectors of the traditions since the nineteenth century have been men – Maori and Pakeha. What was deemed significant has been edited and reconstructed throughout the process of recital and writing. Orbell suggests that the collection of Maori myths by Pakeha men, combined with the overwhelmingly male recital of them by Maori, consolidated a picture of Maori tradition that very rarely, if ever, includes Maori women.[36]

If you look hard enough, women are present in the waka traditions recounting migration of Maori from Hawaiki to Aotearoa New Zealand. Maori women often represent or symbolise nature or natural features. In particular, they bring fire and protect and plant kumara. Although Maori women are located as part of 'nature', they are also cast in the role of protector. It is deemed 'natural' that their supposedly inherent nurturing capacity should place Maori women in a role that emphasises the universal feminine qualities of care and protection. There is, therefore, an implicit connection between nature, the realm where women's activities are confined, and nurture, where women's role as assistant, protector and helper is recognised. 'While most of the main protagonists in the myths are men their success generally depends upon the assistance of women. Female relatives are the most common helpers, kinship being such an important factor, but wives sometimes fill this role.'[37] Traditionally, Maori women are often depicted as assisting and protecting men who are unknown to them. Female protection of strangers allows an emphasis on women's nurturing capacity, suggesting their ability to nurture outside kin relationships.

Further entrenching the link between women and nature, some waka traditions associate women with water. In mythology, women are usually swimming through water to catch or save someone, or else they use water as a threat against others. Araiteuru, a female taniwha at Hokianga, is sometimes said to have escorted the waka Mamari during its voyage from Hawaiki to Aotearoa New Zealand; others claim it was the Takitimu that she escorted and protected, accompanied and guided.[38] Thus, the ocean is not merely the physical environment for migration; it is also a constant motif associated with Maori women in mythology and tradition. Unlike western scholarship and tradition, in which the ocean is the male space of adventure, many Maori myths and traditions depict the sea as female. In many east coast traditions, too, some of the ocean's protectors or guardians, such as taniwha, are female.[39]

The women represented in the waka traditions are not captains or leaders, but are associated with specialised nurturing skills. In particular, they are the cast as the protectors and planters of kumara. As Orbell notes,

> most of the main protagonists in much-loved stories of tribal origins are male; less is said about the wives who accompany them. There is one notable exception. In numerous traditions it is a woman who is responsible for introducing the highly prized kumara, or sweet potato. This was the main crop plant, and women played an important part in its cultivation. Generally, it is the main wife of the captain of the canoe who brings the kumara. One particular woman, Whakaoti-rangi, was so famous in this connection that five different tribal groups claimed her as an ancestress, and her prudence and industry were proverbial. According to one story, when her companions ate their seed tubers on the voyage, she kept hers tied up in a corner of her basket. She planted them in the new land, and they flourished.[40]

Whakaotirangi, a passenger on the Arawa waka, is said to have brought the kumara from Hawaiki, planting it at Maketu. Te Kete Rokiroki a Whakaotirangi, the dining room on Te Awhe marae, is named for her, thereby embodying the memory of the bringing of kumara to the shores of Aotearoa New Zealand and its planting.[41] In traditions relating to the Aotea waka, Rongorongo, the wife of the captain Turi, planted eight kumara seeds she had brought from Hawaiki and in autumn they harvested eight hundred basketsful.[42] Both Whakaotirangi and Rongorongo are said to have been allocated the special care of the kumara.

Whakaotirangi appears in the waka traditions of Tainui and Te Arawa. In both she is the main wife of the captain, and her function is the same: she is the carrier and protector of the precious kumara seeds from Hawaiki to Aotearoa New Zealand. In the Tainui tradition, she is a wise and forward-thinking woman who, while the rest of the crew ate theirs, saved her kumara seeds and planted them on the shores of Aotearoa New Zealand. They flourished, thereby providing the source of kumara in the Tainui rohe. In the Arawa tradition, Whakaotirangi is the wife of Tama: he stole her from one of his crew members, Ruaeo. On the voyage of the Arawa waka, its tohunga, Ngatatoro-ti-rangi, in revenge for Tama seducing his wife Kereroa, sent the waka to Te Parata, the whirlpool at the end of the ocean, but, on hearing the cries of the women and children, prevented the waka and its passengers from being swallowed by the black hole. While the waka was in this position, some of its cargo was lost, including the kumara seeds. However, Whakaotirangi was able to save her seeds by fastening them tightly in a corner of her basket.[43] She planted them in Aotearoa New Zealand where they grew prolifically. Consequently, Whakaotirangi is remembered for her wisdom and foresight, and is repeatedly cast in the role of protector and nurturer. The few kumara that she was able to save is now used by Arawa as an apology when limited food is available.[44]

Traditions associated with the Mataatua waka recite accounts about three leading women. These women included Muriwai, sister of the captain Turoa, and his daughter Wairaka, who saved the waka from floating away at Whakatane, using the strength of a man. While preoccupied with exploration, Turoa neglected to perform the required ritual to mark their safe arrival. It was left to Muriwai to carry out the ritual, even though it was not the role women performed, to ensure success in the future.[45] From Hawaiki, Wairakewa, the mother of Muriwai and Turoa, travelled to Whakatane on the trunk of a manuka tree, which she planted on the mound of the foreshore after she arrived. It became a mauri of the Mataatua people (a force referred to in songs and healing rituals).[46]

Margaret Orbell has found that Maori women are present in waka traditions as either sacred or profane – tapu or noa. They caused or were involved in a crisis on the voyage or they helped to resolve it. Often it was the breaking of tapu by a woman during the voyage that initiated a disaster or crisis.[47] Therefore, in a number of traditions, when a waka encounters a crisis or is on the brink of destruction a woman is usually at the centre. This casting of women as potential destructors of waka is the direct opposite of their more positive and feminine roles as helper, protector and nurturer.

Ngahuia Te Awekotuku offers one explanation for this binary treatment of women in Maori tradition, arguing that Maori society is patriarchal; it is governed by tapu, on which rests the belief that women are the negative and destructive element, the inferior and the passive. In particular, women's sexuality is presented in a number of traditions as a potential destructive element in waka voyages. Marama Kikohura was a woman of high rank on board the Tainui waka. When the vessel got stuck in the process of crossing the bar into the Manukau Harbour, Marama sang a chant confessing adultery with a slave. The confession loosened the waka and it was able to land.[48] As Antony Alpers notes, possibly as a result of her transgression, it is Marama, the moon, who is remembered for helping to free the Tainui waka from the bar. Once settled, Whakaotirangi, the principal wife of Hoturoa, planted her kumara and they cropped abundantly, along with her gourds and mulberry trees; in contrast, Marama's crops grew the wrong way, her gourds turned into weeds and the mulberry tree became a whau tree.[49] As mentioned earlier, Tama, the captain of the Arawa waka, sent his crew member Ruaeo on a task so he could seduce Ruaeo's wife Whakaotirangi. Collectors of waka traditions often expunged any reference to female sexuality or adultery from the narratives. Jennifer Garlick argues that George Grey's editing and alteration of tradition served to obscure the significance of Maori women's roles as powerful agents in the realm of the gods, and in maintaining tradition.[50]

In the traditions relating to the Horouta waka, the breaking of tapu by a woman is a central motif associated with destruction and violence. The waka leader, Paoa, instructed that the kumara on board was not to come into contact with fern root, but a woman named Kanawa disregarded his orders, stole fern root from Ahuahu and hid it on board. This breach of tapu angered the gods who, in response to Kanawa's indiscretions, sent a storm to the edge of Whakatane. In the throes of the storm, Kanawa was flung into the water, but she clung on to the bow of the waka and the vessel overturned. Kanawa died in the storm and the bowpiece was damaged. Orbell suggests that Kanawa's death and the damage done to the bow of waka serve as a warning of disasters that would follow if tapu restrictions were not observed.[51]

Tradition is retained through recital and oratory as well as ceremonial ritual. From the nineteenth century Pakeha began collecting and recording waka traditions, as did Maori. One of the enduring and controversial subjects of these writings has been Maori origins and migrations. In children's literature, however, they have been neglected, or ghettoised, often badly written or taken out of their cultural context. Between 1900 and 1930, in an attempt to create a body of indigenous stories, much Aotearoa New Zealand children's literature consisted of fairy stories and legends – especially Maori myths.[52] Apart from suggesting that Maori traditions are suited only to children's literature, Orbell argues that such attempts at historical interpretation have led to the neglect of figures other than warriors and voyagers.[53] The women of myth and tradition who have been widely remembered, read and written about are those who have been described in terms of their beauty and those who undertook 'male' heroics. Ngahuia Te Awekotuku, offering the example of Wairaka who saved the Mataatua canoe,[54] argues that if a woman challenged or contravened the patriarchal ruling she became a legend or a culture heroine, often because she acted as a man would have done in the same situation.[55]

Waka that sailed to Aotearoa New Zealand often belonged to Maori women. Antony Alpers recounts the tradition of the Aotea waka, the second of two canoes built by the master waka builder Toto on Hawaiki. The vessel belonged to Turi's wife Rongorongo, daughter of Toto and sister of Kura Marotini, the female owner of the first waka.[56] In migration traditions a waka is usually described as arriving from Hawaiki under the command of a male captain or leader, who becomes the founder of a tribe.[57] However, written accounts of waka traditions often neglect to emphasise that women, along with men, were founders of one or more hapu. For example, from the children of Rongorongo and Turi came the tribes of the Whanganui district and Ngati Ruanui.[58] In short, although waka traditions do not always explicitly acknowledge the migration of Maori women, they were important not only to the mechanics of leaving Hawaiki but also because, on arrival, they became the originators of particular iwi groups.

Waka have a resting place. In a number of traditions, a waka turns to stone, creating an identifiable landform for those who trace their descent to it. There is, however, an exception. Ngati Ranginui in Tauranga say that when the Mataatua canoe entered their harbour it went aground on a sandbar near the entrance. In order to prevent disaster an old woman on board offered herself as a sacrifice to Tangaroa, god of the sea. In this tradition, her body became the skid over which the canoe moved forward to safety, and Te Kuia, the Old Woman, is now a rock near the entrance to the harbour, to which fishers offer gifts in exchange for luck and protection.[59]

Rosemary Madden's argument about Maori women and mythology differs from Orbell's view. Madden states that the 'deeds of ancestors, handed down through the generations within the traditional narratives, provide the models for correct behaviour. These models do not support a view of female inferiority but confirm a female status and authority which is equal to but different from that attributed to males.'[60] She argues that throughout Maori mythology and tradition, one can find examples of Maori women who are equal to men because of their difference. A different view of the gendered significance of waka traditions is provided by Aroha Mead, who suggests that the marginalisation of women and families in waka traditions represents the stagnation of modern Maori leadership: 'we created heroes out of the captains of the waka with scant attention for the collective bravery and commitment of the crew and the invaluable expertise of the navigators. Without them, the captains would merely have been in charge of a fleet of sinking canoes.'[61]

WAKA ON THE LAND

Because waka traditions are associated with the ocean, their land-based importance can be ignored. It is reasonable to suggest that, owing to the relative marginalisation of the ocean in our historical scholarship, waka traditions have not been fully explored for their historical, social and cultural significance, and particularly for their relationship with space, place and the environment.

The environment and landscape have long been key areas of historical, geographical, artistic and literary inquiry in Aotearoa New Zealand. Francis Pound suggests there is an artistic nationalism that 'has been inextricably intertwined with the depiction of land'.[62] And Claudia Bell argues that, from colonisation, New Zealand settlers integrated land into national identity.[63] This environmental character of national identity is also claimed by Keith Sinclair and Miles Fairburn.[64] Similarly, historian Giselle Byrnes, addressing the issue of identity through a discussion of the idea of space in relation to landscape, argues that the 'New Zealand landscape has been repeatedly invoked as a central motif signifying our cultural distinctiveness and imparting a sense of national identity'.[65]

In historical terms, we have been less interested in the marine environment of this country. In fact, the environmental literature, both in Aotearoa New Zealand and overseas, is characterised by the marginalisation of the marine and coastal environment and a preference for the landscape. A large number of Aotearoa New Zealand books, whether research, academic, popular or pictorial, focus on national parks, tramping and travel.[66] The small amount of environmental history that has been written in Aotearoa New Zealand tends to reflect the national obsession with land rather with the sea, possibly because it is easier to associate issues of Pakeha identity with the land. This historical neglect of the ocean is more surprising given Aotearoa New Zealand's very long coastline, and the fact that it consists of islands surrounded by vast oceans.

Although the migrations of Maori men, women and children to Aotearoa New Zealand from Hawaiki took place on the ocean, it is on the land that the waka traditions remain alive. As feminist geographer Linda McDowell notes, '[i]n all sorts of disciplines, scholars are writing about migration and travel, borders and boundaries, place and non-place in a literal and metaphorical sense'.[67] Furthermore, McDowell suggests migrations are about a type of movement that changed the 'relationships between individual and group identity, everyday life, and territory or place'.[68] McDowell allows us to see that movement through space can be both physical and metaphorical. Therefore, it is not surprising to find Maori scholar Ngahuia Dixon characterising waka traditions as 'oral survey pegs', a reference to the ways such traditions are connected with spatial boundaries. In doing so, Dixon questions the Pakeha understanding of place as associated with physical and geographical materiality, and offers an understanding of place that is more abstract and personified.[69]

The recent publications of the New Zealand Geographic Board, *Nga Tohu Pumahara: The Survey Pegs of the Past* and the *Maori Oral History Atlas*, reveal the spatial dimensions of Maori tradition, illustrating the ways in which iwi are connected through space, place and oral tradition.[70] Further, the authors of *Nga Tohu Pumahara* remark on the way in which waka traditions are relived through place names.[71] In fact, waka traditions are always being reinscribed and reinterpreted through the journey of people and groups through space and place. These publications emphasise the physical and metaphorical aspects of migrations and of the traditions that encase the journeys. These migrations not only took place in the physical movement across the sea to Aotearoa New Zealand: they continue to be experienced within Aotearoa New Zealand, by men, women and children as they travel throughout the country.

Spatiality is, therefore, an important component of Maori oral traditions. For the authors of *Nga Tohu Pumahara*, place names carry meaning and memory, and thus act as the oral survey pegs of human history. Moreover, names in landscape act as survey pegs of memory and the daily use of names means the traditions are always present, always available and always travelled, so reinforcing the histories of the people of a particular place.[72] The spatial dimension of waka traditions and the movement they embody, that of migration, are revealed in the following statement by Sir Tipene O'Regan, speaking about Ngai Tahu:

> Each time we voyaged onwards we rolled up our legends, our whakapapa and our place names, and carried them with us to be unrolled in a new place and fitted to a new landscape . . . They brought with them the intellectual order, the mental maps, of the Polynesian world. Maps in the form of stories, songs and place names: the frameworks that bind together the natural and spiritual world; which order the relationships within the natural world; and hold together past, present and future generations. The Atua of the Pacific were used to people the spiritual world of this new land; the creation stories, carried in the minds of the voyagers, were unrolled and stretched to fit the mountain peaks, the contours and the coastal configurations of this island.[73]

Conclusion

Today Maori women play essential roles in remembering heroines of the migrations, such as Wairaka, Whakaotirangi and Wairakewa. Through storytelling and karakia, kuia weave images of the heroines and heroes of tradition in words.[74] The karakia recited on the Aotea waka is still sung today by girls and women, who re-enact the voyage, with poi taking the place of the paddles.[75] At the same time, a place name embodies a tradition on the land, allowing all New Zealanders to relive the waka traditions as they migrate from place to place within the country. However, the depiction of waka traditions as great adventurer narratives has masked the significant roles of Maori women, especially as migrants and colonisers. Moreover, although many scholars have suggested that the waka traditions and question of Maori origins are a well-trodden path in New Zealand scholarship, I believe there are, in fact, many aspects that deserve further investigation. In particular, as this chapter has revealed, there has been a dearth of material connecting women with the traditions of migration. A considerable part of this chapter has been concerned with Pakeha representation of waka traditions; more thorough research into rich oral history is required to reveal the complex roles of Maori women in waka traditions.

2
Women at Sea, 1870–1885

David Hastings

It was pouring with rain on the morning the migrant ship *Hermione* sailed from London bound for Auckland in 1883. But late in the afternoon, as the ship travelled down the Thames and reached Ramsgate, the weather cleared to reveal a glowing sunset and a new moon hanging in the sky. In the second-class cabin that day, a young woman called Emilie Letts wrote the first instalment of a long diary letter to her parents. Her record of the departure shows her mood swinging to mirror the sudden change in the weather. At first she was excited as she described the sunset, the moon and the 'simply splendid' sea. But her excitement was blown away by a gust of melancholy. 'How I wish you were all here to enjoy it all with me,' she wrote. 'I cannot forget the dear old home, and the tears will come when I think of you all and your love and kindness.'[1] Most of the tens of thousands of women who migrated to New Zealand in the 1870s and 1880s must have felt similar contradictory emotions, the heightened sense of excitement tugging them in one direction and a 'great wrench of the heart' tugging them in another.[2] Yet typical as Letts's state of mind may appear, we should not assume that she was a typical migrant woman. As a second-class passenger paying her own way, she was one of the privileged few. Most women came to New Zealand on assisted passages jammed below decks in the steerage compartments. They were the beneficiaries of an ambitious migration scheme devised by colonial politicians, most notably Julius Vogel, to overcome a serious labour shortage and to bolster the European population.

Colonial politicians were very particular about the kind of people they wanted: hardy types who would help to break in and develop the country. Many of the migrant women were the wives of farm labourers, builders, carpenters, stonemasons and dairy men. The colony also wanted an abundant supply of single women – first to work as domestic servants, cooks, dairy maids and nurses, then to marry Pakeha bachelors, who greatly outnumbered Pakeha women, and produce many children. The need was so pressing that provincial superintendents would order consignments of single women much as they would order cargoes of raw materials for building a railway.[3]

If there were a typical migrant woman, she was more likely to be found below decks among the domestic servants and the wives of farm labourers than in the saloon with the first- and second-class passengers. The experiences of such a woman would differ markedly from those of Emilie Letts. But class was not the only factor to have an important bearing on a woman's experience of the voyage. Her gender itself was significant, as were her marital status, her religion and her ethnic background. For instance, it is a fair assumption that the steerage women, most of whom were driven from their homelands by economic necessity, would have felt the great wrench of the heart more powerfully than the thrill of setting out on the first voyage of their lives. On the other hand, young women travelling in a first-class cabin were likely to feel more excitement than pain. These differences, as well as the tensions they generated, will be discussed in detail below, but before considering them it is worth exploring some of the experiences that were common to all women who arguably made the longest and most arduous migration voyage in history.

It did not matter whether a woman was consigned to the shadows in steerage or to the luxury of the saloon, she would most probably be greeted by scenes of confusion when she arrived on board. Carpenters were often still at work installing the fittings and the deck would have been cluttered with general cargo and provisions. Whatever order there may have been vanished with the arrival of the passengers and their baggage. Adding to the confusion were the numerous bumboat men, hucksters and outfitters who clambered on board in the wake of the passengers and turned the main decks into open-air markets, pressing on the bewildered migrants anything from cutlery and crockery to whisky. On some ships the spirit sellers threatened to tip the balance from mere confusion to chaos. On the *Tweed* in 1874 Elizabeth Brough described how Irish whiskey was bought with 'astonishing rapidity by the sons of St Patrick to quench their thirst ere they ventured on to the salt sea'.[4] Religion had a place in the strident market place too. Missionaries would push their way through the crowds at the last moment distributing comfort as well as Bibles, hymn books and children's scrapbooks.[5]

Before the ship was cleared for the departure, the passengers had to go through one last formality: a medical examination by a doctor appointed by the British Board of Trade that aimed to winkle out anyone showing signs of infectious diseases such as measles or scarlet fever. In the nineteenth century such illnesses were often fatal, especially to children, and there was little chance of controlling an epidemic on a crowded migrant ship. Prevention, then, was everything and the main tactic was the final medical examination. This was a worrying prospect for women driven to migrate by economic necessity. They knew that if one of their children had a rash or signs of fever they stood a good chance of being turned back at the very moment of embarkation. The fear of being rejected at this point was so strong that some mothers went to great lengths to conceal symptoms in their children.[6] Their fears were usually unfounded, however. With up to four hundred passengers embarking at a time, these examinations were necessarily hasty and few people were rejected. Furthermore, the Board of Trade doctors, who would not have to face the consequences of a seaborne epidemic, tended to err on the side of negligence and pass people with the most ominous symptoms such as rashes, spots and fevers.[7]

Once the medical examination was finished it was time to depart. Unlike modern travel, a nineteenth-century departure on a sailing ship was a long, drawn-out process. A ship leaving London would be towed down the Thames to a point where it could set its sails. It then had to tack its way along the English Channel until it reached the Atlantic Ocean, often battling adverse winds and tides for days. Most of the passengers succumbed to seasickness, which hit them at the first hint of a swell and did not release its grip until the ship was on the open sea and settling into the work of the long voyage. When they finally emerged from steerage compartments made foetid by so much sickness, they were struck not only by the fresh sea air but by the majesty of nature. The diarists among them filled pages with their observations. They recorded daytime sightings of flying fish, whales, porpoises and seabirds. In the evening they were awed by the sun as it sank below the horizon like a huge basket of fire. At night it was the stars that captured their imagination. Mary Dobie wrote that from the deck of the *May Queen* the Magellan clouds looked like 'splips of the Milky Way gone adrift'.[8]

The ships' boards creaked and the water hissed by as they worked their way along what was known as the Great Circle route, which began with a zig-zag across the Atlantic. The first leg took them near the coast of Brazil in search of the right winds to carry them southeast towards Africa. Next, they would round Cape Horn and sail down into the roaring forties, where gale-force westerlies would whisk them away to their destinations. It was a voyage that took them from the furnace of the tropics to the ice floes of the Southern Ocean, from the fretful calm of the doldrums to the fury of South Atlantic storms.

Life at sea brought special hardships. Emilie Letts and her family found the heat of the tropics particularly hard to take. 'Oh dear, dear it has been too hot today,' she wrote after the *Hermione* had been becalmed in the doldrums for several days. The family had spent most of their time on deck, clothed as lightly as was decently possible. Still, they were more comfortable than they had been a few days before when a tropical rainstorm had forced them below into their cabins. With the portholes shut against the rain, the heat became unbearable and tempers short.[9] Discomfort was compounded by the stench. Even when domestic duties were performed conscientiously, the atmosphere was often overwhelming. In the single women's compartment on the *Cartvale* in 1874, the toilet and bathroom were dark and dirty, giving off a sewer smell. In the married compartment, where the drains were blocked by passengers' rubbish, the stench was 'most abominable'.[10] Rats and cockroaches were also a constant problem and, like the smell, they were no respecters of class or station in life. Catherine Parnell wrote that the *Caduceus* was swarming with rats, which boldly entered the second-class cabin she occupied with her mother and sister.[11]

As the ships worked their way south it became colder and many of the diarists noted the sailors replacing light-weather sails with heavy-duty canvas in anticipation of storms ahead. This was the turning point, usually deep in the South Atlantic where the ships turned eastwards and the roaring forties pummelled them past Prince Edward Island, the Crozets, the Kerguelens and Australia, all the way to New Zealand. The women, who had been unable to bear their cabins in the tropical heat a few weeks before, now sought refuge there from the Antarctic cold. Steerage passengers stayed in bed for most of the day to keep warm. Christina Macdonald, in the saloon of the *Timaru*, was more fortunate in that she had a fire, but it did not ease her fear of the gales that blew the ship along like a racehorse.[12] Hardier women enjoyed the exhilaration of a storm. Emilie Letts stood on the poop of the *Hermione* admiring great waves like volcanoes but throwing up foam as white as snow instead of lava.[13] Sometimes the storms were too much, even for the bravest soul. In one storm Catherine Parnell wrote that the seas were running 'mountains bad', threatening to engulf the *Caduceus*. The ship's foresail and jib were blown away in the night and with every lurch the passengers thought it was going to capsize. 'Mother, Fanny and myself would have given a good deal to have been on dry land last night for between fright and sickness we were miserable in the extreme.'[14] When storms were this bad the passengers were confined below decks. The skylights were covered with protective canvas, leaving them in gloom, sometimes for days on end. It was difficult to eat because food would fly around the cabin and impossible to sleep because of the noise and fear.

The fear was well justified: shipwreck was an ever present danger. In the mid-1870s, at the height of the migration boom to New Zealand, two disasters attracted widespread attention in Britain. In the middle of one night in 1874, the *Cospatrick*, a Shaw Savill ship carrying 467 people including 423 migrants bound for Auckland, caught fire and sank in the South Atlantic Ocean. Only three crewmen survived. The inquiry into the sinking, including sensational reports of cannibalism in one lifeboat, made a deep impression on people planning to migrate.[15] Jane Findlayson noted it in her diary when *Oamaru* passed the spot of the disaster.[16] The following year another Shaw Savill ship, the *Strathmore*, ran aground on the Crozets, a group of inhospitable sub-Antarctic islands poking out of the Southern Ocean south-east of Cape Town. About forty people, including one woman, managed to scramble ashore where they clung to life for nine months, surviving on seabirds and moss before a passing ship picked them up.[17]

Less sensational but just as dangerous were diseases such as scarlet fever and measles. In the 1870s medical science had no effective treatments for infectious diseases or diarrhoea. Instead, doctors emphasised prevention, first, as we have seen, by keeping infected people from the ships, then through imposing thorough cleanliness and proper sanitary arrangements on board. If the final medical examination was often just a cursory check by doctors who knew they would not have to answer for their mistakes, the public health measures on the ships were enforced with the zeal of martinets by surgeons who knew full well that they would have to give an account of themselves to the colonial government at the end of the voyage. No doubt this zeal did much to keep the death toll down. Nevertheless, there were several tragic epidemics. The *Mongol* and the *Scimitar* lost sixteen and twenty-six passengers respectively. There were similar epidemics on the *Berar*, the *England* and others. The dead were usually children and the causes usually included scarlet fever, measles and diarrhoea.

The perils of disease, shipwreck and fire were shared by everyone on board, but the danger of childbirth was confined to women alone. One male diarist made it clear that he did not approve when a young woman gave birth: 'Well I do not know but I think she might have stayed at home'.[18] It was not as simple as that. Assisted migrants were not in the position to choose their time of departure; they went when called. If a woman were pregnant she would have to face childbirth at sea. Meticulous records kept by Millen Coughtrey, surgeon on the *Chile*, show how fine was the line between life and death when mother and child were at their most vulnerable. Of three women who went into labour on the *Chile*, two were successfully delivered after long and difficult labours. Coughtrey almost certainly saved one of these babies, who entered the birth canal with the umbilical cord around her neck. But the third labour ended in tragedy with the baby stillborn and the mother, who was suffering from tuberculosis, dying a short time later. Apart from giving an insight into the medical techniques of the time – for instance, women in labour were liberally dosed with alcohol – the records show masculine domination of a uniquely female experience. Coughtrey was in charge, although he was at pains to point out in his notes that he was always accompanied by a nurse when attending expectant mothers, especially when making an internal examination.[19]

Throughout the arduous three months of the voyage, life on the ships was carefully regulated according to Victorian values. All on board knew their place and knew what their role was. The three great precepts, class, gender and the family, rigidly dictated how space on the ships was divided. First- and second-class passengers occupied the cabins under poop deck (the highest deck, at the stern of the ship). The assisted migrants were in steerage, which was divided according to gender and marital status. Under the first- and second-cabins was a compartment for the single women. Forward, and as far away from the single women as possible, was a steerage compartment for the single men. Between them was a compartment for married couples and children, giving the family a central position in space, just as it occupied the central position in Victorian social values. The steerage passengers were grouped into messes for the purpose of performing domestic duties which were carried out according to Victorian concepts of gender. The women performed the homemaking chores such as looking after the children, making the beds, washing the dishes, preparing the food and doing the laundry, which was especially onerous in salt water. The men took leadership and guardian roles: they were the mess captains and the constables assigned to take turns on watch at night.

Any particular woman's experience of the voyage was greatly influenced by where she was located on the social map: it influenced how much room she had, what she ate, what work she did, how she was entertained and how much freedom she had. One of the most obvious contrasts was the great difference between the amount of space available to steerage and cabin-class women. Emilie Letts was delighted with her spacious cabin on the *Hermione*; it was the largest on the ship and right next to the saloon.[20] But the space occupied by the Bayes family in the *Famenoth* steerage compartment was not so much a cabin as a cubby-hole. At just 3 feet 9 inches wide and 7 feet 3 inches long (1.15 metres by 2.2 metres) there was scarcely enough space to lie down. The fit was so tight that Joseph Bayes could only just work his shoe between his bunk and the partition that separated the family's cubby-hole from the one next door. Yet four people occupied this space: mother and father on the lower bunk and their two sons sharing the bunk above.[21]

Just as great was the contrast in diet. Migrants in steerage could expect a breakfast of tea or coffee, whitened by condensed milk, followed by biscuits or toast and porridge or preserved meat. In the saloon, the variety was much greater and, by the standards of the time, of far higher quality. As well as the usual tea, coffee and toast, the menu included bacon and eggs, chops and eggs and even curry and rice.[22] At dinner or lunch the contrast was even more striking. On most ships steerage passengers were limited to two dishes for each mess. The main course was usually some sort of preserved or salted meat, either boiled or baked, followed by a pudding that could also be baked or boiled, such as plum duff. Cabin passengers ate more fresh meat and less preserved or salted meat than those in steerage. Catherine Parnell described a dinner on the *Caduceus* of soup, roast beef and potatoes.[23] But even that paled beside the banquets served to Minna Pirie on the *Somersetshire* where the first-class passengers dined on fish, mutton, tripe, beef, ham, cold chicken, sausages, chops and cutlets. On top of that they started with entrées and finished with desserts to make the mouth water: gooseberry and currant pies, oranges and raisins.[24]

With work, the contrasts are not so striking, at first anyway. No matter where they were, all women performed the domestic work required by their status as the linchpins of the Victorian family. Steerage diaries portray the lot of a married woman as an around-the-clock cycle of relentless domestic toil: making beds, preparing food, cleaning, washing the dishes, doing the laundry and looking after the children. But these similarities mask one important difference: cabin-class women had people to do some of the work for them. In the saloon, stewards swept the floors, prepared meals, served the food and washed the dishes. It was also possible for cabin-class women to employ others to take over the especially arduous tasks of child-minding and laundry. The Piries, for instance, hired a 'nice little girl' from steerage to look after their son Cecil. And sailors were available to do the laundry although at five shillings per eighteen garments the price on the *Hermione* was far too high for Emilie Letts.[25]

Steerage migrants were working their passage, whereas saloon passengers were on holiday cruises. The diaries written in the saloon are full of fun and games, with women as energetic participants. These games can be loosely grouped into four different types: deck games, board and card games, parlour games and reading groups. The deck games included the old standards of quoits and tennis. Board games included draughts and chess, but more popular than either were cards, especially whist, which was played during supper parties in private cabins. Then there were parlour games that could involve everyone in the saloon. One hot, tropical night on the *May Queen* the cabin passengers gathered on the poop for a session that included six different games.[26] By far the most popular was a flirtatious game called a philippine. At dinner a person who found a nut with a double kernel would eat one kernel and give the other to someone else, usually a member of the opposite sex; when the two next met, the one who first cried 'philippine' would be entitled to receive a present from the loser. Those cabin-class women who tired of games or who wanted something more culturally uplifting could join a reading party, a small group who would take it in turns to read aloud to each other from magazines or novels. Steerage passengers also enjoyed games at sea but there are few references to women participating. One of the rare mentions is of George Fearnley's wife playing the game Simon Says, hardly comparable to the time-consuming philippines that took place repeatedly on the *May Queen*.[27] Nor was there anything remotely comparable to the *May Queen's* reading parties. This is not to say that the women in steerage were inherently less playful than those in the saloon. The best explanation is that the former, especially those with children, were too busy.

The contrasts in experience were underlined by the physical separation of the women. Steerage women were not allowed on the poop deck, which was the preserve of the saloon classes. And although saloon women could descend to the main deck if they so wished, most kept themselves aloof. The Dobie sisters, for instance, communicated with steerage women only through an intermediary.[28] Minna Pirie, who did descend, went among the steerage passengers as a grand matriarch, ministering to the sick and counselling the poor.[29] On rare occasions these class barriers were taken down temporarily. Every Sunday all passengers were invited to attend the official Church of England service conducted by the captain and the doctor on the poop. Often the dissenters would attend, as well as holding their own prayer meetings in steerage. But the Catholics stayed away and there is no record of any priest celebrating mass at sea. At other times, usually when the ship was in the tropics, there would be a dance on the main deck under a canopy of stars or the passengers would organise a concert. Those on board would have the opportunity to do their party piece, whether it was a comic song, the recitation of a famous poem, a turn on the piano or, in one case, a series of conjuring tricks. Even the sailors, many of whom were singers of renown, were invited to contribute.

One group on the ship was excluded even from these moments of togetherness: the single women in steerage, who were effectively locked away for the duration of the voyage. In most respects, the rhythm of life in their compartment followed that of the other steerage areas: the women were divided into messes and had to prepare their own food, make their beds and sweep the floors. But their mess captains were not allowed to take their food to the galley for cooking as other steerage passengers did. Instead, they had to pass it to a specially appointed male constable who would take it for them. The authorities were determined that there should be no immoral or indecent acts on the migrant ships and that no man, whether migrant, sailor or officer, should 'take improper liberties with the female passengers'. Not only were the single women confined to quarters but no man, not even the captain or the doctor, was allowed to enter their compartment unchaperoned.[30] This explains why Coughtrey was so punctilious in noting that whenever he examined a woman he had a nurse with him.

A matron was appointed to watch the single women like a hawk twenty-four hours a day. Her instructions were to permit no communication whatsoever between her charges and any other member of the ship's company. Unlike other passengers, who were encouraged to spend as much time on deck as possible so their compartments could be properly ventilated for health reasons, the single women spent most of their time down below. This could be an extremely unpleasant ordeal, especially when the ship was wallowing in the doldrums with little breeze and the temperature nudging forty degrees Celsius. When they were allowed up, it was only to visit a cordoned-off section of the poop at set times and, as always, under the watchful eye of the matron. At night they had to retire earlier than the other passengers and, when time came for lights-out, the matron would lock the door of the compartment from the inside.[31] From the moment they set foot on the ships, the single women were effectively imprisoned and their jailers watched over them with a keenness that bordered on obsession.

Often vigilance over the gender divide was so successful that the single women and the single men did not get the chance even to speak to each other. Jane Findlayson, a domestic servant travelling on the *Oamaru* in 1876, wrote that there was no communication with the young men who were in the fore part of the ship, as the women were in the stern and the married people were in between, keeping them as far apart as possible. When the single women held a dance, it was an all-female affair, except for the fiddler who was one of the married men: 'Agnes and I were thinking that we had often heard of young women getting acquainted with young men on board ship and afterwards getting married after landing but that sort of work is utterly impossible here, we only see them at a distance'.[32]

The treatment of single women was in marked contrast to the treatment of married women in two other imporant respects. Like prisoners everywhere, the single women were required to work. Matrons would supervise them in doing needlework on the voyage and, if they behaved themselves, they were allowed to keep the fruits of their labour. If not, it would be confiscated. This was in striking contrast to the needlework done by the saloon women. Although it was work, it was also a form of leisure, which the first- and second-class women would pick up and put down when they chose. In other words, needlework in the single women's compartment was a public matter and a means of social control; in the saloon it was strictly private.

The same general point may be made about sexual molestation. The protection of single women from sexual molestation was regarded as a public matter but what went on in marriage was private. Yet, from the evidence, it would appear that a woman was at much greater risk within marriage than outside it. None of the documents pertaining to hundreds of voyages examined for this study contains any evidence of a single woman being sexually assaulted. There is, however, real evidence that physical and sexual assaults frequently took place within marriage. The medical journal of Millen Coughtrey gives one instance of a husband's attempted rape of his pregnant wife and several of women being physically assaulted by their husbands. Although Coughtrey discreetly helped the victim of attempted rape by moving her into the hospital and away from her husband's unwanted attentions, no official action was taken against any of the men who beat their wives.[33] But the slightest indiscretion – real or imagined – involving the single women would be the subject of excited comment in official reports or even public controversy.[34]

It has been argued that the single women were sequestered as a form of protective custody: to keep them safe from the 'sexual predations' of the men on board, including the captain and surgeon, who might use their positions to improper advantage.³⁵ The regulations support this view, with their insistence that all men in the single women's compartments had to be chaperoned. But this oversimplifies the Victorian attitude to women. On the one hand, women were thought to be pure, weak and in need of protection. But, on the other hand, some women were considered agents of disorder and a threat not only to morality but to the nation itself. Once a woman had been seduced, she was feared as a potential corrupter of innocent young men who would go on to perpetuate a cycle of immorality.³⁶ So, even though the regulations emphasise the protective aspect of the women's incarceration, comments by the colonial authorities suggest there was as much or greater concern about the threat that some women posed. For instance, several women on the *Asia* and the *Woodlark* in 1874 were regarded as 'notoriously loose'. Julius Vogel and the immigration commissioners complained that their drunken and immoral behaviour upset the 'respectable' passengers and was likely to discourage decent people from migrating. Moreover, it was not just a threat to morality but an economic problem. Time and again the commissioners complained of unsuitable migrants who, instead of contributing to the colony, would be a burden. This included several of the women from the *Woodlark* and *Asia* who could not hold down jobs, as well as single women who were pregnant.³⁷

In the cramped and tightly controlled little world of the migrant ships, it was common for tensions to flare into quarrels and sometimes violence. For instance, a quarrel between Emilie Letts and a Mrs Humphreys, wife of the minister on the *Hermione*, forms a central theme in the Letts diary. The break between the two women, who had known each other in England, came after they had been at sea for about a month. Letts wrote that Humphreys publicly accused her of some offence; unfortunately she does not say what. Although Letts was cleared, the tensions between the two women became progressively worse. Letts confided to her parents a series of increasingly outrageous allegations about Mr and Mrs Humphreys. Among the most serious were that Mrs Humphreys had taken a lover and that Mr Humphreys had failed to repay money that he had borrowed. Letts's version of the story held that everyone on board was on her side. Typically, the captain had told her that she had not been invited to the saloon while Mrs Humphreys was there because 'he did not consider [Letts] a fit associate' for a lady.³⁸

Disputes among women could also explode into violence, although not as frequently as disputes among men. A particularly nasty example took place on the *Chile* in 1873. Anne Vesey, a twenty-two-year-old steerage passenger travelling to New Zealand with her blacksmith husband and their son, was a troublemaker of the first order. From the day she set foot on the ship she came to the attention of the surgeon, Millen Coughtrey, as a malcontent who was only too ready to get her way through nagging, false accusations, bad language and threats. Eventually, she resorted to violence. The main object of Vesey's ire was a fellow steerage passenger called Catherine Wall, whom she assaulted twice. The first assault took place after Vesey had been sentenced to a day of only bread and water for disobeying the surgeon's orders. That evening she launched herself unprovoked at Wall, who was chatting to two other women on deck. She grabbed Wall's hair, hit her several times and had her by the throat when the schoolmaster and others intervened.[39] Four days later the two women had an irrational dispute over the cleaning of a table, which quickly escalated with Vesey hurling accusations at Wall, insulting her and threatening her.[40] The surgeon ordered that Vesey be put in irons and handcuffed to the capstan. She put up a violent struggle, broke away from her captors and for the second time assaulted Wall, who was nursing a new-born baby. Before the sailors managed to drag her away she sank her teeth into Wall's hand.[41]

Male diarists were inclined to blame shipboard quarrels on women's petty struggles for pre-eminence. Not only did this ignore the obvious fact that men were just as likely to quarrel as women but it tended to oversimplify the quarrels as personal matters. Certainly personal tensions, magnified by the extremely stressful living conditions on board, were significant. But we should not be blinded to the influence of deeper tensions that had as much to do with conflicts in the passengers' social backgrounds as with the immediate stresses of shipboard life: factors such as class, ethnicity, religion and gender.

Women of different classes occasionally came into conflict, despite their physical separation. A row erupted on the *Ashmore* in 1883 when the first-class women tried to take over the organisation of a dance that had been started by the second-class women.[42] The case of the *Ashmore* showed the second-class passengers playing a defensive role in delineating social space. But there could be aggression too. For instance, on the *Western Monarch* in 1879 the second-class passengers tried to drive steerage women off the quarter deck. There was a furious row which the captain adjudicated by handing the second-class a partial victory: steerage women were allowed to sit on the quarter deck but not steerage men, who were allowed on it only if they were 'doing a promenade'.[43]

Ill will and hard words were also generated by religious and ethnic tensions, most commonly between Irish Catholics and English and Irish Protestants. The Protestants regarded Irish Catholics as savages.[44] They were supposedly dirty and dishonest, and were usually blamed if the passengers became infested with lice.[45] They were also ignorant of the Bible and in need of help, no better than the many atheists on board who lived in 'utter ignorance of the scriptures'.[46] Elizabeth Fairbairn, matron on the *Oamaru* in 1877, was a good example of one who kept the prejudice alive. When she was accused by one of her charges of favouring Protestants over Catholics she wrote, 'Truly if the Roman Catholics wanted me to be favourably impressed with regard to their religion they would have need to behave a little better'.[47] Protestant hostility to the Irish Catholics was returned in kind. For instance, on the *Adamant* in 1875 when an Irish Protestant tried to observe the anniversary of the Battle of the Boyne, a group of Irish Catholics disrupted proceedings by marching around the deck, banging on saucepan lids in a parody of the Orange marches that would be taking place in Belfast on that day.[48]

The religious and political content of these disputes is all too clear. To some historians, religion is of rapidly diminishing interest in the nineteenth century because secular ideology had undermined religious truth. The big debates were no longer about doctrine but about the physical laws of nature.[49] Gone were the days, as in the sixteenth century, when wars were fought over religion and states were defined according to religious precepts. Now it was possible to be an atheist, and many of the migrants travelling to New Zealand were. Yet many of them, especially those who wrote diaries, were devoutly religious and to them the great religious issues of the past, such as predestination versus free will, were as vital as ever. Time and again the diarists refer to tensions arising from religious debates and arguments on the voyage.[50]

The political aspect of the tensions was generated by the oppressive British regime in Ireland. From the Irish Catholic point of view, there was much to grumble about. It has been estimated that about one million people died during the potato famines of the 1840s and millions were forced to migrate. Many of those had migrated to Britain where they had no choice but to work for starvation wages and live in squalor. Along with their pittance, they earned the resentment of British workers they displaced in the workforce. Problems had begun to emerge again in the late 1870s with strident demands for home rule in Ireland and a strong, and increasingly violent, campaign for land reform.[51] To the British the Irish had an indelible reputation for being dirty, slovenly, lazy and untrustworthy. The standard caricature of an Irishman in *Punch* magazine in the mid-nineteenth century was a creature with simian features, a low brow and matted hair, wearing a tattered coat and carrying a shillelagh.[52] This caricature was kept alive in the diaries of women such as Elizabeth Fairbairn.

Tensions of class, religion and ethnicity often lurked in the background of conflicts which diarists reported in purely personal terms. For instance, it is possible that class tensions played an important role in the personal quarrel between Letts and Humphreys. Superficially Letts's account may look like a petty struggle for personal pre-eminence, but she tells us just enough to suggest there was more to it than a mere clash of personalities. Humphreys, as the wife of an Anglican minister, was solidly middle class, whereas Letts's mother was a washerwoman. Emphasising the class distinction was the obvious difference in wealth between the two women: Letts had to do her own laundry because she could not afford the services of the sailors whereas Humphreys had enough money to pay the steward to do everything for her, then have enough left over to spend on ale and spirits.

The battleground for the quarrel was the saloon. It appears from her diary that, as a second-class passenger, Letts did not have the automatic right to enter the saloon. She could go there only by invitation whereas Humphreys was clearly entitled to be there in her own right. But Letts was nothing if not determined. She spent much of the voyage vigorously trying to rise socially. Using her talent as a pianist, she curried favour with the captain until she was a regular in the saloon as first-choice pianist for concerts and church services, apparently having displaced her rival. In her diary entry of 4 October, referring to the Humphreys, she notes triumphantly that 'they have tried hard to have the run of the saloon, and are very annoyed that someone else is asked to play before them'.[53] Although Letts attempted to portray the conflict in strictly personal terms, clues dropped in her own account suggest that the real issue between her and her erstwhile friend was class. In the rigidly structured hierarchy of shipboard life Mrs Humphreys tried to keep her distance and assert her superior social status, which Emilie Letts challenged with all her might and claimed a resounding success.

One part of the ship generated more than its fair share of difficulties: the single women's compartment. This is hardly surprising given that adults who had committed no crime were treated like children, at best, or prisoners, at worst, when they were locked down from sunset to sunrise. It was extremely frightening, especially in storms, when the common fear that a ship might sink was redoubled as the women realised that, if disaster should strike, their chances of reaching a lifeboat would have been greatly reduced.[54] Being locked in constantly was also bad for their health. For instance, in 1875, Dr William Hosking on the *Dallam Tower* noted that the single women's compartment was poorly ventilated. In the morning, it was stifling and sickening and the women suffered from violent headaches.[55] Some doctors tried to alleviate the suffering by improving the ventilation. One recommended keeping the single women's hatch open at night with a grating and padlock to allow ventilation while protecting the virtue of those down below.[56] The grating emphasised the true status of the women as prisoners but at least it would provide them with fresh air, something that was considered essential to preventing outbreaks of disease. Nevertheless, the idea was never taken up. Indeed, another doctor was censured for trying it on his own initiative.[57] Dr Hosking had a far more humane approach: in the tropics he would allow the single women to stay on deck until late. For his troubles, he found himself at the centre of a sex scandal when the ship arrived in Wellington and the matron accused him of improper conduct while the ship was at sea.[58]

Doctors like Hosking were few and far between. Usually the women's health and well-being came a distant second to preserving their separation from the rest of the ship's company. It is no wonder, then, that tensions could escalate to boiling point. Some women, like those on the *Eastminster*, were not prepared to accept such inhumane treatment. After they had been at sea for thirty-three days, they mounted a noisy protest against being locked down at night, shouting, singing and banging tin pots together and refusing all pleas to be quiet. Eventually the captain promised the women he would change the rule and the next day they were allowed to stay on deck until nearly ten o'clock.[59]

More common than collective protests were examples of individual women refusing to accept the restraints placed on them. They chipped away at the rules and regulations, to the perpetual frustration of doctors, matrons and immigration commissioners. Sometimes they even managed to escape. Their offences ranged from minor infringements, such as chatting or writing to the sailors and other men on the ship, to sexual liaisons. On strict ships, even a minor infringement required a great deal of resourcefulness and care. In 1876 a group of single women on the *Cardigan Castle* found out how careful they had to be when the matron spotted them passing letters to a sailor on the poop. The matron snatched the letters and there was a scuffle, during which her knitting and new hat fell overboard.[60] Although this particular challenge was snuffed out, there is plenty of evidence to show that determined women often succeeded in breaking the barriers. Many surgeons complained about single women giving a great deal of trouble. On the *Isles of the South*, the *Apelles*, the *Friedeberg* and other ships, 'familiarities were reported to have taken place' between single women and the sailors.[61] Precisely what these familiarities were is not always clear. At times the term may have referred to no more than casual conversations, but often it implied much more. The familiarities that took place on the *Palmerston* and the *Hindostan* occurred in the forecastle (sailors' quarters), suggesting illicit sexual relationships.[62] Indeed, Christian Christensen, a diarist on the *Palmerston*, stated bluntly that two of the single women were caught in bed with two sailors.[63] The captain responded by whipping the sailors and humiliating the women, who were left standing on the deck in their night attire.

One day, after the *Hermione* had been at sea for thirteen weeks, Emilie Letts heard that land would be sighted within twenty-four hours. She could scarcely contain her excitement. 'Hurrah!' she wrote 'we are to sight land tomorrow. I cannot believe it, it seems too good to be true.' But it was true. The sailors had the anchor ready to drop and Letts started her packing immediately. On the next day there was a general rush for the deck when the mate called out the word that everyone was anxious to hear: 'Land'. It looked like a cloud on the horizon but people lingered on the deck all afternoon impatient to get a clear sight of their new home. By five o'clock Letts had seen enough to write a detailed description. 'It is very rocky and sandy, and white cliffs also. Such grand immense rocks, and on the top we could distinguish the green moss and trees, such a treat I can assure you. You can form no conception of what it is like to see nothing but water all round for twelve weeks.'[64] In fact the *Hermione* had taken a little longer – eighty-five days. But this was still a very good run. A more usual time for the voyage was a hundred days and there were examples of ships taking even longer. When the *Adamant* finally reached Bluff in 1875 it had been at sea for 140 days and provisions had run down to the point where the passengers were starving.

For passengers who arrived on ships flying a yellow flag, to indicate disease on board, the ordeal was not quite over. They would be taken into quarantine, usually on an island, where their clothes and baggage would be disinfected and the ship stripped down, cleaned and painted. They would then have to wait days, sometimes weeks, until the epidemic passed before they were allowed on shore. The lucky ones who arrived on clean ships set foot on land straight away to begin their new lives. Letts disembarked and went to stay with a prosperous uncle and aunt in the Auckland suburb of Kingsland, where she immediately began making plans to open a shop. Jane Findlayson, the domestic servant on the *Oamaru*, would have found work at between fifteen and twenty pounds a year. Anne Vesey, the aggressive woman on the *Chile*, would have gone with her blacksmith husband to a job that paid about forty-five pounds a year all found, including tools. There would have been a ten pound bonus if they stayed a year, such was the demand for blacksmithing skills. In this respect, the steerage-class Veseys were probably luckier than the first-class Piries, who travelled in comfort and with capital but had no clear idea of what they wanted to do. They disembarked in Dunedin and spent their first few weeks wandering north and complaining about the high cost of accommodation, before settling down in Auckland.[65]

3

'No one but black strangers to spake to god help me': Irish Women's Migration to the West Coast, 1864–1915

Lyndon Fraser

In a moving letter written from Goldsborough on New Zealand's West Coast, Ellen Piezzi, proprietor of the Helvetia Hotel, contrasted her own situation in a 'pleas gone to the bad' with the imagined securities of her brother-in-law's existence in California: 'I am quite glad to here of you bene so comforted and have [a] good home for your self. Even if I never saw you I like to here from you. I was glad to here youre sister is nere you. You are great Compny to echoder [*each other*] but poor me. I got no one neder of mey one [*neither of my own*] or Julius but black strangers to spake to god help me.'[1] The peculiar sorrows that pervade Ellen's prose were shaped by the sudden death of her Swiss-Italian husband, Guiglio, when flooded rivers made access to emergency medical treatment for his infected hernia impossible. This cruel blow shattered the domestic harmony that she later described in a letter to her sister-in-law: 'He was a good husband to me and respected his Wife in all his duties to her and Litlones [*little ones*] and kind to them and to his Wife'.[2] Pregnant with the couple's third child, Ellen Piezzi found her misfortunes compounded by bouts of ill health and declining returns on the bush-clad Waimea diggings. The daunting task of running a substantial hotel, keeping long trading hours and caring for young dependent children weighed heavily on the young widow. Although surviving correspondence shows that her 'buoyant spirit' languished temporarily, Ellen's astute financial management and quiet perseverance were eventually rewarded at her 'New plase' in Rimu: 'I am dooing pretty fare traid at present. I got 10 borders and good many coming in and out but if cores it take along time to peell up. The things is so derr and every move is money. I am dooing as Well as any one les and if the betie [*often better*] but I got to ceep 2 girls one to cook and one to other work foitin beds and I got anew billiard tabel.'[3]

The story of Ellen Piezzi and female migrants like her remains 'the largest single lacuna in the history of the Irish in New Zealand'.[4] Despite recent attempts to recover their hidden histories, we know very little about Irish women's migration experiences in local social settings during the nineteenth and twentieth centuries.[5] This chapter aims to remedy this deficiency for one particular region by exploring Irish women's migration to the West Coast of New Zealand's South Island from 1864, when colonisation began, until 1915.[6] The first section establishes the main features of the inflow and the social attributes of its participants, but these characteristics alone cannot convey the human aspects of the migration.[7] This task requires the imaginative exploitation of scattered and fragmented sources, as well as the critical interrogation of oral evidence. I focus here on a few key themes that emerge from the research materials – the role of personal networks, familial mutual support, marriage and religious affiliation – to show that Irish women preserved and adapted certain Old World cultural resources in order to survive in a new environment. Theirs is a complex story involving real hardship and suffering, alongside a remarkable capacity for negotiating modern systems of communication and travel.

I

When Ellen Piezzi sailed to Hokitika from Melbourne in 1870 she entered a landscape quite unlike anything she had encountered in Australia. Beyond the rolling breakers that swept over the treacherous bar at the port's river entrance, Ellen caught her first glimpses of the goldfields capital and its surrounding hinterland. A glance northwards from the open roadstead outside the mouth revealed the back premises of Revell Street, the town's principal thoroughfare, stretching in an irregular fashion along the beach that had been an unmarked wilderness of sand dunes and driftwood before the gold discoveries six years earlier. A vast expanse of rugged coastline led toward Greymouth, the region's second port, and on past the richly auriferous terraces and pakihi that sustained instant mining townships such as Brighton, Addison's Flat and Charleston, to the flourishing commercial centre of Westport, on the north bank of the Buller River. The view from starboard encompassed the grand sweep of south Westland, with its extensive collection of ramshackle towns, abandoned beach-workings and tiny encampments hidden behind a dense mantle of scrubland, flax and ancient rain forest. In the background, a magnificent procession of towering mountain ranges zigzagged in both directions up and down the coastline, their majestic silence contrasting vividly with the crashing waves that assaulted vessels approaching the Hokitika bar. As they rounded the North Spit and reached the sanctuary of the harbour, Ellen and her fellow passengers confronted the brilliant spectacle of Gibson's Quay, the available wharfage tightly jammed with shipping, the riverbank bustling with horses and drays, workmen and messengers, while the shrill cries of scavenging gulls punctuated the incessant clamour from the streets below.[8] Along the winding quayside an array of substantial buildings proclaimed the town's status as a major goldfields emporium and pointed inland toward the Kaniere diggings, clearly visible from upper reaches of the harbour.

An extraordinary mixture of people made up the new society that emerged in this environment during the nineteenth century. On the bush tracks and beach highways connecting the numerous goldfields communities, travellers might encounter French priests, solitary hatters, 'black' tinkers and old hands, together with 'All Nations' parties, domestic servants, prostitutes and small mining gangs from rural villages in Upper Panyu. The cosmopolitan nature of the region's population was also readily apparent in rickety townships such as Charleston and Brighton, where the distinctive accents of Durham coalminers, Norwegian sawmillers and Shetlanders from Unst mingled with the voices of London dressmakers, Cornish engineers and Limerick housemaids. In the streets of Greymouth, Poutini Ngai Tahu of the Mawhera reserve rubbed shoulders with diggers from Dumfries, North Devon and Cape Breton, as well as the merchants and storekeepers of various nationalities who rented properties on their land. As the gold rushes gained momentum, the entire region stretching northwards from Awarua to Kahurangi Point became a meeting place of diverse connections, influences and interrelations.

These cultural complexities were compounded by the rapid expansion of the gold-mining frontier. Crude settlements materialised suddenly on beach ridges or riverbanks when rushes broke out, fresh strikes caused major fluctuations in population and tiny encampments evaporated overnight as restless inhabitants made their way to newly opened alluvial fields or returned to the Australian colonies. The various actors who participated in these dramatic events experienced not only the chronic insecurity associated with sudden changes in fortune but also a disturbed, accelerated sense of time. Even when the region's economy settled into a steady rhythm after the boom years of the 1860s, the ebb and flow of people continued, albeit on a much reduced scale. By the late 1890s, Kumara's parish priest, Denis O'Hallahan, reported that around a district 'going down headforemost' significant numbers had moved to Western Australia, Auckland and Reefton:

> All the young and single men are nearly left for the simple reason that they can get'nothing to do' here so they have to go and look for something elsewhere. Then again young girls can get no situation, as those in business have to do their work for themselves and the consequence is that they also have to leave for Greymouth, Reefton, Nelson and Wellington.[9]

Irish-born women were strongly represented in the richly variegated communities that developed along the bush-lined rivers and alluvial terraces of the West Coast. Census figures show that the Irish component of the foreign-born female population was almost one-third for the years 1867 to 1896, a proportion that fell dramatically thereafter in absolute terms and relative to other groups (Table 3.1). Irish expatriates outnumbered their English-born counterparts until late in the century and retained a significant presence in the region until the First World War. This broad picture is complicated by the fact that a substantial number of Australian-born females recorded by the census enumerators were

Table 3.1 Birthplaces of West Coast's female population, 1867–1916

	1867 %	1878 N	1878 %	1886 N	1886 %	1896 N	1896 %	1906 N	1906 %	1916 N	1916 %
Ireland	32.6	1650	31.7 (17.5)	1503	32.3 (13.7)	1272	30.8 (10.0)	967	25.3 (6.7)	691	17.2 (4.4)
England	34.0	1432	27.5 (15.2)	1355	29.1 (12.4)	1285	31.1 (10.1)	1116	29.2 (7.8)	1365	34.0 (8.7)
Scotland	14.3	585	11.2 (6.2)	653	14.0 (6.0)	604	14.6 (4.7)	516	13.5 (3.6)	755	18.8 (4.8)
Australia	?	1117	21.4 (11.8)	856	18.4 (7.8)	723	17.5 (5.7)	1000	26.2 (7.0)	939	23.4 (6.0)
Cont. Europe	?	294	5.6 (3.1)	170	3.7 (1.6)	147	3.6 (1.2)	122	3.2 (0.9)	89	2.2 (0.6)
Other	?	130	2.5 (1.4)	117	2.5 (1.1)	102	2.5 (0.8)	96	2.5 (0.7)	180	4.5 (1.1)
TOTALS											
Foreign-born		5208		4654		4133		3817		4019	
NZ-born		4222		6292		8595		10,525		11,665	

Notes
1. Sources: *Census of New Zealand*, 1878–1916. The figures for 1867 have been extracted from Murray McCaskill, 'The Historical Geography of Westland before 1914', PhD thesis, University of Canterbury, 1960, pp. 6/17, 6/18, 6/21 and 7/17. McCaskill's estimates are based on a sample of 1600 people whose birthplaces were recorded in the annual reports of the Hokitika, Grey River and Reefton Hospitals between the years 1866–74. These figures do not distinguish between males and females.
2. The percentages displayed in brackets record the respective proportions of the foreign-born components in relation to the entire population.
3. Although Scottish-born women outnumbered their Irish-born counterparts across the entire region in 1916, this pattern does not hold for the provincial district of Westland. Here, females of Irish birth comprised 25.0 per cent of the foreign-born population compared with a much smaller proportion of Scots (13.0%).

first- and second-generation children of Irish home backgrounds, some of whom had accompanied their parents across the Tasman Sea. We can also assume that the New Zealand-born contingent featured a sizeable minority with Irish parentage, and that the published data for England and Scotland contain a small number who were descended from Irish migrants to Britain. The Irish women in goldfields communities, then, were differentiated by generation, as well as class, religion, age, marital status and parenthood. In total, the entire group comprised between one-quarter and one-third of the female population in Westland and Nelson South-West over the years 1864 to 1915.

Further analysis of the census evidence highlights the distinctive pattern of Irish women's settlement on the West Coast. Although newcomers were dispersed widely throughout the region, the balance of numbers between men and women varied over time and from place to place for both the Irish-born and Roman Catholic populations. In the boroughs of Greymouth, Westport and Ross, Irish-born females maintained a rough parity with their male counterparts in every census decade other than the 1890s, when many unemployed single men were attracted to the Australian colonies or other places. By contrast, Hokitika featured a gender imbalance in favour of women until the early 1900s, and the counties of Buller, Inangahua, Grey and Westland contained an overwhelming preponderance of males. Among the Roman Catholic population, on the other hand, the numerical dominance of females over males in the five urban boroughs is quite clear and reinforces the impression that the diasporic label 'West Coast Irish' is best understood in multigenerational terms.

Two critical observations can be made on the basis of the extant census listings. First, although it is true that the region's Irish-born population was dominated by men until well into the twentieth century[10] – they were attracted by the extractive industries of gold, coal and timber based on heavy manual labour – localised clusters of women and men had profound effects on the social character of the region's various scattered settlements. In Hokitika, for example, first- and second-generation Irish Catholic women would have had a more limited choice of marriage partners within their own denomination than their co-religionists resident near Okarito or in the Grey Valley.[11] Presumably mixed marriages (between Catholic and 'non-Catholic') in migrant households had less impact in the larger towns where newcomers constructed a wide array of formal structures such as churches, sectarian schools, confraternities and welfare networks. For women living in more remote locations, however, the struggle to fulfil their own spiritual duties and ensure the religious allegiance of their children must have presented a far greater challenge. Such was the case for Ellen Piezzi who sent her eldest daughter, Helvetia, to St Mary's Convent in Wellington '[to] be taugh[t] her fathers langus and musick and brought up better than be[ing] around the publick house door'.[12]

Second, the comparison of gender ratios in different census districts indicates that the region's urban centres had a much higher proportion of Irish-born and Roman Catholic females than the goldfields and agricultural areas. In the main towns this imbalance reflected the incessant demand for female domestic servants, an occupation that was particularly attractive to young Irish women. The rural and alluvial mining areas, on the other hand, provided fewer opportunities for paid employment and required considerable numbers of male workers. Women's labour was in continuous demand and remained in short supply across the region, whereas the earnings of their male counterparts were often irregular and subject to chronic fluctuations in external markets.

In attempting to illuminate the complex mobility of Irish women settlers on the West Coast we face problems: the original census manuscripts have not survived and the shipping lists for the region lack sufficient detail. Nonetheless, we do have access to historical data that can help build 'windows into the past'.[13] Especially when used in conjunction with other sources, death certificates provide an alternative basis for reconstructing the migrant populations. The

Table 3.2 Demographic characteristics of West Coast Irish at date of arrival in New Zealand, 1864–1915

	Pre-1860	1860–64	1865–69	1870–74	1875–79	Post-1880	Not known	Total
Sex distribution of Irish migrants								
Female								
N	50	130	271	127	76	64	17	735
%	6.8	17.7	36.9	17.3	10.3	8.7	2.3	100.0
Male								
N	82	425	437	107	88	72	135	1346
%	6.1	31.6	32.5	7.9	6.5	5.3	10.0	100.0
Marital status of adult females								
Single								
N	26	58	141	66	40	40	14	385
%	65.0	50.4	54.4	57.9	57.1	67.8	-	57.8
Married								
N	14	57	118	48	30	19	7	293
%	35.0	49.6	45.6	42.1	42.9	32.2	-	43.2
Marital status of adult males								
Single								
N	68	376	367	79	61	55	103	1109
%	89.5	88.7	84.4	75.2	72.6	79.7	-	85.2
Married								
N	8	48	68	26	23	14	5	192
%	10.5	11.3	15.6	24.8	27.3	20.3	-	14.8

Sources: Registry of Births, Deaths and Marriages (Lower Hutt); Probate Files, CH 171, National Archives, Christchurch; Passenger Lists, IM-CH 4 and IM-15, National Archives, Wellington. Additional information on individual migrants was obtained from genealogies, newspaper obituaries and cemetery transcripts held at the West Coast Historical Museum. The data on Irish males have been taken from death certificates for the period 1876 to 1910.

following analysis is based on a study of 735 Irish-born women whose deaths were registered on the West Coast between the years 1876 and 1915.

As Table 3.2 shows, an overwhelming majority of Irish women made their way to the colony after 1864, with almost two-fifths (36.9%) disembarking at the height of the West Coast gold rushes (1865–69). In contrast to their male counterparts, comparatively few female migrants (17.7%) voyaged to New Zealand in the early 1860s. Differences in the timing of migration for both genders are also apparent from 1870, when more women arrived in the colonies. This evidence indicates that the region's Irish female population came largely from the eastern Australian colonies. The general trend of this movement is hardly surprising given that the West Coast's physical isolation from the rest of the South Island helped to turn the region into 'an economic dependency of Victoria' during the 1860s, and made the capital, Hokitika, into 'a trans-Tasman suburb of Melbourne'.[14] Although many Irish men spent time on the Otago

Table 3.3 Age distribution of Irish female migrants to the West Coast at date of arrival in New Zealand, 1864-1915

	0-14	15-19	20-24	25-29	30-34	35-54	55+
			Females (N= 568)				
N	30	83	166	157	105	119	31
%	4.3	12.0	24.0	22.7	15.2	17.2	4.5
	(14.2)	(20.4)	(35.6)	—— (18.3) ——		(9.3)	(1.2)

Median age: 26.6 (21.2)

Notes
1. All data obtained from the same sources as Table 3.2 except the figures displayed in brackets, which record total age distribution of emigrants from the whole of Ireland – as listed in *Commission on Emigration and Other Population Problems*, 1948–1954, Dublin, 1954, pp. 122, 320.
2. The median age for Irish male migrants to the West Coast was 28.5 years (n = 1175) compared with 22.5 for those listed by the *Commission*.
3. There are significant differences in the median age of women by denomination: Roman Catholic (26.3), Anglican (28.9), Presbyterian (28.0).

goldfields, a temporary sojourn in that province was much less common for women, most of whom sailed directly to the West Coast from Melbourne. The available documentation suggests that they were two- or three-stage migrants who had served extended colonial apprenticeships in Australia.

What of the migrants' ages and marital status? Predictably, the ages of Irish female migrants reflect the fact that many had migrated to other colonies before they reached the West Coast. As a result, these newcomers were considerably older on arrival than their counterparts who left Ireland for various global destinations during the nineteenth and early twentieth centuries. As Table 3.3 reveals, the median age of the Irish women in the sample (26.6) differed notably from the average of 21.2 recorded by the *Commission on Emigration and Other Population Problems* for the whole of Ireland between 1852 and 1921.[15] There were relatively few Irish female children in the inflow compared with the wider exodus and those aged from fifteen to twenty-four were significantly underrepresented. Migrants in their late thirties and forties were quite prominent. About three-fifths (61.9%) were aged between 20 and 34, a proportion that is less than that reported in Terry Hearn's study of Irish-born housewives arriving in Otago before 1871 (79.5 per cent).[16] Conversely, the West Coast Irish female population contained a much larger proportion of migrants over thirty-five (21.7%) than the southern goldfields (5.1%).[17] Both inflows reflected the distinctive colouration of Irish women's migration to Victoria in the 1850s and the complex linkages of kinship and mobility that tied goldfields communities to eastern Australia.

Most surprisingly, perhaps, married women and widows comprised a majority of Irish female migrants when they arrived on the West Coast. This contrasts markedly with one of the key features of Ireland's post-Famine exodus: a relatively high outflow of women, in which single females travelling in sibling networks were predominant. Of the 678 migrants to the West Coast for whom we have reliable information (see Table 3.2), 293 were married at some stage in their lives overseas (43.2%) and a further fifty had married in other New Zealand destinations (7.4%). There are striking parallels here with the proportion of married Irish females sailing to Port Chalmers and Dunedin from Victoria between 1861 and 1864 (47.1%).[18] When we examine the places of marriage for the West Coast sample, we find that more than two-fifths of the unions formed outside New Zealand were solemnised in Victoria (46.4%). Smaller numbers took their vows in New South Wales (8.5%), Tasmania (2.0%) and South Australia (1.0%), while a few celebrated marriages in England (2.4%) and the United States (0.7%). Of those who married in New Zealand, an overwhelming majority did so in the province of Otago. The high incidence of marriages in both that province and in Victoria further underlines the critical importance of Melbourne in the transfer of Irish-born women to the West Coast, either directly or, in some cases, via Port Chalmers and Dunedin. This impression is reinforced by the experiences of the ninety-five female migrants in my sample who married in Ireland (32.4%). We may never know the individual circumstances surrounding the departure of these women from their local communities and we can only speculate that, for some, marriage and emigration 'represented an alternative to the traditional Irish match'.[19] But it is clear that many sailed to the Australian colonies with their spouses alone and most arrived on the West Coast with families that included children born in Victoria. These women, and their contemporaries who married in such places as Ballarat and Geelong, were the mothers of a substantial portion of the region's Australian-born population.

The crucial importance of Australian antecedents among female migrants to the West Coast is reflected in the pattern of geographical origins and religious affiliations. Figure 3.1 depicts the relative numbers of women from each Irish county who came to the West Coast between 1864 and 1915. Although all thirty-two counties were involved, the migration was selectively regional in nature and not a random or universal phenomenon. As we might expect, the migrant streams were centred upon a cluster of south-midland counties with strong Australian connections. Clare, Limerick, Tipperary, King's and Kilkenny accounted for about two-fifths of the inflow (41.5%), a preponderance that greatly exceeded their share of Ireland's total female inhabitants in 1861 (14.5%). Thus a substantial proportion came from an area that was relatively prosperous by Irish standards and, after the Famine, had made a particularly rapid transition from labour-intensive cereals to livestock production in response to changing market prices. This rural transformation was certainly evident in Clare and Tipperary, which together dominated Victoria's intake and consistently provided the largest share of newcomers in absolute numbers and relative to their respective

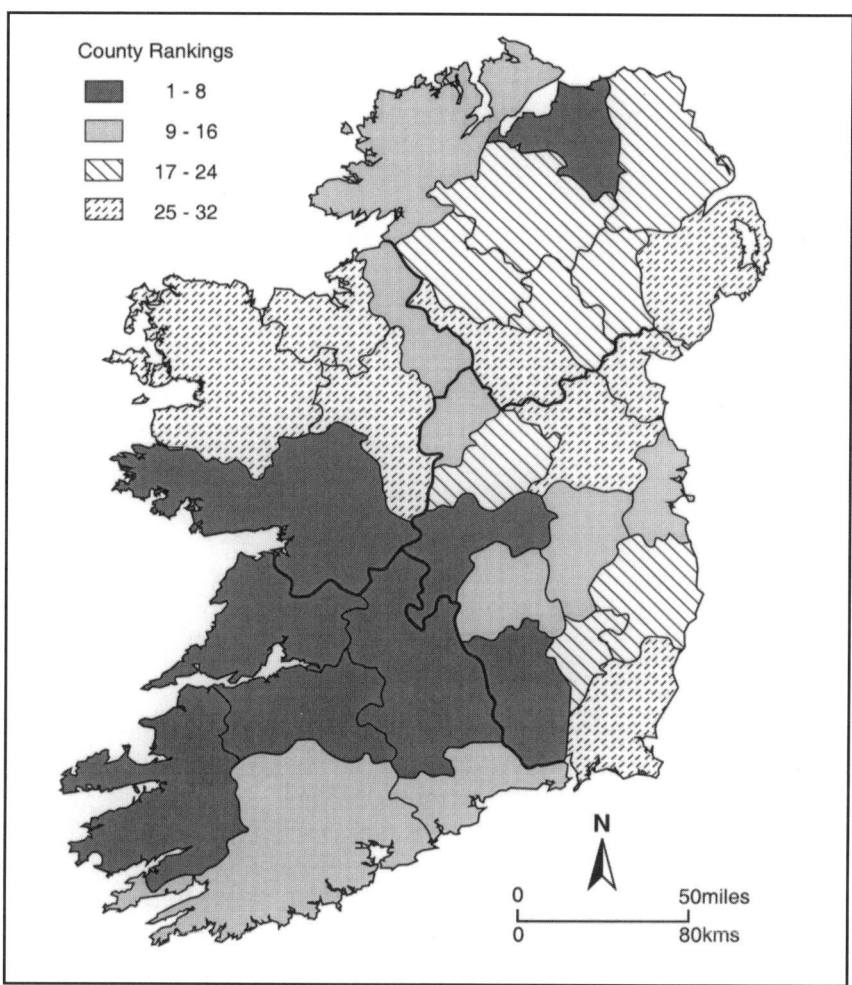

Figure 3.1 County origins of West Coast Irish women, 1864–1915.

populations. This marked southern orientation, as shown in Table 3.4, is further accentuated when we consider that Munster's proportional representation (51.3%) was almost twice that for its population distribution (26.0%). Migrants from Ulster and Connaught were under-represented, although the western seaboard counties of Donegal and Galway were important exceptions to this wider pattern. The distinctive geographical origins of the West Coast's Irish female population best explain the divergence between the Catholic/Protestant breakdown in the region (80/20) and New Zealand as a whole (55/45), along with its close resemblance to the balance of religious affiliations recorded in 1901 for Victoria (70/30), New South Wales (71/29) and Queensland (72/28).[20]

Table 3.4 **Regional proportions of West Coast Irish female migrants by date of arrival in New Zealand, 1864–1915**

	Pre-1860	1860–64	1865–69	1870–74	1875–79	Post-1880	Not known	Totals
Ulster								
N	2	20	44	23	17	14	6	126
%	8.3	19.4	19.8	23.2	25.0	26.4	-	21.1
Leinster								
N	3	24	49	9	10	8	5	108
%	12.5	23.3	22.1	9.1	14.7	15.1	-	18.2
Connaught								
N	5	12	23	7	5	4	0	56
%	20.8	11.7	10.4	7.1	7.4	7.5	-	9.4
Munster								
N	14	47	106	60	36	27	15	305
%	58.3	45.6	47.7	60.6	52.9	50.9	-	51.3
Totals								
N	24	103	222	99	68	53	26	595
%	4.0	17.3	37.3	16.6	11.4	8.9	4.4	100.0

Notes
1. All data obtained from the same sources as Table 3.2.
2. The denominational percentages for the West Coast sample were as follows: Roman Catholic (79.6%), Anglican (10.6%), Presbyterian (6.0%) and Wesleyan (0.8%). Data on religious affiliations were unavailable for 3.0 per cent of female migrants.

What strata of Irish society did the migrants come from? This question cannot be answered conclusively without access to reliable data, but death certificates contain some useful information, especially after 1875 when local registrars were required to list the occupation of the dead person's *father*. A close analysis of the surviving documentation shows that, although all social levels of Irish society were represented, women migrants came largely from agricultural backgrounds. The farming sector dominated the inflow (65.4%), and a small but significant minority was drawn from families associated with pre-industrial trades. Women from agricultural labouring households, on the other hand, were under-represented relative to the proportion in the Irish population and compared with the corresponding rates for Irish wives who travelled to the Otago goldfields.[21] These complexities are heightened when we consider that many of those from such backgrounds as hotel-keeping and retailing belonged to the rural female workforce. Despite its limitations, the evidence allows us to conjecture that newcomers were drawn disproportionately from among the ranks of middling tenant farms and the families of an emerging post-Famine élite of prosperous farmers, shopkeepers, merchants and traders. Although more research is needed to confirm this hypothesis, it accords with local fieldwork and the observations of such contemporaries as Father Nicholas Binsfield who claimed that Catholic miners came from '[the] well-to-do classes at home'.[22]

The most plausible explanation for this pattern lies with the character of Irish migration to Victoria, which attracted a majority of unsubsidised settlers before 1860.[23] Without state assistance, the poorest or least experienced migrants with few resources would have been unable to afford the passage, which ranged from three to five times the rate for a transatlantic crossing in the 1850s.[24] The fact that substantial fares of this nature were sometimes funded from private sources such as dowry payments underlines the relative affluence that some newcomers had enjoyed within Irish society. This was certainly true for many female workers who participated in the self-financed movement from Melbourne to the Otago and West Coast goldfields during the 1860s and 1870s. We can think here of Ellen Walsh, the daughter of a comfortable Kilkenny artisan-tenant farmer, or 'the Limerick girls', Ann Diamond and her cousin Johanna Weir, whose mossy gravestones in the Notown cemetery obscure moneyed backgrounds in Adare.[25] For women such as these, the decision to leave Ireland was a family one and represented a logical and practical option in a rural society where opportunities for undowried females were quite limited.[26] Whatever their personal motivations, David Doyle's recent assertion that 'strong and medium farmers' daughters had, at worst, intelligent choices imposed on them' seems a more realistic view of their migration than the fanciful depiction of an independent flight from patriarchal oppression.[27] The complex negotiations that preceded the departure of young women from the households of smallholders, labourers and urban artisans, on the other hand, remain inaccessible. Case studies of West Coast migrants from less affluent backgrounds, such as Catherine Bourke, Margaret McGirr and Maria Phelan, suggest that state funding was used as part of their families' economic strategies, but we may never know how many newcomers received subsidies or the extent to which their fares were supplemented by private benefactors.[28]

II

Regardless of their social origins or marital status, Irish women seldom travelled to the region as isolated individuals. The colourful folklore surrounding female miners such as 'Sugar Annie' Rankin and Bridget Goodwin, or the shadowy world of prostitutes such as Tipperary Mary, Overland Kate and Leaky Liz, forms an important part of the West Coast's historical landscape, but their stories are unrepresentative.[29] As we have already seen, most newcomers to the region were married women and widows, and many arrived in family groups with children born in Victoria and New South Wales. Most were accompanied on their journey by kinsfolk or followed the paths of relatives and friends who had already settled on the West Coast. Ann Diamond (*née* Gleeson) of County Limerick, for example, spent three years in Dunedin with her husband, Patrick, and friend Mary Maloney, before moving to Red Jacks, a remote Westland mining camp in which they established a substantial hotel and store. According to family tradition, the two women travelled to Victoria in the late 1850s with Ann's cousin, Johanna Shanahan (later Weir), on passages that had been paid by the Gleesons.[30] Johanna stayed in Melbourne with two of her brothers until 1865, when she agreed to join the others at Diamond's Hotel, a 'carefully furnished' establishment that featured 'coloured prints of Wolfe Tone and Robert Emmet', and corner backets 'decorated with green velvet plush and hearts and shamrocks'.[31] She assumed responsibility for general management of the hotel and acted as the cook, producing 'excellent meals from an enormous stone fireplace equipped with iron hooks for hanging heavy iron pots and cauldrons, and a spit for roasting'.[32]

The migration pathways of single women featured a similar reliance on kinship networks. Typical in this regard was Catherine Minehan of County Clare, who sailed to Sydney aboard the *Spitfire* in 1863. Accompanied by two brothers, Patrick and Sylvester, her departure was part of a much wider movement of family and friends from the parish of Kilcredan to New South Wales that began soon after the Famine and continued unabated until the 1870s. She was reunited in the colony with four elder siblings, Martin, Bridget, Jeremiah and Denis, and later joined by her younger brother, Michael, as well as numerous cousins and Old World neighbours. Catherine Minehan worked as a domestic servant in Sydney before venturing across the Tasman with four of her brothers in the late 1860s. It seems likely that she lived with Patrick and his Kilredan-born wife, Honora White, during the years immediately before her marriage to Patrick Dunn at Ross in 1874. The couple later returned to Australia and settled eventually at Kyabram, Victoria, where they ran a hotel.[33] Such examples highlight the importance of family and neighbourhood networks in the migration of Irish women to the region and indicate that these connections often spanned the Tasman Sea in both directions.

The persistent insecurity of gold-mining settlements promoted a dependence on personal networks of friends, siblings and other relatives.[34] In practical terms, Old World social ties provided an important source of companionship, material assistance and information for new arrivals and considerably reduced the risks involved in moving to the West Coast. Johanna Weir, for instance, gave birth to seven children, six of whom were delivered by her cousin, Ann Diamond, at a time when the Notown doctor, John Grattan, suffered from acute alcoholism.[35] At Rimu, a widowed Ellen Piezzi arranged for Helvetia's education in Wellington through her sister, Mary, and managed two hotels with the assistance of male siblings: 'I got my brothes minding the other plase for me and i go home oust Week for cupel of dayes setel up overthing for them and go back again'.[36] In a more abstract way, however, Old World connections could preserve notions of familial duty prescribed by Irish society. Migrants of both sexes constructed complex webs of association, stretching from Nelson Creek to Ballarat, and from south Westland to distant parishes in County Clare. These intimate connections were strongest between adjacent generations, but they also stretched backwards and forwards through time, as shown, for instance, by the letters from Kate Phelan in Limerick City to her Greymouth-born niece, Cecilia Horan.[37] The enduring significance of personal networks based on ties of kinship and acquaintance is clearly evident in surviving migrant correspondence, which expresses a 'dialogue of moral persuasion' similar to that described by David Fitzpatrick in his widely acclaimed study of Irish-Australian letters, *Oceans of Consolation*.[38] Like their male counterparts, female letter writers were particularly concerned with major problems of familial organisation such as the dispersion of households, marriage and the support of ageing relatives.[39] Catherine O'Toole of Inagh, County Clare, for instance, penned a moving account of parental vulnerability in an attempt to elicit 'a little gift' from her married daughter, Susan Hogan of Maori Gully:

> Your long wished for letter of the 30th May last came to hand on yesterday. It was at James Cassidy's some days before I got it. You have no idea how delighted I was when I got it & when it was read for me. I assure you I shed tears of joy when I knew that yourself dear husband & little children being well. If you knew the many anxious days & nights & even months & years I expected to get a letter from you. Picture to yourself if one of your dear children left you & went to a foreign land & that you would not hear from that dear child for a long number of years. Would you not feel sore at heart? I know you would & poor Parents in general would so you see it's no exception in my case. You ought at least write me a few lines occasionally so that I can know that ye are all right. It would Console me in my old age.[40]

Although the migration of women such as Susan Hogan to the West Coast undoubtedly placed additional strains on familial bonds already disrupted by movement to the Australian colonies, it is wrong to assume that mobility led inevitably to weak kinship networks. Such connections played a key role in shaping colonial population movements and maintaining social relations across large distances.[41]

In the chronic instability of everyday life in the region's goldfields communities the paid and unpaid activities of women were essential. Whether they lived in isolated mining camps or larger urban centres, the daily lives of Irish female migrants were shaped by work and the family-centred concerns of childbearing and child-raising. Like Johanna Weir at Red Jacks, married women kept cows and poultry, made their own butter and jam, cared for the sick or those in trouble, nurtured children and carried out routine household tasks such as cleaning 'by strenuous scrubbing with wood ash on a damp brush'.[42] These activities must have been especially onerous in the wretched living conditions of the mining townships. Bad weather damaged vegetable gardens or saturated crude homes, and sudden floods or blizzards drowned fowls, ruined supplies and temporarily severed communications with other places. The harsh climate, the heavy burden of domestic labour and the constant battle with rats, mosquitoes and bush flies extracted an enormous physical toll on Irish women. And this workload increased dramatically when men were incapacitated or injured, leaving wives responsible for the economic welfare of their families. The high mortality rate among adult males on the goldfields ensured that many women spent a portion of their lives as widows, often scratching out marginal existences in remote inland communities. In both cases, family survival depended on strong women and the economic interdependence of the conjugal unit. As a result, female migrants enjoyed far greater power within marital relationships than in Ireland: for example, they played a major part in the disposition of property in wills.[43] This apparent recognition of Irish women's contribution to their husbands' prosperity is evident in the bequests made to widows such as Bridget Scanlon of Westport, who received the residuary interest in the estate of her partner, Michael, along with all his coal, gold-mining shares and a hotel in Palmerston Street.[44] For these women, emigration was a source of empowerment rather than 'a passive experience to be borne stoically'.[45]

The isolated nature of frontier settlements like Maori Creek and Red Jacks broke down ethnic or cultural barriers. Such was the case in the south Westland wilderness clearings of Arawhata and Okuru where Mary Nolan of Queen's County reared ten children on a property situated alongside the farming families of various nationalities.[46] Yet the limits of frontier pluralism were also clear. Sarah Gillin discovered its outer edges when she nursed a 'Robber Chinaman' ill with pneumonia at Notown Creek and earned the opprobrium of local residents alarmed by the actions of a 'Chow lover'.[47] The boundaries of social interaction were also plainly evident in the context of marriage. As with their counterparts in the Australian colonies, the choice of marriage partners by Irish migrants on the West Coast presented a formidable challenge to the unity of family networks.[48] Writing from Killarney, County Kerry, around 1900, Mary O'Connor bluntly reminded her son, William, that the 'affection you have for you[r] child ought to make you think of your mother that nursed yourself.' Yet she seemed pleased with the photograph of her new daughter-in-law, Theresa Knowles: 'She is a nice mild looking Woman and a nice Handsome Woman. All of us are proud to be able to show it to all [our] friends.' After seeking further information about Theresa's family, Mary hinted at certain omissions in the retrospective announcement of her son's wedding: 'I suppose she was not an empty girl'.[49] These bonds of reciprocity were most likely to fracture on the West Coast when women married across religious lines and turned away from, or were ostracised by, their own families. The Catholic/Protestant divide was often permeable, as Johanna Weir's union with the son of an Ulster Presbyterian minister shows.[50] But increasing condemnation of mixed marriages by clergy and the rise of sectarian tensions during the late nineteenth and early twentieth centuries ensured that these lines were more sharply drawn then than in the early years of colonisation.[51]

Marriage was central to the lives of Irish women who came to the West Coast. Of those who arrived as single women, more than 95 per cent married at some time, most within their first two years in the colony. Although the surviving demographic records are incomplete, an analysis of all marriages involving Irish-born females for the years 1881 to 1889 shows that most were in their early twenties on their wedding day. This finding corresponds with the age-group distribution pattern of the migrant stream reported earlier and matches recent estimates of the median age at marriage for Irish women in rural areas of the United States.[52] Furthermore, the West Coast evidence undermines the view that the peculiarities of Irish culture played an important role in matrimony.[53] Irish-born women in the region were just as likely to marry as women of any other nationality and formed unions at similar ages to their foreign-born counterparts. Once married, the great majority of migrants became mothers and helped to sustain the high level of reproduction typical of newly settled communities.

What was the extent of intermarriage among Irish female migrants on the West Coast? A close examination of the 221 extant marriages from the period 1881 to 1889 shows that nearly three-fifths of all newcomers married Irish-born men (58.8%), and a large minority selected husbands from outside the boundaries of their own nationality. This significant finding suggests Irish women were not always confined by ethnicity in their choice of marriage partners. Nevertheless, this analysis treats female migrants as an undifferentiated whole and obscures as much as it explains. A much more revealing picture emerges when we consider the influence of religious affiliations. Of the 169 marriages involving Roman Catholic women, more than two-thirds (69.2%) married Irish-born husbands, and one-tenth found partners outside the faith (10.7%). The remainder formed unions with second- and third-generation men from Irish backgrounds (11.8%) or wed Catholic males of various nationalities (8.3%). The evidence suggests that relatively few Catholic female migrants on the West Coast in the 1880s crossed the religious divide and married Protestants. Where these lines were transgressed, Irish women tended to marry in local registry offices or private homes rather than Protestant churches: Annie Mahoney of Kilcommon, for example, married an English-born miner, Samuel Furness, at the Reefton home of her brother-in-law, Stewart Montieth.[54]

There are, however, striking differences between the marriage alliances constructed by Catholic and Protestant females. Although the number of cases is very small, Protestants were overwhelmingly inclined to take spouses from the non-Irish male population (71.4%). Most, though, still chose husbands with the same religious affiliations. Put another way, the evidence reveals that 162 marriages involving Irish women during the 1880s took place before a Catholic priest (73.3%), with a further twenty before Anglican clergy (9.0%), and another fifteen before Presbyterian ministers (6.8%); twenty-three were held in registry offices (10.4%). These figures are remarkably similar to the balance of religious affiliations reported for the group in first section of this chapter. Overall, we can conclude, tentatively, that, throughout the 1880s, Irish women migrants on the West Coast overwhelmingly married men of the same religious background as themselves, and that Roman Catholics were by far the most likely to select Irish husbands.

The role of informal social networks based on ties of kinship, neighbourhood and religion was undoubtedly critical in shaping the marriage alliances of Irish women. Female witnesses at weddings were generally drawn from the same locality as the bride, as were the grooms and their male witnesses. In cases where family members signed the registers, the brothers and sisters of couples usually assumed this responsibility. Jane Clohessy of Addison's Flat, for example, witnessed the marriage of her sister, Catherine, who wed a Galway-born miner, Patrick Kane, at the township's Roman Catholic chapel in 1881.[55] Other migrants, such as Mary Walsh, Margaret Kiernan and Ellen McMahon, called on Irish-born friends at their weddings, a pattern also common among their male counterparts.[56] The selection of marriage partners inevitably redefined and extended local social networks and their transnational connections, even though most Irish women selected companions with similar religious values. For Protestants, family ties seem to have been rapidly superseded by the wider social networks of the host society. Among Catholics, on the other hand, immediate kinship groups were less easily diluted, and, indeed, strengthened by friendship ties, living close together and baptismal sponsorship.

Transplanted churches presided over some of the most significant events in the lives of Irish women on the West Coast. As in the United States, Canada, the Australian colonies and other parts of the British Empire, Catholic females were part of global Irish educational and religious networks that stretched out 'infinitely and in all directions'.[57] The rapid development of parish churches, chapels, parochial schools and convents in the region after 1865, along with the growth of confraternities and mutual-aid organisations, enveloped them in a powerful institutional structure. The reach of these networks of association was extraordinary, given the isolation of many West Coast mining communities. Parish returns show that poor communications prevented priests from regularly administering the sacraments to Catholics in remote districts and forced them to construct a series of stations in private households.[58] The supporting role played by women such as Mrs Warren at her residence in Barrytown, where Father Denis Carew celebrated mass for a number of 'forlorn diggers' from the mountains and beaches, was crucial in perpetuating Catholic religious practices in the region.[59] In some places, female parishioners competed with one another to provide accommodation for roving clergy, their success celebrated in names like 'The Bishop's Room' at Frances Sullivan's home in Stafford or 'His Grace's tea-set' in the possession of Ann Diamond's descendants.[60] Others gained considerable status by raising sons who became priests, while most ensured that their children were baptised, even though births were not always registered with the agencies of the state. On the other side of the religious divide, Protestant Irish women constituted a small but significant minority within the mixed congregations of the region's Anglican and Presbyterian churches. Although these migrants left behind far fewer records than their Catholic counterparts, we can still recover fragments of their life stories through family histories and the surviving registers of baptisms, marriages and burials. The extant materials are fragmented and difficult to interpret, but they do suggest that many Protestant women infused their surroundings with some degree of meaning and coherence through religious practices transposed from the Old World, which connected them with various strands of British Protestantism throughout the world.

A sympathetic understanding of the religious dimension to Irish women's lives on the West Coast does not obviate the need for proper critical scrutiny of power relations within local denominations. Among Catholics, for example, the religious experience was sharply divided on male/female lines, a pattern that found symbolic expression in the seating arrangements at mass in Greymouth as late as the 1940s: 'men on one side of the church, women on the other, men crowded in the church porch'.[61] But there was a much more positive side to the spiritual lives of female migrants than an attempt by men to impose prescriptive ideals of mothering and 'home-building' on women's lives. When they arrived on the West Coast goldfields, Irish women confronted a volatile society marked by incessant social change, public drunkenness, high mobility and frequent isolation. Yet they exerted some degree of control over their circumstances by appropriating and re-creating religious practices and traditions from the Old World. Religion allowed female migrants to make sense of their new lives and provided the institutional connections essential for survival in a strange land. They were not passive ciphers manipulated by rigidly patriarchal churches or blind followers of tracts on blissful domesticity. Newcomers resisted clerical bullies, protected the reputations of drunken priests and valued the high standard of spiritual care given by other clergy, as well as nuns and teaching brothers. Irish women participated in wakes, baked for church fairs, assisted the poor and the sick, enrolled their children in an extensive system of parochial schools and helped to curb the worst excesses of the region's male drinking culture. On a more intimate level, however, the experience of personal faith enabled female migrants to reckon with isolation and the pain of displacement. Perhaps the most enduring image of this deep religious sentiment is that provided by Mrs Ryall of Barrytown, who walked the beach each night saying the rosary 'because she believed the breeze blew straight from Ireland'.[62]

III

We are now in a position to reach some conclusions about the main features of Irish women's migration to the West Coast. The movement was part of a massive exodus driven by an incessant demand for migrant labour in the English-speaking world during the nineteenth and early twentieth centuries. The uneven geographical distribution of the migrants, with a clear bias towards the region's urban centres, shows that, in certain places, their labour was needed more than men's. Most women performed routine tasks, unpaid, in the household, while single females in their late teens and early twenties usually found employment as paid domestic servants in the main towns. In terms of their social characteristics, the majority were two- or three-stage migrants who sailed directly to the region from Melbourne after serving extensive colonial apprenticeships in Victoria. The regional origins of the inflow reflected this general trend and turned upon the key centres of Australian emigration such as Tipperary, Clare and Limerick in Munster, Galway in Connaught, and King's and Kilkenny in Leinster. Newcomers were considerably older than their compatriots venturing abroad between the Famine and the First World War and more than half had married before their arrival on the West Coast, three-fifths in the Australian colonies. As might be expected, the balance of religious affiliations among the Irish-born closely matched the patterns found in Victoria and included a similar proportion of females drawn from agricultural backgrounds. The strong presence of well-heeled women from rural Irish families underlines the fact that the migrants were differentiated by class, generation, religion, and parental and marital status. Finally, we may surmise that Irish women were highly visible on the West Coast, given that the entire multigenerational group comprised about one-third of the total female population between the years 1864 and 1915.

The migrant stream that flowed into the region differed in several crucial respects from the corresponding movement of Irish women to other New Zealand destinations. The predominance of Roman Catholics, the high proportion of married females, the critical importance of Australian connections and the relative insignificance of state assistance set the West Coast apart from the provinces of Canterbury and Wellington. Irish women were among the earliest arrivals on the goldfields and formed part of a diverse 'charter group' with a powerful role in defining the nature of local community life.[63] Yet the circumstances that they faced in the ramshackle towns and mining camps of the region during the nineteenth and early twentieth centuries presented a far greater challenge than those encountered by their compatriots in Timaru or Christchurch. To survive the harsh isolation and chronic instability of everyday life they were impelled to preserve and adapt various Old World cultural resources such as family ties, informal social networks and religious traditions. Historians have identified similar mechanisms at work in other diasporic locations, and we need to be aware of these resemblances.[64] But we must also keep in focus the specific nature of Irish women's experiences on the West Coast and the varied responses that they made to their rapidly changing social world. The findings reported here remind us of the importance of context in shaping the socio-cultural adaptation of female migrants and the distinctive tonalities of their lives.

4
Pink cheeked and Surplus: Single British Women's Inter-War Migration to New Zealand

Katie Pickles

During the 1920s, in co-operation with Britain, the government of New Zealand ran a scheme that offered free passages to British women aged between eighteen and forty, who were 'bona fide' domestics – general servants, cooks, housemaids, parlourmaids, waitresses, laundresses and nursemaids. They were required to have worked in such jobs for two years, either for an employer or in their own homes. At the time, an estimated 90 per cent of New Zealand homes employing domestic labour had only one servant per household,[1] and there was an overwhelming demand for general servants (had more servants been available, many people would have preferred two servants). After passing a medical examination, each woman signed a document to say that she would undertake domestic service for twelve months, not marry during this time and stay in New Zealand for at least five years. Along with the free third-class passage, a two pound gratuity was provided as an extra incentive.[2]

The recorded 4504 British women who chose to migrate to New Zealand (see Table 4.1) represented only approximately 5 per cent of the estimated 100,000 women who left Britain during the inter-war years as assisted domestics. By far the greatest number (approximately 80%) chose Canada; while about 5 per cent made the journey to Australia.[3]

At the end of the First World War, newspapers in Britain wrote of the 'enormous excess of women' owing to the deaths of so many men in the country's worst blood-letting in history.[4] From the Colonial Office, Leo Amery cited figures that showed there were more than a million more women than men in Britain. According to historian Dane Kennedy, Amery considered these 'surplus' women to be 'wasted resources', who were 'fated to husbandless, childless, unsatisfied lives, and liable to distress and discontent as demobilized soldiers replaced them in the workforce'.[5] Well before 1918, British officials were busy considering what to do with these 'surplus' women. Since there was a 'surplus' of men over women in the dominions, especially in the country districts, in 1917 the Dominions Royal Commission on Population called for

Table 4.1 Domestics who arrived in New Zealand, 1920–1932

Year	Nominated	Assisted	Total
1920			1
1921			No data
1922			655
1923	126	424	550
1924			649
1925	181	436	617
1926	104	400	504
1927	124	465	589
1928			338
1929			232
1930			180
1931			155
1932			34
Total			4504

Source: AJHR 1920–1932, D-1.

'adjustment'.[6] It was considered that the men who were returning to civilian life deserved decent jobs; such employment should not be taken up by women filled with new-found confidence after their time in the auxiliary services or in wartime industrial work. The 'surplus' women would be sent to the British dominions, thereby solving colonial domestic labour problems and, at the same time, strengthening the empire by contributing to population growth and market development. As Stephen Constantine puts it, female migration would confirm women's traditional place 'and the satisfaction of masculine needs; it would preserve British culture and political predominance in the dominions by the breeding of new generations from fresh British stock, and it would sustain economic production and prosperity through the stimulus of more marriage, higher birth rates, population growth, and larger markets'.[7]

The idea of 'surplus' women was, of course, not new in the twentieth century. In Britain the myth of redundant women was in popular usage from 1851,[8] and gathered momentum with the long period of migration before the First World War, when more men than women emigrated from Britain. Female migration during this period, and its integral connection with labour, has received considerable attention from historians.[9] For New Zealand, Charlotte Macdonald's history of single women as immigrant settlers in the nineteenth century juxtaposes the presence of a 'sex-imbalance' in Britain with a shortage of female domestic servants in New Zealand.[10]

It was considered wasteful and unnatural to have more women than men per capita. In an age where people were 'stock', there should not be a surplus of either sex. In contemporary studies of the European colonisation of New Zealand the concept of an excess of men over women is often asserted, with the principle of reaching for a balance of the sexes forming an underlying heterosexual principle. The assumption of patriarchal society, the family unit, and of colonial helpmeets and a 'man's country' is well documented by historians of New Zealand, if often implicitly.[11] Charlotte Macdonald has suggested recently, however, that 'the conclusion, then, is not to deny the existence of the population imbalance but to give it greater specificity, and to question the degree to which it can be used as an unproblematic dynamic of gender'.[12] The British colonies were seen as a frontier man's zone, a harsh place for taming indigenous peoples, clearing land and building new societies that looked to the 'old country' for their models of social order. This meant setting up a domestic society with women in the 'private' sphere of the home and family and men in the 'public' sphere of trade, commerce and the land.

Domesticity was clearly central to colonialism in the case of the surplus women of the 1920s. Domestic service was the paid occupation for which the dominions most required young women and this pragmatic demand was combined with the view that domesticity was women's 'true' unpaid vocation and the recognition that women were essential in human reproduction. New to the post-war years was the extent of state involvement in attempting to carry out the imperial objectives based on these views and beliefs.

As part of Britain's grandiose post-war emigration plans, single women became a target group in the 1922 Empire Settlement Act, which authorised assisted passages and land settlement for British people to emigrate to current or former British territories, especially Canada, Australia, New Zealand and, to a lesser extent, South Africa. The act was initially for fifteen years, with three million pounds allocated each year.[13] In the plans for settlement there was much negotiation between Britain and the receiving countries. The preference for the types of migrants to be supported was worked out after consultation with the dominions at the 1921 Imperial Conference in London. Both Britain and New Zealand, cautiously, hoped that a great new wave of migration was about to begin. New Zealand, and the other former British colonies, agreed to meet half the costs and to take on more official responsibility in the selection and settlement of immigrants. The structure of the Empire Settlement Act assumed that the heterosexual family was the fundamental social unit, and included a pragmatic rural emphasis. Under the legislation, the more desirable the migrant, the greater the assistance offered. Single agricultural labourers, married couples, juveniles aged fourteen to seventeen and domestics were the major target groups.[14] Nearly two million emigrants were recorded from 1920 to 1929. By 1936, 405,230 people had migrated under the act: 46 per cent to Canada (186,524), 43 per cent to Australia (172,735) 11 per cent to New Zealand (44,745) and a mere 1226 to South Africa. Approximately a third of migrants were males over twelve years, a third females over twelve and a third young children: a favourable reflection of the objective of encouraging families, women and children.[15]

Overall, historians have judged the Empire Settlement Act a failure. Explanations often echo the sentiments of the architects of the legislation, who regretted the relatively low numbers of migrants in comparison with the pre-1914 years, far fewer than the planners had envisioned. Any remaining hopes were dashed by the Depression.[16] Such analyses have overlooked those who chose to migrate. Another important factor in explaining the act's 'failure' was the strong degree of autonomy in the dominions, and increasing uncertainty about the strength and value of the empire.[17] Well aware of the post-war push factors in an economically depressed Britain, the dominions carefully vetted any British plans to 'dump' people. Although willing to operate within the empire where it was beneficial, the dominions put their own interests first,[18] and were mindful of their own trade unionists and war veterans who feared attempts to flood the labour market.[19]

At the time, so-called 'British stock' was considered the unquestioned 'race' with which to populate the dominions and create a vaster and more successful British empire. A social imperialist doctrine of the time saw the dominions as an opportunity for economic development and a means of renewal for a 'British race' polluted by industrial urbanisation.[20] It was believed that there were vast expanses of land, especially in Canada and Australia, waiting to be populated with fresh 'British stock'.[21] Not only could the dominions absorb surplus British people, but they needed to do so if they were to develop their political, economic and social lives to the best advantage, and to play effective roles in imperial defence.[22]

In the quest to ensure that British people migrated to British territories, and especially the dominions, all possible destinations were assigned positive environmental qualities. In Canada, the cold northern climate would promote self-reliance, initiative, individualism and strength – a hardy northern race created by a stern and demanding climate.[23] Meanwhile, South Africa was considered the 'lungs of Empire', its hot climate beneficial for any number of ailments.[24] Australia was the land of the redeeming and strengthening sun. And migrants would adapt easily to New Zealand with its climate comparable to Britain's. Indeed, a 1926 New Zealand publication, titled *New Zealand: The Better Britain*, emphasised a new Britain under the Southern Cross: a land British in tradition, British in ideals, and closely reproducing the features of the land from which they came. The immigrant, as we know from experience, readily adapts himself to the conditions of life in New Zealand. In no country of the Empire is this process of adaptation to new surroundings so free from difficulty.'[25] New Zealand was a 'progressive, prosperous land' that 'holds out the promise of reasonable comfort and prosperity to all classes of immigrant – the man on the land, the artisan, workers of both sexes in the factory, and women in domestic service.[26]

As has been mentioned, the shortage of domestic servants in New Zealand was perceived to be acute and immigration was considered a way of alleviating the situation. The Department of Immigration's 1919 report stated that 'At the present time there is a great demand for domestic servants, and an endeavour is being made to arrange for a steady flow of this class of immigrant, as soon as the necessary accommodation is available'.[27] Meanwhile, the Dominion Office in Britain agreed that 'the absence of domestic assistance in the homes of New Zealand is a matter of national importance'.[28]

Immediately after the war, the 'servant shortage' situation reached alarming proportions. In 1919 the M.P. for Auckland East, A.M. Myers, asked in parliamentary question time 'if in view of the great shortage of domestic servants he would instruct the High Commissioner to arrange for regular batches of domestic servants by each boat leaving England for New Zealand?' So acute was the shortage perceived that 'a number of domestic servants should be imported at each possible moment'. Prime Minister Massey replied that 'the earliest possible moment would be when all the soldiers had returned'.[29] Myers was not alone in his fears. The M.P. for Gisborne, W.D. Lysnar, suggested the chartering of special boats to bring more British emigrants who would relieve the 'serious shortage of labour in New Zealand particularly in regard to domestic service, the shortage of which is causing serious inconvenience and in some cases the actual loss of life through want of proper assistance in carrying on domestic duties'.[30] A concerned New Zealand *Herald* in 1920 declared that 'Home life in New Zealand was suffering because of the shortage of domestic help', and suggested a potential solution: 'Yet the excess of women between the ages of fifteen and forty five in the United Kingdom, numbered 566,000 in 1911, now stands at 1,266,999'.[31]

It was mostly men, however, who were the immediate post-war targets for repatriation, and then immigration. The New Zealand government's immediate priority was to repatriate soldiers: bringing home the troops was reported to be taking up all the shipping available through 1919.[32] Massey promised that once these men were back in New Zealand the government would 'bring the country whatever immigrants were necessary'.[33] Men continued to be the focus of migration: up to the end of 1922, under the Returned Servicemen Scheme 86,027 British people – 39,419 returned servicemen and their families – left Britain for new opportunities in the dominions. Approximately 43.7 per cent (37,576) went to Australia, 31.3 per cent (26,905) to Canada, 15.5 per cent (13,349) to New Zealand and 7 per cent (6064) to South Africa.[34] Attention then turned toward the newly minted Empire Settlement Act and the priority it gave to single female domestic servants. The act greatly bolstered the New Zealand government's scheme, through the Department of Immigration, which had been assisting a small number of British women to emigrate as domestic servants since 1920.

Although the ideas of surplus women and servant shortage were nineteenth century in origin, in many ways the post-war years were a new era for women. Many glimpsed new horizons and experienced attitudes brought about by the results of first-wave feminism, which saw the entry of women into higher education and previously male occupations, and new work opportunities arising from technological and industrial change.[35] As an occupation, in inter-war New Zealand, domestic service belonged to an earlier era of servitude. Women were seeking higher wages and better working conditions, and were moving into higher paid work in commerce and factories and into middle-class occupations such as teaching and nursing. Between 1918 and 1939, work in factories, offices and department stores gradually took over from domestic service as the primary employment of women.[36]

The idea of women migrating as domestics may have been old-fashioned, but the implementation of the scheme itself displayed some new initiatives that belonged to the 1920s. Up to the First World War voluntary women had taken primary responsibility in the assistance of women migrants.[37] Although, in the 1920s, for the first time in British history, 'the importance of women to any comprehensive strengthening of the empire was fully accepted by the government',[38] it was still believed that women were best able to care for female migrants, so women's voluntary organisations continued their maternal work. Although both the British and dominion governments were increasingly involved in migration between the wars, private agencies were still important, and other women were considered the most suitable supervisors of migrant women.[39] At the same time, though, women were slowly entering paid positions within government, and in the move away from voluntarism toward professionalism some gained key bureaucratic positions in the migration area.[40]

An example of increasing state involvement was the Society for the Oversea Settlement of British Women (SOSBW), a half-voluntary, half-state organisation that aimed to increase the number of British women in the British empire. It was founded in Britain in 1919 by amalgamating previously influential women's voluntary emigration societies: the South Africa Colonization Society, the Colonial Intelligence League and the British Women's Emigration Association. In 1920 the SOSBW was recognised as the Women's Branch of the Oversea Settlement Department of the Colonial Office, though its staff remained voluntary.[41] Its rhetoric echoed the sentiments of the Colonial Office, with the SOSBW's second annual report asserting that, 'At the present time the question of the better distribution of British population is of paramount importance. While the Mother Country is over-populated and with a large majority of women, the dominions have vast empty spaces and more men than women.'[42]

In receiving migrants, the dominions followed a pattern of bureaucracy similar to Britain's, with government immigration departments setting up special women's branches, while the bulk of the work continued to be done by women's voluntary organisations such as the Girls' Friendly Society, the Young Women's

Christian Association (YWCA), the Victoria League and the Imperial Order Daughters of the Empire (IODE).[43] The Salvation Army and the Overseas League were also of great importance. The very women involved, society matrons, were likely also to benefit personally from a larger pool of domestic labour.

At the end of the First World War delegations of the British Government Oversea Committee were sent to New Zealand, Canada and Australia to enquire into post-war conditions for the migration of surplus women. In 1919, Misses F.M. Girdler and G. Watkin from the SOSBW toured New Zealand to investigate the possibilities for single British women. Their rationale, set out in a memo to the YWCA in New Zealand, was that 'at the conclusion of the War 181,000 women were working as members of the Women's Auxiliary Services. On demobilization many will return to their homes and many to their former occupations, but there is a certain proportion who have expressed a desire to come out to one or other of the Oversea dominions, some of whom have specifically asked to be sent out to country districts.'[44] They were confident 'that a new era in immigration is about to open'.[45] Optimistic about New Zealand opportunities, they reported many openings for industrial and domestic workers, especially for domestics on farms. They also saw opportunities for women to work on the land in sharemilking, beekeeping, orchardry and poultrykeeping. Their detailed report encompassed the high expectations of post-war British migration.[46]

The post-war plans emphasised the importance of continued and improved protection of single women migrants. Girdler and Watkin suggested 'a system which will ensure protection during the journey, reception upon arrival, assistance in obtaining employment and the establishment of some form of welfare work which will follow them up and form a link with the central organization'.[47] The delegation was concerned with the arrangements for the reception, temporary housing and distribution of the new arrivals. There were grand plans for establishing small residential hostels as depots for women arriving from overseas; these would also provide permanent homes for a certain number of daily workers.[48] In accord with the imperial rhetoric of populating vast rural colonial expanses, there was ample recognition that country positions needed to be made attractive. According to the SOSBW delegates, the existence of hostels and clubs in the small towns would 'offer the strongest inducement for young women to go into country homes, knowing that they have in their nearest town a Club and Hostel where a personal interest will be taken in their welfare, and where some social life will be available'.[49]

The Department of Immigration reported upon Watkin and Girdler's tour, but in 1920 the minister stated that 'I am of the opinion that there is not a great deal of scope to place women settlers, other than domestic servants, in this Dominion',[50] and the infrastructure suggested in the report did not eventuate.

The plans for networks of hostels to welcome and care for an influx of single British women became an indicator of unrealised hopes.

The New Zealand government was pragmatic about the servant shortage and required women migrants to be domestics, but the middle-class women's organisations throughout the empire shared with the SOSBW a faith in a broader imperial agenda. They regarded empire settlement as an opportunity for British women of their own class to migrate. Women who would never have considered entering domestic service in Britain were co-opted for such work overseas with the promise that it was an avenue toward a better life. In the mid-1920s, for example, parties of educated British girls went to Australia to work as domestics under a scheme assisted by the Victoria League, a voluntary empire-wide women's organisation. The scheme offered an assisted passage for women aged eighteen to thirty-five years, and a year of domestic employment at a fixed minimum salary in Victoria; the new arrivals would keep in touch with the Victoria League. In contrast to other domestic labourers, the league believed that an 'educated woman in the country districts will often find that she shares the work with the members of the household, and also takes part in their social life'.[51]

The Victoria League and other middle-class women's organisations pinned their hopes on migration schemes as ways to 'strengthen the ties which bind the women of the Empire together'.[52] In rural settings, it was hoped that the migrants would make social connections and marry in the community. An early 1920s booklet, *Australia Invites the Domestic Girl*, stated that 'the healthy, wholesome British domestic girl, is the girl who in some capacity can help in the home as a first step towards entering in to a home of her own. For Australia, above everything, is a land of home-making, and for the rapid multiplication of homes she needs more and more of the right type of girl, and there are not enough of the native-born to go round.'[53] Here, in the healthy antipodean environment, a thriving British woman would first gain an apprenticeship in a respectable Australian home, before establishing her own, fulfilling her natural role as wife and mother, and ultimately contributing to the national and imperial good.

Despite the attention that their work received from the SOSBW, the number of middle-class women migrants was very small. No tax on resources, the migration was able to continue during the late 1920s, when the domestics' scheme was waning. The SOSBW reported the Victoria League as looking after settlers 'with undiminished goodwill and kindness'.[54] In 1929 the league placed ten 'educated girls' in Christchurch as 'home helps', an increase from the three who were selected and sent in 1928.[55]

As suggested in Girdler and Watkin's report, with increased state involvement came more attention to protection. British stock must be respectable and women's virtue protected. Women's organisations stepped up their maternal

Table 4.2 Regional destinations of domestics after they disembarked in Auckland and Wellington, 1923–1932

Year	Auck	C'bury	H Bay	Marl	Nelson	Otago	S'land	Taranaki	Wgtn	Westland	Total
1923	147	64	19	4	9	31	5	11	254	6	550
1924	169	84	38	9	17	45	5	11	267	4	649
1925	177	88	28	3	17	31	10	13	245	5	617
1926	123	69	33	0	1	34	11	7	225	1	504
1927	160	84	42	3	8	47	9	9	223	4	589
1928	92	49	23	2	0	20	1	7	140	4	338
1929	55	30	11	2	4	16	1	4	102	7	232
1930	50	17	6	0	2	8	0	4	87	6	180
1931	36	16	4	0	0	9	1	1	87	1	155
1932	6	3	0	0	0	3	0	0	22	0	34
Total	1015	504	204	23	58	244	43	67	1652	38	3848

Source: AJHR 1922–1932, D-1.

role as surrogate mothers, guiding 'daughters' to another part of the family in the empire's big happy home. Proper protection during the voyage out was a major concern of the SOSBW.[56] In the danger zone of the port, hostels in Britain provided lodgings to protect women from unsavoury characters before their departure. On Canada-bound ships matrons, called conductresses, were organised as chaperones;[57] the 1921 report of the SOSBW claimed a 'complete system of protection of all unaccompanied women in Canada'.[58] The longer journeys to New Zealand, Australia and South Africa posed more problems. In 1924 a conference urged that on-board conductresses should be appointed for single girls, in addition to matrons. From 1926 there were permanent conductresses, as well as sewing materials (as in mid-Victorian days) so that needlework classes could be held on board, fostering domestic virtues.[59] In 1926 the SOSBW made the claim that 'a matron appointed by the New Zealand government travels in each steamer in charge of domestic servants proceeding under the free passage scheme'.[60]

In comparison with the other receiving countries, the New Zealand reception and placement of domestics had a small and relatively orderly history. The machinery for placing domestic servants was well organised, perhaps unrivalled by Canada and Australia, although New Zealand had the clear advantage of being a smaller country and having fewer arrivals. Table 4.2 shows the arrivals and destinations of the women domestics. As in the nineteenth century, there were two types of migrants: nominated and assisted. Nominated migrants were sponsored in Britain by relatives or future employers in New Zealand; assisted migrants applied directly through the New Zealand High Commission in London. In the case of domestic servants, the distinction between nominated and assisted migrants was nominal only. Because of the demand for domestic labour, conditions for both categories of migrants were the same and, aside from some groups of children, women domestics were the only nominated group to qualify for a free passage. New Zealand nominators could be both family members and employers: women migrated to work for their relations.

In 1920 the YWCA wrote to the New Zealand government offering to look after all arriving assisted single British women, and setting out its conditions. The association had a strong record of helping women migrants in the years before the First World War, when it had received 150 pounds per annum for its work of meeting ships and providing temporary accommodation. A contract with the government gained cabinet approval on 15 November 1920. The YWCA was to be available at the four ports of Auckland, Wellington, Lyttelton and Dunedin to receive women immigrants upon their arrival in the dominion. Women officers would meet all ships and trains, when and where requested by the Department of Immigration, and conduct the domestics to hostels. Temporary accommodation would be provided in the hostels, the first twenty-four hours of board and lodging free. A specified number of guaranteed beds in hostels in Auckland (25), Wellington (30), Christchurch (10) and Dunedin (10) would be set aside. Further, the YWCA would generally advise and assist the new arrivals. They would be offered full free YWCA membership for three months, and the association would attempt to keep in touch with the women.[61] For its work, the YWCA was to receive a sum of five hundred pounds per annum, half of what it had initially asked for.[62]

Along with other women's organisations and the SOSBW, the YWCA considered its work of wider significance than merely the placement of domestic labour. In requesting the subsidy, the New Zealand YWCA president evoked nation-building and the aspirations of empire settlement: 'Dear Sir, You will of course be aware that the War has brought "girls" into much greater prominence and shown how much more important they are than has hitherto been conceded, whether they are looked upon as workers only, or as the prospective mothers of a generation which will be called upon to bear a heavy burden'.[63] Women could be useful in contributing to creating good citizens through their maternal capacities and, if the British women were well cared for, they would become good national and imperial citizens. Hence the YWCA extended 'the human touch': each migrant received 'a warm and courteous reception and each girl is made to feel she is an individual come to a branch of her Mother Country and in whose mind the idea is implanted that she is part of a British working community helping to build up a part of the British Empire and in this way is her self respect appealed to'.[64]

Such rhetorics of race, empire and nation were ever-present in the YWCA's correspondence with the New Zealand government. In 1926 the secretary wrote to the under-secretary for immigration thanking the government for a 250 pound instalment of the subsidy and 'trust[ing] that our Association in its turn is doing its share to help make these girls into good New Zealanders'.[65] Each arrival was given 'a posy of flowers and these flowers are so cherished that, in some cases, they have been sent back to the beloved Home Country to their families as a token that they have found friends here and others have put them between the leaves of books to be kept for always'.[66] The work with immigrants was part of the YWCA's more general inter-war concern with citizenship. Its Girl Citizen movement paralleled other youth movements of the time, such as the Girl Guides, who were also concerned with moral and physical fitness.[67] The YWCA sought to mould the migrants into model citizens: 'it is the first months of life in New Zealand that set a girl's standard of living'.[68]

Generally, as British stock, the domestics were highly regarded and their qualities for becoming good New Zealand citizens were emphasised. Referring to a continuation of colonial New Zealand's pioneering past, the *Auckland Star* reported of the first arrivals in September 1920, that this 'advance guard' were

> all keen and intelligent women. One of them is a housekeeper with references extending over five or six years, and a widow with a little girl to support. It is to make a place for her and to get the little girl out that she has come so far and had the courage to land in a strange country with only a pound behind her. It is by this kind of woman that the Dominion has been built, the English women of unsurpassed courage in the face of difficulties.'[69]

In 1927 the YWCA report for Auckland recorded 'A fine type, nearly all young, from 17-25 years of age and very eager to take advantage of the opportunities offered them in this country. They are attractive in appearance generally, and underneath their surface lightness almost all are ready to absorb all the new impressions in this country.'[70]

Given the propaganda of the British and New Zealand governments, bolstered by women's organisations, why did only 4504 women migrate to New Zealand? Domestic service was not a popular occupation at the time, and there was a shortage of such workers in Britain, as well as in the dominions: one did not need to migrate in order to find work as a domestic. In terms of the scheme in general, Janice Gothard argues that Canada attracted the largest group of migrants because of its proximity to Britain and the importance of chain migration – that is, following family members who had already migrated.[71] Marilyn Barber has suggested that the attraction of higher wages and better opportunities in Canada was a motive;[72] Gothard concurs that 'the promise of higher pay for lighter work, an attractive climate and a more democratic society were the ultimate draw'.[73] Publicity could also be an influencing factor. Interviews by Paula Hamilton with women who chose Australia reinforce 'the role played by government publicity in the decision to migrate'.[74]

It was not a new phenomenon for New Zealand to receive lower numbers of British migrants than other countries.[75] Not only was its population smaller but it was the furthest country from Britain. This led to much caution on the part of the New Zealand government, which enforced strict conditions. The

1921 Department of Immigration report stated that 'Because of the fact that New Zealand is situated at such a great distance form our base whence our supply of immigrants is drawn, it is essential that none but the best quality should be despatched to our shores'.[76] There was mention that the high commissioner had received 1500 applications for passages under the scheme that year, indicating that many applicants were rejected.[77] A few of the recruitment sheets that survive from the New Zealand High Commission in London suggest that, in accordance with the scheme, only those with experience as domestics were accepted, and those with other skills, such as masseuses and mental nurses, were rejected.[78] Free passages were offered as an incentive, but there was no aid with the fare to reach the port of departure. According to the records, the New Zealand authorities were recruiting almost entirely in Scotland and the north of Ireland. It was suggested that heavy rail fares to ports of embarkation prevented 'particularly women for domestic service' from migrating.[79]

For all destinations, it appears that a significant number of families used the scheme for reunification.[80] As well as a woman applying independently for an assisted passage under the scheme, any person living in New Zealand, family, friend or future employer, could nominate (sponsor) a woman for migration. In the case of domestic service, both direct assistance and nomination qualified for the free passage and gratuity, and were subject to the same conditions. This meant that family members already in New Zealand, and as in need of domestic assistance as the next person, were able to nominate female relatives and reunify their families without having to pay. For New Zealand, the number assisted in the early 1920s was higher than those nominated but, as the scheme waned, nomination took over. In 1927 the YWCA commented that there were fewer girls in their buildings as the department was sending to New Zealand only those who already had friends or relatives there.[81] A free passage, then working for relations, was a convenient way for women joining family in New Zealand to migrate.

The shortage of domestic labour in New Zealand, combined with the relatively small numbers of British women migrating, meant that sophisticated labour bureaux were not needed. In 1921 the YWCA commented that 'every time there is an arrival of an immigrant ship our Association is besieged with inquiries as to whether we have any of these girls'.[82] There is evidence that arriving women were snapped up at the ports. In 1920 Harriet Morison reported that the Women's Labour Bureau had been swamped with hundreds of enquiries for domestics from Auckland housewives 'ever on the alert to secure help'. Each one, she said 'could have been placed a dozen times over'.[83] There were also reports of some New Zealand women who sought servants by going directly to England to recruit and then nominate suitable women. They met the migrants as the ships arrived in New Zealand and whisked their help away.[84] Discussion about reopening labour bureaux surfaced during the 1920s, but in 1930, the small number of migrants were still being 'placed quietly' by the YWCA.[85]

Because there was such a shortage of domestics, migrants could afford to be choosy. First, most stayed in town. Table 4.2 shows the vast majority in the Wellington region, followed by the Auckland region. Canterbury, presumably with Christchurch as the largest place of employment, was third, and Otago, presumably with Dunedin absorbing most of the domestics, fourth. Furthermore, the women were able to demand good positions in grand homes, preferably with a friend or another servant. In 1923 the Dunedin YWCA commented that the scheme 'has been fairly simple to manage, though a good deal of time is often involved finding work to fit in with the ideas of the girls themselves. This is specially the case in a town such as ours with very few large homes and therefore a small number of places available offering work for two girls at once.'[86] Domestics saw cities as places of safety, providing companionship in numbers. This is understandable, given such evidence as Mary Findlay's account of domestic service during the Depression which reveals the vulnerability of young women in private homes, and the real dangers they faced.[87]

It was hoped that up to 2500 domestics a year might be absorbed, but this figure was never realised. In the peak years of 1923 to 1927, 651 was the greatest number to arrive in one year (see Table 4.1). The situation was so disappointing that, rather than being overworked, the YWCA actually profited from the government subsidy and by 1924 felt that it was not using the subsidy honestly. From Auckland the YWCA's general secretary wrote to the business secretary in Wellington:

> I think I have already written to you saying that I do not think that we are dealing quite fairly with the Government in the use of their subsidy. Our own immigration Committee feels this very strongly. They feel that we have no right to receive any money from the Government unless we are expending the whole lot of it in immigration work.[88]

Despite constant threats of discontinuation, the government realised it was getting value for money and did not stop the subsidy until April 1931, after which the YWCA billed for its work on an ad hoc basis.[89]

Much of the YWCA's work drew upon its maternal identity, and providing 'homes away from home' was part of this. A 1927 report from Wellington suggested that 'The home on Boulcott Street is truly the home of the overseas girls. There they come for help, counsel, and advice; there they meet their friends and there, time after time is the bugbear of homesickness driven away. To many girls the arrival of the Home mail is received with mingled feelings ... many feel lonely again.'[90] When the government subsidy was finally stopped, the YWCA wrote a letter to the Minister of Immigration listing the extent of its labours. Its work included assisting women to find employment, arranging for accommodation between jobs, readdressing letters for some hundreds of women, enquiring about women on behalf of relations, setting up clubs and providing lounges and restrooms for Sundays and afternoons off duty and organising welcome parties and social reunions (at Christmas time and other times of the year), sometimes for as many as 150 women.[91]

Not all help was for positive events. The YWCA also dealt with 'impecunious circumstances',[92] such as visiting girls in hospital with fruit and flowers. A 1930 report told of 'one girl [who] was married some time ago, lost her husband, has been in ill health and now with her little boy is being cared for at Holiday House'.[93] The Auckland report for 1927 noted 'nervous depression for one overseas girl'. After a spell in hospital, she went to the Holiday House to convalesce, and was able to start work again after a couple of weeks' rest. Another girl whose 'mental balance has become strained, was befriended and arrangements made for her return to her people in Scotland'.[94] The 1930 report told of 'one girl, through an accident to her finger resulting in septic poisoning was disabled for life. She has been given practical help. Two girls became so ill that they were not fit to work and they were returned to their own country; also to others, whose folk were in ill health.'[95] Canada was an eager deporter of unsuitable migrants,[96] but from the YWCA evidence it appears that New Zealand's distance from Britain led to a concerted effort to work with those who were seen to be behaving inappropriately. For example, a 'girl who had fallen into bad company and had been ill for some weeks was transferred to Wellington, as it was thought to have her under the direct supervision of Miss McLean, and away from her associates'. The few specific references to troublesome migrants were to Irish women. There was, for example, the 'red' hot little Irish girl who objected to work for a Jew'.[97] A 1930 Auckland Report suggests that 'a rather young inefficient and difficult group of girls' had arrived the previous February: 'Two of these have been constantly under medical attention (provided free in such cases). Another who is 18 was causing difficulties with petty thefts and wanton behaviour and has been put in a home by Miss MacLeod. Two more of ignorant Irish type have found it hard to fit into positions, one has been in six places in nine months.'[98]

What do we know about these women's experiences? Marilyn Barber has suggested that 'for the most part, the lives of the immigrant domestics remain obscure, and it is impossible to determine how many married, went into other employment, or returned to their country of origin'.[99] As much disturbing recent attention has revealed, a number of adults and children suffered brutal abuse under 'empire settlement' schemes.[100] There is reason to suspect that domestics were also subject to abuse. Mostly working alone in private homes, women were dependent upon the goodwill of their employers. Immigration authorities considered the women under threat until they arrived in New Zealand 'marriageable' and employable, according to the morals of the time, and during the 1920s they went to great lengths to control domestics, implementing increased protection and surveillance. Migrants were encouraged to correspond with the SOSBW in Britain but only positive letters were printed in the organisation's reports; it is likely that those who were unhappy in their new situations did not put pen to paper. The usual formula ran: 'New Zealand [or Australia or Canada or Rhodesia] is a wonderful country'. Then came a paragraph about the amazing hospitality and friendliness of the local people, followed by an account of travel through the country and the observation of 'natural' wonders.[101] A letter written about New Zealand 'pays tribute to the YWCA in New Zealand, to whose care the society commends many new settlers'. 'A.F' continued that

> the YWCA is doing a very good work here amongst the oversea girls. They sent one of their secretaries to meet us at the wharf and took care of us till we were settled with situations. I am pleased to say I have an excellent situation here and have found a great many friends here that are very kind to us ...[102]

Another correspondent wished

> to express to you again my gratitude for assisting me to come out to the colonies. I am very very happy despite the hard work on a farm. I am well in the backblocks ... This district is composed of newly cleared land all up and down, great deep gulleys utterly impossible to wholly cultivate. I am keeping house for my nephews and the boys are so thankful to have a comfortable house and good meals. We all appreciate your kindness.[103]

In contrast to the SOSBW propaganda, there was some concern in New Zealand about the 'quality' of the immigrants being sent. The 1927 Report of the Annual Meeting of the Women's Division of the New Zealand Farmers' Union (WDNZFU) recommended 'that the Government be urged to exercise a more careful scrutiny of migrants, particularly from the point of view of public health', and 'be asked to enquire much more carefully into the bona fides of nominators of immigrants, thus eliminating the indiscriminate and comparatively unchecked nominations of unsuitable persons'.[104] It was also suggested that nominators were not coming through with promised work, so that the women 'become a burden and a tax upon the people and the land'. The president of the WDNZFU asked the YWCA about its scheme, and commented that there should be better selection and more agents in Britain.[105]

The concerns of these country women were centred on the migrants' ability to seek and adapt to rural conditions. The YWCA itself reported that the women migrants were often 'delicate and inexperienced and never want to take country positions'.[106] There was a feeling among rural women that migrants were neither aware of nor prepared for country life. In the WDNZFU's opinion, the YWCA should 'ascertain the number in the family, the room the girl would have to sleep in, the distance from a church, and what part of the country the girl would go to'. Echoing the sentiments of other middle-class women's organisations, they suggested 'middle-class girls to help build up the Empire, to help women on the land'. The WDNZFU report mentions that 'a lady in Timaru had told her two girls came out under this scheme, and they were getting 35/- a week in the country. They stayed two months and said they could not stand it any longer. This question could with advantage be discussed at Branch meetings.'[107]

Officials at all levels of 'empire settlement' were well aware of the problems of untrained domestics and of the difficulty of adapting to new environments, which, despite the claims of empire unity, could be very different. One remedy was to set up domestic training hostels. Although the post-war London Khaki University of Canada, set up by the Canadian government to prepare British war brides for Canadian housekeeping and life, was never replicated, more attempts at pre-departure and post-arrival training were made as the 1920s progressed. In Sydney in 1923, a Mrs Macdonald attempted to establish a domestic training hostel through her Domestic Immigration Society, where up to 150 single women migrants could be trained in cooking and housework before being dispatched for employment in New South Wales country districts. It proved too costly, however, and the topics were thought better handled before arrival in Australia.[108] To meet such pre-departure demand, a British training centre was established in Market Harborough in December 1927.[109] There is evidence that, despite its hard and fast rule of accepting only experienced domestic servants, New Zealand began to make use of the centre for 'certain cases who could not show the necessary two years' preliminary employment in Great Britain or their own homes'.[110] But by the time there was more interest in the dominions for domestic training in Britain, and pre-boarding hostels and training places were gaining momentum, the effects of the Depression were setting in, and efforts were short-lived.[111]

The 1925 case of Margaret Little and Annie Meldrum illustrated the hopes of the migrants, as well as the confidence and forthrightness that they could display. The two women arrived in Auckland, then proceeded to Dunedin. When the YWCA charged them board after their first free night they wrote to the high commissioner in London to complain about their treatment. He then wrote to the Department of Immigration to ask about the procedure for charging domestics and whether it was necessary for maids going to towns other than Wellington to secure their own situations. 'In the past I advised approved applicants that upon arrival in New Zealand they would be accommodated at the YWCA Hostel until the first domestic position was found by the authorities and the charges would be born by the department. Would you please have me informed whether or not this is correct.'[112] The YWCA replied that Little and Meldrum had refused general positions, wanting housemaid jobs, and that the twenty-four-hour free rule is 'hard and fast' as 'often girls are very difficult to place, they refuse to go where there are children unless they get every night out and every Sunday. Often thay are not keen to start work after the long voyage and want to hang around while the boat is in port.'[113]

The British women who migrated under the scheme were no different from their New Zealand counterparts, moving out of domestic service at the first opportunity. At the time, domestic service was still the single largest employment area for women, but it was older women, trained to do nothing else, who predominated. The fifteen to twenty year age group entered commerce as much as domestic service. It appears that, if at all possible, the British migrants completed their year of service and did no more. Although in 1922 a domestic might earn twenty-two to twenty-five shillings a week, the pay could be as little as five shillings. Meanwhile, in industry, the average minimum weekly wage was forty-two shillings for a tailoress and forty-seven shillings for a boot worker. A cook in a hotel could expect seventy-eight shillings and a housemaid sixty shillings a week.[114] Sandra Coney has suggested that 'it was no wonder that domestic work, even though some homes now had vacuum cleaners and gas or electric cookers, was an unattractive proposition'.[115] Perhaps because it was so unpopular among New Zealand women, the YWCA found that 'many of the Oversea girls take up mental nursing'.[116]

Ironically, it was race – being of British stock – that allowed the women access to the same occupations as other New Zealanders. The only exception to the demand for British domestics at the time was in South Africa, where, from 1900 to 1939, more black servants were employed, and the demand for British domestic labour declined. Rather than offer an incentive, the introduction of labour-saving devices was retarded in South Africa by low-status labour: 'The face in the kitchen was black not white'.[117] In New Zealand, the idea of Maori as domestic servants was briefly mooted. Some thought that the Queen Victoria School 'ought to be a source of trained maidservants for Pakeha ladies', but overall such rhetoric was rejected.[118] Because Maori women shunned domestic service and Pakeha did not turn to Maori as domestics, New Zealand's path diverged from that of South Africa.[119]

Despite what the propaganda suggested, domestics were not always treated as part of the family. Some faced local resentment for fulfilling one of the broad objectives of empire settlement: reproduction of the population. In her novel *Nor the Years Condemn*, Robin Hyde mentioned

> the pink cheeked English and Scotch Lassies who came out under the immigration schemes ... staffed the public institutions and half the private houses, and were cordially detested by the New Zealand girls, who felt a growing rivalry over the service jobs they did not want for themselves, and feared, moreover, that the immigrants might carry off their future husbands. Husband hunting, they called it; coming out as bold as brass, most of them without a penny in their pockets, swanking about towns, expecting to be everybody at a moment, and talking loud in those broad, ridiculous accents.[120]

The evidence points toward marriage as the eventual, if not immediate, lot of the majority of surplus women, as it was of most New Zealand adults at the time. Some met their future husbands on the voyage out, or through immigrant networks.[121] After all, the British scheme was based on such reproductive hopes. With the demand for domestic service, however, it was in the New Zealand government's interest to keep women in domestic service for as long as possible. This was reflected in the stipulation that girls not marry for a year, and in the government's insistence that the passage money be repaid if the contract were broken. YWCA records show that some women married within a year of arrival in New Zealand, sometimes breaking their agreement with the government. In 1930 the YWCA was still organising weddings: during that year five girls were married, and it was 'necessary for three girls to go into the Maternity Home'.[122] If the British women who came to New Zealand were similar to those who went to Canada in 1920, most married. As the director of the Women's Branch of Canada's Department of Immigration commented, 'there are times when I think that I am just running a matrimonial bureau'.[123]

The domestic servants' scheme represented ideas that belonged to a bygone era. In the 1920s women had newly earned political status, wider work experiences and were demanding more challenging employment opportunities. In comparison with Canada and Australia, New Zealand was able to maintain a well-organised scheme, but the small number of migrants meant that the impact was limited and the scheme misplaced. The 4504 women who did migrate and stayed in New Zealand blended into wider groupings of British migrants. Labelled 'homies' and 'oversea' migrants, they became a part of the general fabric of New Zealand society.

Domesticity was at the forefront of plans for empire settlement. It was considered the 'natural' occupation for women as reproducers of the next generation of citizens, and the 'servant shortage' meant it was also a convenient, paid, interim occupation that women could use to migrate. Ironically, the more bureaucracy that accompanied migration, the more choices women migrants possessed, and the more they could support or subvert the imperial and national objectives of migration. Those who chose to migrate sought opportunity and happiness. Unwittingly, the notion of surplus women may have helped them in their pursuit of self-betterment. Where the women have become well-known figures, such as Connie Birchfield, the scheme itself is not explicitly mentioned.[124] Perhaps this can be taken as evidence of the gap between imperial and national rhetoric and personal achievement. Women exerted an often unconscious and unassuming control over grandiose and pompous imperial plans based on the belief that an uneven distribution of the sexes was somehow wrong and unnatural, and definitely wasteful.

5

Refugees from Nazism, 1936–1946: The Experiences of Women

Ann Beaglehole

> Nobody wanted us. New Zealand did not want us and neither did anyone else.
> – Gerty

In the years 1933 to 1939, Jewish refugees enquiring about immigration to New Zealand were informed by the New Zealand High Commission in London that it would be hardly worth their while making an application.[1] The legislation determining New Zealand's immigration policy at this time was the Immigration and Restriction Amendment Act of 1920. It allowed free entry to immigrants of British birth or descent, but required other people to obtain entry permits. In particular, the act aimed to restrict the entry of 'race aliens': Chinese, Indians – and also Jews.[2]

It is uncertain how many refugees from Nazi Europe, many of whom were Jewish or had a Jewish background, were declined entry to New Zealand or were discouraged from even applying for a permit.[3] Unlike the United States or Australia, New Zealand did not have a quota for refugees. Nor did it have a set of rules that applied in every case: each application was 'treated on its merits'.[4] The guidelines adopted for processing applications and the way these were interpreted ensured that most refugees were prevented from entering New Zealand. One of the most important considerations was 'the suitability of the immigrant for absorption into the Dominion's population'.[5] E.D. Good, Comptroller of Customs during this period, was quite explicit in his interpretation of this guideline: 'Non-Jewish applicants are regarded as a more suitable type of immigrant'.[6] Walter Nash, who was Minister of Customs, held the same view.[7]

Despite these restrictions, about 1100 refugees from Central and Eastern Europe settled in New Zealand in the years between Hitler's rise to power and the outbreak of the Second World War.[8] Precise information about the numbers of women applying to enter New Zealand, and the numbers declined and accepted, was not collected. However, on the basis of census birthplace figures, alien registrations and data about the marital status of refugees in New Zealand in 1945, it is possible to estimate that the numbers of women and men who settled in this country were roughly equal.[9] The extant data on marital status shows that 309 females had married fellow refugees, eighteen were married to British subjects and 180 were single, widowed, divorced or married to a partner living outside New Zealand.[10] The majority of male partners were employed in the professions or business, and a few of the women had themselves obtained professional qualifications.

Although most of the refugees had some connection with Judaism, their self-identification was diverse and complicated.[11] Some identified strongly as Jews. Others were connected to Judaism only by birth, the origin of a grandparent or by marriage. They were mainly middle-class, well-educated city people, accustomed to a culturally heterogeneous environment and the cultural and social amenities of Central European cities. New Zealand cities, and the cultural life that existed in them, reminded these newcomers of small provincial towns in Europe. Not surprisingly, most refugees experienced a profound sense of dislocation. They responded to their plight by trying to put the past behind them and by working hard at fitting into New Zealand society.

This chapter focuses on the early settlement experiences of female migrants, including aspects of their lives during the war years when refugees from Germany and Austria were classified as 'enemy aliens'. It is based on official papers and on oral histories of thirty-two former refugees, undertaken in the mid-1980s.[12] The topics covered in the interviews included the different experiences of women and men at work, in homes and in families. I did not, however, consider the influence of gender on questions about the decision to escape or the subsequent adaptation of refugees, and carried out little analysis of the interviews from a gender perspective. This chapter does not seek to determine whether there were significant gender differences in refugees' experiences, but simply to focus on the accounts of the women, revealing their strengths and their struggles to settle in a strange country.

Escape to New Zealand

Refugees who succeeded in reaching New Zealand were often asked 'Why did you come to this country?' This question reflected a lack of understanding: it is the absence of choice about leaving home and one's future destination that distinguishes the refugee from the migrants. Most refugees in the study fled Germany and Austria in response to direct threats: 'If you're not out within twenty-four hours, you'll be in a concentration camp'.

Their eventual destination, New Zealand, was not usually a choice. Refugees migrated wherever a permit was available. Permits were obtained through connections often found by chance, coincidence or good luck, and the entry documents often arrived just in time: further delay would have meant certain death. 'New Zealand was the first realistic offer of immigration. Other countries' quotas were full. We had tried everywhere,' recalled one woman, echoing the experience of others.

The pressure of events forced families apart. Some family members received permits, while others did not, and having close relations in New Zealand did not ensure permits for other kinsfolk. As a consequence, fragmented family groups or refugees travelling alone faced the trauma of leaving their homes and the problems of settling into a new country with little or no familiar support. Many people delayed plans to emigrate, hoping that their situations might improve. Others were reluctant to leave relatives, especially elderly parents who would not, or could not, escape. Eva, from Berlin, who arrived in New Zealand at the end of July 1939, had found it very difficult to make all the arrangements required to emigrate. The question of money was crucial: 'If you had money, you couldn't take it out [of Germany]. If you had no money, they wouldn't take you.' She had also delayed her departure for as long as possible. 'I am an only child and I didn't want to leave my parents. Then finally I got the permit and had to dash away. It was hard. I left in the nick of time before the outbreak of war. I can still see my parents standing on the platform as the train pulled out.' Subsequently Eva tried to obtain permits for her parents to join her in New Zealand, 'but it was impossible. New Zealand didn't want old people.' Her parents were later taken to Auschwitz. Alice from Breslau, Germany, received a permit in 1939 to come to New Zealand as a domestic servant. 'When I received the permit I was so excited. But actually leaving was very hard. The night before my departure, I was lying in my mother's arms. It was terrible because I knew I would never see her again or my sister and her little boy.'

Gerty from Czechoslovakia came to New Zealand in 1939 with her brother. She was only sixteen at the time. Gerty's mother was determined to arrange the emigration of her two youngest children.

> My mother said, 'the sooner the better'. She literally just pushed us out. New Zealand was one of the prize places to go to, but incredibly difficult to get into. Nobody wanted us. You had to be very clever at having connections of an important sort to be able to get out and to be able to get in anywhere. People tried desperately hard to get out, to go *anywhere*. Getting here was a mixture of coincidence, luck, a fair amount of machination and skill and a certain amount of money. There was absolutely no chance for my parents to come to New Zealand too. In fact, after I left, they tried to get to Brazil, but I had another brother who by that time had been arrested and was in a concentration camp and my parents wouldn't leave without him. My mother was a tremendous battler and she did everything from bribery to anything whatever to try and arrange his release, but failed. In the end my parents were arrested and they didn't survive.

Esther was born and brought up in a small town not far from Frankfurt. It was in places like this that 'much of the cruelty and pushing round of Jews happened at first'. When Esther's father was beaten up, the family decided to move to Berlin. While their furniture was being packed into a van, the person who had bought their house grabbed a table from the van saying, 'I'll have that.' The day before, this man had tried to push Esther's father down a flight of stairs. Incidents of these kinds were very common, especially in the rural areas. In that small town not one Jewish person survived.

Those last months before departure were lived in fear. Alice remembered the situation in Breslau:

> In November 1938, they started smashing up all the Jewish shops. That was a horror night. We could hear it being smashed up and all the cameras and perfumes were thrown on the road. We thought that we were next. We had the blinds down and between the blinds we were watching. When I couldn't stand it anymore, I hid behind the wardrobe. The following day, early in the morning, my brother-in-law was taken away to Dachau [concentration camp]. He didn't even have time to put his socks on before they took him away. My nerves were torn. I never knew what the next day would bring.

Ingrid left Vienna for New Zealand in September 1938. She had many memories of the threats and intimidation that were part of everyday life at that time: 'they treated Jews like animals. We lived in fear. You never went out on the street without a toothbrush in case you were picked up. When there was a knock on the door, one didn't dare open it.'

By the late 1930s, people were frantic to leave, but they faced enormous difficulties in arranging their departure. Aside from the financial obstacles already mentioned, Ingrid recalled that 'they tortured people with red tape, with regulations impossible to fulfil. To get a passport, you might have to stand in queues all night. Then the SS would come and make you go to the end of the line again'. New Zealand's own 'red tape' also endangered the lives of the refugees. As several interviewees recalled, 'the authorities were ignorant of the urgency of our situation. New Zealand wasn't really aware that they had to save people.'

The survival of refugees depended on chance happenings, strokes of good fortune and individual acts of kindness. Anna had a lucky encounter, which probably saved her own life as well as those of her husband, Peter, and their small daughter. Late in 1938, she was desperate to leave Vienna for a neutral country.

> I remember hundreds and hundreds of refugees standing outside the Swiss Embassy. I was waiting there surrounded on all sides by people wanting a permit to enter Switzerland. People were crying. Eventually a man came by – tall, very good looking, well dressed. I thought he must be an official. As he went into the Embassy, people tried to waylay him. He waved them away. I went behind him, not quite aware of what I was doing. It looked as though I was his secretary and I was allowed through the door. It turned out that the official was the ambassador. I talked to him. I showed him a picture of my one-year old child. I said to him 'you know what will

happen to us, to my child, if we don't get out of Vienna?' And he said, 'I can't tell you how much I feel for you. I would do anything to help but my hands are bound'. Then I cried and he asked me to return at 5pm that day. 'I will take a risk to help you,' he said. So we prepared for departure and returned to the embassy at 5 o'clock. But only the ambassador's deputy was there and he asked 'what do you want?' I told him that the ambassador had promised to help us, but this man, a Nazi, was about to throw me out. Just then the ambassador arrived and told the deputy this was not a concern of his and asked him to leave. Then he handed me the permits. With the last of our money we took a taxi to the station and boarded the train for Zurich.

HOPES AND FIRST IMPRESSIONS

New Zealand's distance from the conflict in Europe appealed to many of the women. Some imagined life would be easier in a small country. Others hoped for a haven for Jews, a place free from anti-Semitism. Supporters of Weimar and left-wing political ideologies were excited by the prospect of 'going to a country with one of the first labour governments of the western world', a government that was introducing important social legislation. New Zealand's reputation for beautiful scenery – forests, mountains, and beaches – attracted others. There were also expectations of a country with a moderate, benevolent climate, a subtropical island or a 'land of eternal spring'.

Most were prepared to take New Zealand on trust. 'I didn't mind what New Zealand was like. I was just so pleased to be somewhere. I was sick and tired of moving around. I just wanted to settle down,' Gisi recalled. She had come to New Zealand with her husband and young son from Ausburg, near Munich, Germany. 'I felt very lucky to have got to New Zealand' was a statement frequently made by female interviewees. It reveals that this country offered what was most important for these women and their families: a home at last, somewhere in the world.

Some hopes and expectations were met during those first weeks and months in New Zealand; others were abandoned forever. Wellington's harbour and the views from the hills, for example, met the expectations of some wanting to find a beautiful landscape. Later the hills seemed bleak, sparse, raw, rough, overwhelming and enclosing. Refugees were struck by the poor, dilapidated appearance of the cities and the countryside. There was no obvious poverty as in Europe, but everything looked unkempt and unpainted. Lily travelled to New Zealand from Czechoslovakia in January 1940 with her husband Frank. Wellington did not feel like a city to Lily; it reminded her of the countryside that one visited on vacations. Yet the landscape was 'wrong'. She recalled a friend saying that being in Wellington was like being on summer holiday. All the greenery around contributed to this impression, but the holiday was not 'right' – it was somehow 'spoilt'. The small, wooden houses, the lack of cafés and restaurants, everything shut by late afternoon – these facts were a surprise for some refugees and a major shock for others. Auckland was the first New Zealand city that Vera from Czechoslovakia had seen. She arrived with her husband, Kurt, and two small children in 1939. 'We walked round the streets and looked up at the shops. We were in Herne Bay. At that time it was very shoddy.'

Encounters with New Zealanders featured prominently in the early impressions of refugee women. Helga was struck by the kindness of New Zealanders. She arrived in Wellington from Czechoslovakia at the end of 1939. Her last memory of Europe was the rudeness and arrogance of the officials to the migrants. Arriving in New Zealand, the passport officials greeted her with a friendly 'How are you?' and 'Are you all right?' 'It was such a relief: it was as though a great burden like a stone dropped from your heart.' Ingrid was also impressed by the friendliness of the officials she first encountered. Arriving in trepidation on a four-week visitors' permit, she was told by the customs officer who examined her arrival papers, 'You can't see our wonderful country in four weeks', and he stamped six months on the permit.

Some women's first contacts with New Zealanders were less positive. Lily became aware that a local shopkeeper was making comments against foreigners. When she confronted the woman and offered to buy her bread elsewhere, the shopkeeper protested, 'Oh, no, no, it's quite all right'. Other early impressions mentioned were different foods, peculiar smells, strange colours, old-fashioned clothes, drunken people in the streets and much else. The significance of these recollections lies not in the importance of any *one* of them: it was the cumulative effect of all the differences that overwhelmed refugee women. As one pointed out: 'It is not the important things that actually seem to get you down in the so-called culture shock, but the small things which make you feel completely strange.'

NEW SETTLERS

Finding somewhere to live was the most urgent task faced by newcomers. Friends and relations, guarantors and the Jewish Welfare Society assisted with searches for accommodation. The society appealed to Jewish community members to provide temporary dwellings.[13] In Wellington, four rooms behind the synagogue were available for the refugees.[14] Magda from Salzburg, Austria, arrived in Wellington four days before the outbreak of war. She came with her two small children, her husband and sister-in-law. The family lived in two rooms behind the synagogue for six months. This already cramped accommodation became even more crowded when the family were obliged to share the space with other refugees also needing urgent temporary accommodation.

Initially some new arrivals stayed with relatives or friends, who were often recent migrants themselves. Eva boarded with a cousin. 'They were very hard up. I didn't have my own room, but slept on a couch in the living room. I had to pay board because as I said they were not rich. My cousin had been a lawyer in Germany, but here he worked in a factory.' Several of the women who came to New Zealand unaccompanied by family found jobs with live-in accommodation. For Alice, the housekeeping job she held until her marriage was a chance to earn a living and it provided a roof over her head. It also afforded a degree of security and helped to improve her English. Rental accommodation was in short supply and frequently unappealing.

Several women spoke of how uncomfortable they were in their first New Zealand dwellings. Franci ventured to New Zealand from Germany in February 1940 with her husband and young daughter. In the family's first flat in the Wellington suburb of Northland there was only one electric point in the entire house, in the kitchen. There were two fireplaces, but nowhere to plug in heaters or lamps by which to read in bed. For several women, accustomed to central heating, one of the worst aspects of local housing was its unsuitability for the climate. Kati, who came here from Czechoslovakia with her parents, remembered sitting in front of a little bar heater and freezing: 'It was assumed that you could survive indoors in temperatures very like those outdoors. Houses were not insulated; they were simply made of weatherboards. The floors were just floorboards on top of nothing. The outside temperature and wind came right into the house.'

A number of the women described the houses they first lived in or visited in New Zealand as 'primitive'. Some, from comfortable middle-class backgrounds, noticed the absence of objects and comforts that they took for granted at home – Persian carpets, ornaments, pictures on the wall and, above all, warmth and comfort. Their observations of dwellings devoid of comfort or attractiveness were based on their encounters with working-class conditions in New Zealand. This was certainly so for Vera and her family. Forced to leave Auckland because of a lack of employment opportunities for her husband (he was a geologist), the couple headed to a South Island mining settlement. In an unpublished account, written many years later, Vera vividly described the conditions that they had encountered. She wrote of the black coal range and of an outbuilding used as a washhouse with its wooden tub, copper and bath: 'The water had to be scooped in and out of the bath with a bucket as there was no sewerage. There was a water tank for rainwater from the roof piped into the kitchen sink, and an outside toilet to be emptied. There was no telephone or radio.'

For women from prosperous, middle-class backgrounds, life in these 'primitive' dwellings meant having to do housework and cooking, usually for the first time in their lives. They had been accustomed to receiving assistance around the house. Some had employed maids, chauffeurs, cooks, gardeners, someone to do the washing and someone else to assist with the children. In New Zealand, they were not in a position to afford help in their homes straightaway and demand for domestic workers was always greater than the supply. When the war started, and jobs with better pay were readily available for women, it became even more difficult to find domestic help. Some young immigrant women filled this gap themselves and earned a living as maids during their early years in New Zealand.

Overall, refugee women embarked on their new lives with energy and enthusiasm. In order to appreciate the scope of the task faced by them, one needs to understand that even in the cities, household appliances such as fridges, washing machines, vacuum cleaners, gas or electric stoves were not common until the mid-1950s. Helga had hardly ever set foot in a kitchen before coming to New Zealand. In Europe, a cook and a maid had done all the household chores. She could not cook or iron, but now had 'three men to look after, a basket full of socks to wash and three men's shirts to iron. How to wash dishes or cook a meal? It was all a problem.' She decided to seek the assistance of the man at the Chinese laundry. 'He laughed his head off, but he taught me how to iron shirts. I stayed there an hour and from then on, I could iron shirts. I can still iron a man's shirt in five minutes.' As a novice cook, however, Helga made some mistakes. On one occasion, she placed some antique silver dishes into the oven and was dismayed to find that they melted.

Herta, an amateur violinist before emigrating from Vienna, prepared herself for her life in New Zealand by obtaining recipes from her cook to bring with her. Because the demands of cooking and housework dominated her day, she gave up music. She could not combine being a musician with these household routines. Herta also thought that her hands were no longer good enough to play as well as she had done in the past. To earn additional income for her family, she started a small business baking continental cakes and sweets.

Rose had never cooked before either. Before departing for New Zealand alone in 1940, she had been a secretary in Berlin. Rose first worked as a cook and domestic servant in this country, a role she managed by studying recipes every evening before attempting to prepare meals the next day. Gerty was also quite unused to cooking and cleaning: 'I had never held a broom'. Her guarantors found her a job at a residential nursery for children. 'It was a harsh, grim place, with no toys for the children', where cleanliness and tidiness brought about by 'elbow grease' prevailed and were regarded as the greatest virtues. 'How I learned to work in that place! Not only hold a broom, but to scrub floors, and never to use disinfectant, but soap and a scrubbing brush and lots and lots of elbow grease.'

In the South Island mining settlement, Vera 'tried hard to get used to the way of life of a miner's labourer'. At first the family boarded with a miner's family from Lancashire. From her kind, helpful landlady Vera learned how to make barley soup. She also encountered a round roast for the first time: 'I undid it, took out the skewers and string and boiled it up for soup.' Vera attended meetings of the Women's Institute and participated in competitions for the best scones and the best blooms. Sometimes she made Czech buns (*buchty*) with jam, which were very much liked by the other women. The task she disliked the most was cleaning that black stove, the coal range. 'At home, I had a maid for the hard work and we had a Dutch tile stove which didn't need to be polished every week. Here, there was a paste called Zebo that you used for polishing the stove and it had to shine! I remember cleaning this black coal range, the tears mixing with the soot on my face.'

Not all of the women had been sheltered from housework before coming to New Zealand. Alice had helped her mother in the house and had also assisted others in the family with cooking and household tasks. The transition to doing domestic work in New Zealand was not a new way of life for her, but it did mean that she had to learn some of the basics of local cuisine, such as how to make sponges and pikelets.

For the newcomers, a minor, though not insignificant, adjustment in domestic life was the need to become accustomed to a less varied diet. Some familiar foods tasted different. Others were unobtainable. Salami and European-type sausages, a range of cheeses including cottage cheese and yoghurts, spices, caraway seeds, real coffee and rye bread were the foods most missed. The refugees disliked mutton, especially its smell in butcher shops. Some foods were strange but not unappealing: porridge and Weet-bix and Christmas cake made with suet. Women often made the foods they were unable to obtain in the shops. Some made their own bread from rye flour ordered from the South Island. Others made yoghurt. Continental cuts of meat could not be bought from New Zealand butchers, but women adapted available cuts to their own needs with little difficulty.

Another example of the energy put into adapting to the new country was the effort many of the women put into learning or improving their English. Although some spoke the language fluently, many were proficient in a literary version inadequate for everyday communication, or knew English 'by the book', a knowledge that did not relate closely with how it was actually spoken. Helga started to learn English en route to the new country. She began by memorising Macbeth's speech 'To-morrow, and to-morrow, and to-morrow', as well as some poems by Rupert Brooke. On her arrival at Wellington, she noticed the inscription of Brooke's verse on the cenotaph.

English classes for new arrivals with little or no English were organised by the Workers' Educational Association (WEA) and by the Jewish Welfare Society. Those of school age learned the language at school, though not in special classes, as the government made no provision for newcomers to learn English. Mostly refugees were left to their own resources. Usually people learned at work. Women at home had to find other means of learning. Vera borrowed *The Forsyte Saga*, which she had already read in translation, from the library.

All refugees shared the desire to acquire at least adequate English as quickly as possible, but their attitude to their first languages and to German culture generally was diverse and complicated. German was that 'filthy tongue', a language 'infested with great bestialities' and 'polluted' by Hitler.[15] It was also the language of a beloved literature, of Goethe, Schiller, Kleist and Heine. Attempting to reconcile the best in German culture, a culture most refugees had identified with and admired, with Hitler's regime led to contradictory and conflicting attitudes towards the language they had recently experienced as a roar of hate.

Gerty tried to forget that German was her own tongue and would not speak or read it until many years later. Eva wanted to free her children from the burdens of the past and have them grow up as New Zealanders, fully belonging in the new country. She saw the use of English in the family as a key to achieving these objectives. Rose, who married a non-German speaking New Zealander a few years after her arrival, avoided that language as a means of 'minimising splits in the family'.

When Vera spoke occasionally to her children in Czech, her husband was cross. 'He wanted us to speak English with the children all the time, so that they didn't get behind local children in their school work.' He also complained if Vera spoke too much Czech at home as he believed his own English, which he needed for his work, suffered. 'So we tried to speak English all the time ourselves and to bring the children up in English.'

The inadequacies of their own English did not deter many refugees from using it as the family language. 'Better the worst English, than the best German' was a common attitude, but not everyone adopted this view. Ingrid decided that the children could not learn proper English from her. She taught both of her sons German, which they learned to speak very well. Many children, even when brought up speaking Czech or German, eagerly adopted English as soon as they went to school. Lily's son, born in 1941, was brought up to speak Czech. 'When he went to school, he complained he couldn't understand his schoolmates.' From that moment on, Lily and her husband spoke English to each other and to their son. At that time, they saw Czech as having little relevance or application in New Zealand. Vera thought differently. After the family moved to Wellington from the mining settlement in the early 1940s, she attempted to teach Czech to the children of other refugees. She established a conversation class at the Wellington Czech Club. 'Perhaps eight children went, but the classes only continued for a few weeks. One by one people dropped out. The parents had no interest in it. Everybody wanted their children to get on and become New Zealanders.'

SOCIAL LIFE

Compared with the intensely active cultural life they had enjoyed in their cities of origin, the limited range of activities available in New Zealand greatly disappointed the refugees. Professional theatre, ballet, symphony orchestras and chamber music hardly existed. Cafés and restaurants were not yet a common feature of New Zealand city life. But there were professional musicians,[16] amateur theatre,[17] touring theatre companies and visiting musicians from overseas. There was also the cinema. Although many women missed the activities they had once enjoyed, most agreed that, set against what they had escaped from, these were small losses indeed. Alice, who settled in Hamilton, explained: 'Breslau where I am from was a beautiful city with a Jewish community large enough to sustain three or four synagogues. The city had lovely parks, concert halls, theatres, an opera house, restaurants. But I didn't miss all that in Hamilton. I had enjoyed that life while I was young. [After the troubles started] I just wanted to be safe.'

Female refugees were determined to be good settlers and tried to appreciate the forms of cultural life and entertainment that were available. For Rose, books, plays, dance classes, learning to play the piano and generally making one's own entertainment were rewarding experiences. Vera's social life and entertainment consisted of the *New Zealand Herald* in the morning, the books available in the small local library, the meetings of the Women's Institute and the occasional pictures or dances held in the local hall. Long hours spent working meant that there was little time to participate in the cultural life that was available in New Zealand. Magda recalled that in her early years in New Zealand, with small children and all the housework to do, she did not have the time to like or dislike her new life.

For women with the spare time and energy for socialising, the absence of places to meet friends – especially coffee houses and restaurants – was a disadvantage. 'It is the little things which make your life that you miss the most,' recalled Anna. 'The coffee house is really very important because it is your social life and your home into which people can come [without a formal invitation]. Without coffee houses you have to invite people and prepare for them.' The necessity to formally reciprocate hospitality was hard for people who could not do so for health or financial reasons. Anna explained: 'In a Viennese coffee house you can still sit all day and read newspapers from different countries, see your friends but spend very little money'.

Gisi, like Rose, enjoyed what was available. She fondly remembered going to the cinema with friends and afterwards to a milk bar for an ice cream or a cup of tea. 'For somewhere special, we went to the St. George Hotel and sat in the lounge. There would be nobody there. We called it the "Palm Lounge."' The milk bars were 'so funny' and so strange for refugees accustomed to cafés. When Wellington's first coffee house, the French Maid, was eventually opened in Lambton Quay refugees gathered there to meet friends and drink good coffee, the availability of which coincided with the arrival of United States servicemen.

Another meeting place, recalled by Gerty, was the Czech Club, known to refugees as the 'Coffee House'. Here people played cards, and there was music. Sometimes picnics were organised. Social occasions such as weddings were celebrated. Members helped each other trace relatives and shared information about matters of mutual concern. They also participated in various 'patriotic' activities such as celebrating the Czech national day and singing Czech songs. Especially in wartime, the Czech Club was a great refuge for people who were not Czechs at all but Jewish refugees of German or Austrian nationality.

Many women relied on each other for their social life and social support, but others were determined not to do so, even at the very beginning. Becoming fully integrated meant having New Zealand friends. Initially these local people were their sponsors or guarantors, and later work colleagues, fellow students and neighbours. Valuable contacts and sometimes friendships developed through involvement with Plunket, play groups and other voluntary associations relating to children and their diverse activities. New Zealand acquaintances were generally regarded as kind, helpful, friendly and tolerant. After their dismal experiences in Europe, refugees did not expect kindness and seemed especially grateful whenever they encountered it. When she first arrived in Hamilton, Alice boarded with a New Zealand family 'who were like mother and father' to her:

> They put a hot water bottle in my bed at night and wrapped my nightie around it. I taught them German songs and we sang them together at the top of our voices. They washed my hair, took me for drives and said to me, 'Always feel at home with us'. Their two small daughters would get into my bed in the weekends and taught me English from their little reading books. These people became my lifelong friends.

While appreciating the kindness of certain people, some women were aware of a lack of 'common ground' between themselves and ordinary New Zealanders. Social class accentuated these differences. Gerty's first job at a residential nursery isolated her from both her fellow refugees and New Zealander intellectuals.

> I was a great reader at home, in philosophy, literature and matters of social concern. Ideas were very important to me. When I came here, I found that no one knew about the things I had been reading about and were important to me. I had to bury my thoughts. The hardest thing was to suddenly realise that not only people you've known, family and friends are gone, but suddenly you, yourself are nil. Everything you have known is irrelevant. What is in your mind means nothing to the New Zealander. It can't be shared. What is homesickness? It isn't missing food; it is the thoughts you can't share, the conversations you can't have. So I buried everything that was of no interest to anyone else.

Shared interests did in fact sometimes provide a common ground for friendships between refugees and some New Zealanders. Quite often these locals were themselves alienated from the mainstream by their intellectual and cultural interests. 'As a foreigner', one refugee observed, 'you were wanted. You were somebody who had been to the theatre and to the opera, who had done things, who came from a different place.' Some New Zealand writers, musicians and scholars eagerly sought out the newcomers from Europe. In this way refugees found congenial New Zealand friends and the New Zealanders gained support, encouragement and an audience.

Despite goodwill on both sides, sometimes there were misunderstandings. In several cases, refugee women were unable to move beyond superficial relationships with New Zealanders, whose reserve Franci felt, made it hard to become friends. There were few invitations to New Zealanders' homes in the early years. 'When you invited them, they didn't invite you back', said Magda.

Those refugees who became acquainted with Maori observed an ease and closeness in social relationships not encountered in the wider society. Rose lived and worked in a Maori community for several months during her third year in New Zealand.

> In some kind of way, I felt more at home, and particularly comfortable with the Maori people. I found it very moving the way people want to get to know each other, the voluntary togetherness, the warmth, which [wasn't] really in existence anywhere else in New Zealand, to that extent. It is something to do with really being accepted, no matter who you are.

Similarly, Vera was accepted by and made friends with the Maori women she met in the mining settlement. Many thought that she had Maori ancestry on account of her dark complexion and dark hair. Cooking, housework and children provided the links for these friendships to develop. Alice, on the other hand, worked as a housekeeper for a Scottish couple and felt rejected by them at a time of personal tragedy:

> My parents and sister and her son were taken to Theresienstadt and later Auschwitz where they were killed. When I got the news of their death through the Red Cross, I lay on the bed and cried and cried. The Scottish woman, my employer, came and asked, 'What is the matter? Why do you cry?' I told her what I had just heard and she said, 'You cry like a foreigner'. She meant I cried too loud, with too much abandon, that British people show proper reserve – they wouldn't cry in such an uncontrolled way. But my heart was breaking, so I cried, with my head down on the bed.

DIFFERENT WORLDS

Refugee women's observations of the strange characteristics displayed by the New Zealanders they encountered were partly accurate, but they also reflected their initial cultural bewilderment. For instance, their inability to correctly place people in the social hierarchy resulted in the mistaken view that New Zealand was an egalitarian society with no significant class divisions. Alice noticed that men were more likely to help in the home that in Europe. Helga thought that 'women were less likely to put men on a pedestal but nagged at them and ordered them about'. She also noticed that married couples did not touch or demonstrate affection in public. 'At home we would never walk through the street without being arm in arm. You never saw that here.' Gisi found the behaviour of men and women at social gatherings quite unusual. The men stood on one side of the room, women on the other. Both were stiff and full of inhibitions. Among the men there would be much talk of beer and sport. The drinking habits of New Zealand males astonished Helga, who arrived in Wellington just before Christmas in 1939. She was accustomed to the quiet, festive celebrations at home, but in Wellington, the Christmas spirit was evident in the number of drunken people on the streets. Helga's neighbour asked her to hide several bottles of beer from his wife who was trying to stop him getting drunk.

In the eyes of New Zealanders, the refugees were a curiosity. 'People stared at me in the bus because I knitted a different way, because my shoes were a different style,' Hannah from Germany remembered. Gerty, who boarded at the nursery where she worked, had to endure the comments of other residents each time she did her washing and hung out her clothes on the line. 'Did you see Gertrud's washing? All those little bits, ha, ha, ha.' The 'little bits' referred to her underwear, which were small and modern compared with the big bloomers worn by New Zealand women at the time. Kati also remembered neighbours' comments about her family's belongings. 'They would inquire about our big pillowcases and duvets. After a while it got on one's nerves.' Refugee women were also irritated by conversations occasioned by buying food different from that usually eaten by New Zealanders. This invited wonder and questions about how it was cooked. Although curiosity was sometimes annoying, it was not necessarily unpleasant. Nonetheless, the insularity of some New Zealanders led to unpleasant comments about people who looked different or who behaved differently from themselves. When Esther hung out her washing on Good Friday, her first in New Zealand, a neighbour yelled over the fence: 'These foreigners, they don't know our customs, hanging out the washing on our holiest day'.

Work

Sewing, cleaning, cooking, childcare, shop work – whatever their previous background, many of the jobs refugee women did when they first arrived fell into one of those categories. Men who were young and healthy had a far greater variety of jobs to choose from. Newcomers did have opportunities to train and to study, but these were also more limited for women than for men. By 1945, 657 refugees were said to be 'engaged in fulltime gainful occupation', with 'one-third of the married women ... supplementing the family income with fulltime or part-time work'. The main occupations of the refugees (their gender not stated) were as follows:[18]

- 123 own businesses, including 22 women working in the family business
- 166 working in one of the professions
- 80 health professions
- 16 nursing
- 251 mainly in domestic duties
- 12 domestic helps
- 15 mechanics
- 19 other skilled
- 18 other semi-skilled
- 15 clerks

As already mentioned, when they first arrived several single women without families in New Zealand obtained work in institutions that offered accommodation. Entering the totally foreign environment of these places was an overwhelming and disorientating experience. When Gerty arrived in New Zealand aged sixteen, she spoke no English and had no practical skills. She believed she had no choice but to accept a job at a residential children's nursery. It was a strict, tough place with few toys for the pre-schoolers, although 'care and kindness' for the residents and the staff were not 'totally absent'.

Domestic service was another avenue of employment for newly arrived refugee women, especially as these workers were in short supply in New Zealand. Rose, who had been a secretary in Berlin, began her working life here as a maid. 'At my first job I was supposed to keep very much in my place. I was not permitted to mix with friends of the family or with the family. I was discouraged from talking to my employer's friends and had my meals in the kitchen.' Although Rose could not cook at first, she started offering dishes such as *wiener schnitzel*, which soon became very popular with the family and their visitors.

Alice worked as a milliner during the day and as a domestic in the evening and during the weekends. In return for doing washing, dishes, putting out trays and making toast for the other residents, her room at the boarding house was free. It was very hard to juggle two jobs, but being young she somehow 'managed it all'. Eva had some experience as a dressmaker, but her first job sewing in New Zealand was still a struggle. 'I could sew', she explained, 'but what was expected of you in New Zealand was different. They gave you a bundle a cloth and it was up to you to put it together'.

Franci's first job was in a cake shop where she learned to make New Zealand cakes, scones and pies. She was her family's main breadwinner when they arrived. Her husband, who had been a judge in Germany, faced enormous difficulties in this country, as did other members of the legal profession, because requalification as a lawyer involved five years' university study.

> He tried, at first, to give German lessons for a living but people would agree to have lessons, then they would cancel. Of course, when war broke out, no one wanted

lessons at all. We were told by a member of the Wellington Refugee Committee that for my husband there were only two possibilities to make a living: the first was to be a 'married couple' in the country, the second to buy a dairy. But my husband couldn't have done the man's job of being a 'married couple', which was gardening. He didn't have the health or the strength. So it had to be a dairy, not just a shop but a dairy. We were advised not to buy a grocery shop, where people have a choice to go to a New Zealander. There had to be no competition. People had to be forced to go there.

With the help of the Refugee Committee, the couple bought a dairy and the skills Franci had acquired at the cake shop were put to good use.

Several refugees with entrepreneurial skills, ingenuity and willingness to work hard established businesses that became successful in the years ahead. The ventures were quite novel for New Zealand and led to a valuable diversification of the economy. Women played a crucial part in the success of these new businesses. The aim of building a secure future for the next generation provided motivation for the drudgery involved. Eva recalled the struggle to establish her family business – a drapery and family outfitters:

> Our two bedroom flat was filled with boxes of clothes for sale, stored under the bed. [My husband] was out all day, Saturdays too, from seven in the morning until late at night, carrying six or seven suitcases. And, he wasn't young, a man already in his fifties. It was very, very hard. That's how we started the business, with nothing. My husband worked to become again what he was before. And if you have a child, as we did, you work for him too. We wanted our son brought up properly. We didn't want to leave him in the lurch without anything. So we worked! If you want to achieve something you have to work very hard.

Ingrid and her husband also built a family business from small beginnings. 'My husband obtained goods, which were in short supply, from refugee friends living in Wellington and sold them in Palmerston North where we were living.' He was away all week selling elastic, combs, candles or whatever else was a scarce and sought-after commodity. As well as caring for her young child, Ingrid contributed to building the business in a variety of ways. On one occasion, she had to iron three hundred blouses in preparation for selling them. Another story of a married couple working together to build a successful business is that of Anna and her husband. Although the couple faced a precarious financial situation, they opened a shop specialising in imported goods and commodities 'catering for the continental taste'. It was the first shop of this type in the city. 'It became a success from the word go' and brought them a great deal of satisfaction.

Women not only struggled to become doctors, teachers, nurses and physiotherapists, but supported the men who undertook courses to requalify in their professions. Their experiences in gaining admission and acceptance were quite diverse. Nurses, for example, received a warm welcome. The profession

Above: Steerage passengers in the 'tween decks, *Illustrated London News* 17 April, 1850. Migrant women travelling to New Zealand from Britain and Ireland during the nineteenth century were more likely to be found below decks among the domestic servants and the wives of farm labourers than in the saloon with the first and second class passengers. *(Canterbury Museum, ref 8353)*

Below: John Pearse, 'Doings on the Duke of Portland [1851]. Gally [sic]'. *(ATL, ref. D-P455010-EF11-)*

Above: Arthur Lagden Haylock (1860–1948), the *Chile* at Timaru, *c.* 1879. The medical journal of Millen Coughtrey, a surgeon on the *Chile* in 1873, provides evidence that physical and sexual assaults took place within marriage on nineteenth-century voyages to New Zealand. *(ATL, ref. F-151215-1/2-)*

Below: This photograph by William Williams (1859–1948), shows crew and passengers on board the *Pleione*, *c.* 1880s. *(E.R. Williams Bequest, ATL, ref. G-25553-1/1-)*

Above left: Kilkenny-born Ellen Walsh (1849–1922) ran the Helvetia Hotel in Goldsborough with her Swiss-Italian husband, Guiglio Piezzi. Ellen married Dennis Maher at Rimu in 1883, seven years after Guiglio's sudden death, and moved to Wellington in the late 1890s where she continued her involvement in the hotel trade. *(Courtesy of Teresa O'Connor)*

Above right: Bridget Pfahlert (*née* Quinn) of County Clare married her German-born husband, Ernst, at All Saint's Anglican Church, Hokitika, in 1868. By the 1880s it was extremely rare for Irish Catholic women to marry in Protestant churches. *(West Coast Historical Museum, ref. 5918)*

Below: This photograph shows Ellen Maher (Walsh-Piezzi) in the doorway of the Helvetia Hotel at Goldsborough c. 1895. The three children from Ellen's marriage to Dennis Maher are standing beside her: (L to R) Ellen, John and Veronica. *(West Coast Historical Museum)*

Above left: Jane Ryall of Barrytown is said to have walked the beach each evening saying the rosary 'because she believed the breeze blew straight from Ireland'. She is pictured here with her husband, Denis, and their children. *(West Coast Historical Museum, ref 997)*

Above right: Emele-Moa Teo Fairbairn's father, Teo Tuvale, in his official uniform, probably in the 1890s. He was Chief Justice and Secretary to Government during the German Administration of Samoa. *(Courtesy of Peggy Fairbairn-Dunlop)*

Below: 'A group of lady immigrants appear satisfied with their first impressions'.
(Source: New Zealand Government Publicity Office, New Zealand: The Country, Its People and Resources, *Wellington, 1926, p. 8.)*

Emele's mother, Naitua, was the daughter of Tanugamanono and Tapasu from the Tofaeono Aiga at Siumu. 'My parents met on the ship going to Germany in the late 1890s. My father Teo Tuvale was part of the official delegation to Kaiser Wilhelm's celebrations, and my mother was a member of the cultural group accompanying the delegation. This photo was taken in the 1920s, after Teo had passed away.' *(Courtesy of Peggy Fairbairn-Dunlop)*

Left: The beginning of Emele-Moa Teo Fairbairn's big adventure. 'I had to chase the children for this photo because they were so scared of the camera and because they didn't want to go to New Zealand. Even when it was time to go out to the boat, I couldn't find Ian. Jim had gone first to New Zealand and had our house ready for us in Kilbirnie. [*L to R*] Jimmy, Mabel, Rex sitting on my knee. Alfred leaning against me, and Ian on the right.' *(Courtesy of Peggy Fairbairn-Dunlop)*

Below: Letty Brown is shown here with her husband, John, and their four children, c. 1968. *(Courtesy Aroha Harris).*

Right: Mrs Sai Louie outside her family home in Parnell, Auckland, *c.* **1905. Although there were no specific laws against Chinese women's immigration, archival records show that women were regarded by the New Zealand authorities as potentially more menacing than their men, because they could procreate.** *(Courtesy of Manying Ip).*

Below: Chinese women in Edwardian fineries. *(Courtesy of Manying Ip)*

Above: 'Some of the party of 30 Chinese refugees from the Canton area who have been brought to the Dominion by relatives in New Zealand'. The escalation of the Sino-Chinese War in south China led to the temporary opening of New Zealand to the wives and minor children of Chinese men who already had permanent resident status. *(*New Zealand Herald, *11 October 1939, p. 13.)*

Below: Opening ceremony of the New Zealand Chinese Women's Association, Auckland, 1995. Manying Ip is pictured 'dotting the eye of the lion'. *(Courtesy of Manying Ip)*

acknowledged a shortage in nursing staff and encouraged the government to lift restrictions that had limited the number of foreign nurses admitted to New Zealand to only ten persons annually. For trained nurses who settled in this country, arrangements were made to 'open the doors' of the profession by giving them one year's experience in a hospital training school before sitting the state examination.[19] Mary Isabel Lambi, director of nursing between 1931 and 1950, wrote personally to Gerty offering her assistance and welcome to the profession. Physiotherapists, on the other hand, attempted to place restrictions on the number of refugees admitted for re-qualification. Dentists also met considerable opposition from the New Zealand Dental Association.[20] It was the medical practitioners, however, who faced the most difficulties in re-establishing themselves in New Zealand. The need to undertake further study to re-qualify as a doctor imposed a huge burden on refugees. Lack of financial resources was only one of the obstacles for Maria, who had German and Italian medical qualifications that she had hoped would be accepted in New Zealand. When they were not recognised, she was unable to spend three years in Dunedin obtaining further qualifications. Maria had a small child and her husband's job with its very modest salary was in Wellington. Emma was one of several women who supported families while their husbands re-qualified as doctors. As her son recalled:

> In the first years of the war, my mother could still give one or two concerts and sing on the radio. After that, German music could not be performed in public, though she still sang privately. She earned money by giving German lessons, music lessons and by running a boarding house for students. What my parents did was to rent a large house, live in two rooms of it and sublet the rest of the house. There was also a big yard, which my mother turned into a vegetable garden. We were able to live in part on what she grew and on the rent the students who lived with us paid. These sources of money and my mother's lessons saw us through. My mother told a story from this period of her life in Dunedin. At this time she was still giving a number of concerts. One morning, a journalist from the *Evening Star* arrived to interview her. He came to the door asking, 'is Madame … at home?' My mother, who had been scrubbing the stairs and had an old tracksuit on, answered the door. She said to the journalist, 'I'll go and see if I can find her'. She then went upstairs and changed her clothes and came down again.

CHILDREN

The hard work and the struggle to become re-established was for the next generation. Women's work and energy went into the creation of new families and ensuring their well-being and security. For refugees who arrived in New Zealand with small children the difficulties of settling were particularly acute. Combining paid employment with caring for children, finding suitable accommodation, a trustworthy doctor, a good school and many other aspects of daily life required immediate attention. Anna and her husband both needed to work and had to find someone to care for their young daughter. She noticed a newspaper advertisement in which a New Zealand family offered 'to take a refugee child and to look after it till the family is settled'. Anna hoped that this was the solution to their problems, but the arrangement did not work out as her daughter was 'a nervous child because we had moved so often from one place to another' and did not settle with the family. She 'cried whole nights'. Moreover, the local family did not behave particularly generously for 'when the woman's own son had a birthday she gave him a big present, but nothing to [my daughter] living in the same house'.

Several women became new mothers in the first few years after arriving in New Zealand. For Ingrid, managing without the support of an extended family was the greatest difficulty. 'It was hard to have a baby and only strange people around you.' She found the hospital care and the Plunket nurses 'wonderful', yet her husband was frequently absent as he struggled to earn a living and Ingrid spent a great deal of time alone with the new baby. 'When the baby cried, I thought it was ill; when not crying, I thought it was dead.' Despite the struggle, the birth of children in the early years of settlement symbolised roots being planted in a strange land. The activities associated with raising a family helped refugee women to achieve a sense of belonging in a new country.

From Refugee to Enemy Alien

Tensions aroused by the settlement of the refugees increased when war began. There were calls on the government to set up an administrative system to identify fifth columnists from the resident aliens in New Zealand. Refugees from Nazi Europe were among those regarded as potential fifth columnists. The Alien Emergency Regulations, under which the government could deport, intern and set up authorities and tribunals to investigate and classify aliens came into being in October 1940, and the accompanying administrative machinery was set to work in the following months. Most refugees from Germany and Austria were classified as enemy aliens, which meant that they escaped internment but were subject to certain rules. These included restrictions on the possession of articles such as arms, maps, radios with shortwave reception, cameras and x-ray equipment. Some places of residence were forbidden for enemy aliens. They had to register with the police and if aliens in a restricted area were moving more than twenty-four miles from their usual residence or if expected to be absent from there for more than twenty-four hours they had to obtain a permit. Refugees also faced restrictions on their employment and, most significantly, were excluded from service in the armed forces.[21]

The system of classification that was set up did not usually inflict great hardship on the refugees. In part this was because, coming from Germany and

Austria, they were accustomed to registering and reporting to the police, so the requirement to do so in New Zealand was not unexpected. It also seemed understandable that refugees, who a short time previously had been living in enemy territory, should now come under close scrutiny. The hardship that refugees did suffer during the war years was due less to the wartime regulations than to the hostile and suspicious attitudes of employers, colleagues and neighbours. Although some women escaped hostility and harassment, for others the climate of suspicion affected every aspect of their lives.

The police investigated all refugees on behalf of the Aliens Authorities. For refugees from Czechoslovakia this was usually only an informal chat with the local policeman. Kati recalled that the policeman 'came to the house, had a cup of tea and said, "I'm sorry, this is what I have to do. Now you tell me how to fill out these forms and I'll do it".' Refugees from Austria and Germany were supposed to undergo a thorough investigation. Some did so. Gisi and her husband were both interviewed at length by the police: 'They were very suspicious'. Alice, however, recalled only the kindness of the New Zealand police who questioned her.

> When I had to report to the police station in Hamilton, I was very anxious and frightened and my English was very bad. But there was such a lovely inspector there. He offered me a cup of tea. The station was a cosy place. There was a bird singing in a cage. The inspector said to me, 'Don't need to worry now, you are in New Zealand'. From then on, I never had any worries about being safe here.

Later on in Wellington, where she was working as a housekeeper, the police approached Alice again. 'My employer became very agitated: "A policeman, a policeman at the door!" But I was calm, not worried. I hadn't done anything. After the Nazis, the New Zealand police didn't worry me.' At the Wellington police station, Alice again met with kindness.

> There was a detective sitting there, typing what I said. He had tears in his eyes and said, 'My dear little girl, the best thing is for you to get married. Marry a New Zealander, become a New Zealand citizen and you never need worry again.' I protested that my English was too bad for that, but he said, 'Oh no, you don't need to worry, my dear, as long as you know what "I love you" means.'

Emma's son recalled that his parents had only 'nice stories to tell about the police in Dunedin' and that the inspector in charge of aliens became a close friend of theirs.

> We had trouble with suspicious neighbours who thought that we Germans must be spies. We lived only 100 yards from the beach and when we went swimming or walked on the beach, some very 'patriotic' people would ring the police saying we were sending messages to German submarines and other accusations of this kind. Every time the police received such a complaint, they had to investigate it, at least in a perfunctory kind of way. My mother would say to me: 'the Inspector has rung

to say, "[Madame . . .] I have reason to come and visit you again to ask you a few questions. I'll be round tomorrow, which will give you time to bake a nice apple cake." He used to love my mother's apple strudel. He would come and eat and drink, ask a few questions, and write a report. This was no real trouble to my parents. I don't think they ever felt persecuted. They were very philosophic about such incidents because, in general, people were very friendly.

By contrast, some refugees had a hard time. Hannah from Germany moved to a small South Island town in 1943 with her husband and small baby. She was aware that under wartime regulations a change of residence had to be notified within twenty-four hours. But because of the baby's illness, bad weather and other difficulties, she was late reporting to the police by a few hours. For this she received a summons. The magistrate refused to suppress her name and she was fined for infringing the regulations. Frightened by the publicity and the disgrace, it seemed like the worst moment of her life.

Ruth from Germany, who worked at Hanmer Hospital, had considerable difficulty with the wartime regulations. 'To go further than a certain distance, one needed a permit, yet I had to go to Christchurch to get a permit ... I needed a permit in order to get a permit.' Although she infringed the regulations through no fault of her own, this young woman came under the constant scrutiny of the authorities:

> Police kept questioning the people I stayed with in Christchurch. I had to give up going [there] to spare them the trouble. The police would ask my friends questions such as 'What did I think of the British Army?' All my letters were censored, but not my parcels. If a friend wanted to send me something, she would send the message in a cigar box.

At times, the close surveillance of the police amounted to harassment. When she was holidaying in Rotorua, the police came to her hotel every day, asking questions. 'I think they took advantage of my being a woman on my own'.

One very serious consequence of the enemy alien label allotted some refugees was the difficulties faced by men in participating with New Zealanders in the war effort against their common enemy. For women, the situation was easier. Their efforts on the home front were usually acceptable to New Zealanders and the fact that they were spared the long separation from husbands, fathers or brothers at a time of struggle in a new country must have been a relief for them.

A serious consequence of the enemy alien label for women was dismissal from their jobs. This was a bitter experience for refugees as many had already suffered such a fate in Hitler's Europe. Elisabeth, who had been teaching for several years at a school in a provincial town, lost her position when the parents of local pupils urged the headmistress to dismiss her because it was rumoured that she was signalling to the enemy. Other pupils, however, wrote to her subsequently to say how sorry they were about her dismissal.

In a similar vein, the superintendent of Hanmer Hospital came under pressure to sack Ruth, who had been working there as a physiotherapist for four years. 'Sometime after war broke out, the superintendent called me into his office and showed me several letters he had received from people saying I shouldn't work at Hanmer, which was a military hospital. But I didn't lose my job. However, shortly afterwards I got married and resigned.' Eva, smoking in her lunch hour on the roof of the building where she worked, was accused of photographing ships in the harbour. Her workmates believed that her cigarette case resembled a camera. Self-employed refugees suffered too. Franci and her husband were advised to take out glass insurance for their dairy in case her status as an enemy alien aroused the wrath of neighbours.

The hostility of neighbours impacted badly on some of the refugee women. 'My son was only a small child,' recalled Gisi. 'One day my neighbour with a threatening face said to him "You scum of the earth".' The family had a flat in the Wellington suburb of Hataitai, from where it was possible to see the harbour. 'People said we had taken that house so that we could spy on the shipping. Later on, we had a house built, also with a harbour view, and again we were accused of choosing that location for spying purposes.' These kinds of encounters with hostile New Zealanders featured prominently in the recollections of some women, not because such incidents occurred often but because of their devastating effect at the time. Yet the bad experiences must not be overemphasised. As Esther noted, 'Even during the war, we felt safe [here]. With our background of being treated like low-grade persons as we had been, we lost that feeling here. We never felt we were outsiders such as we had been in Nazi Germany'.

PUTTING DOWN ROOTS

New Zealand's prewar restrictions on alien immigration continued after the war and impacted on the efforts of refugees to bring out their relatives who had survived the Holocaust. The prolonged separation from their families made some women feel that they would always be outsiders in New Zealand. Naturalisation helped to foster a sense of belonging to their adopted home. It was also needed to remove barriers to employment in the public service, banking and in other professions.[22] Franci, as one member of a deputation on the future status of refugees in this country, spoke to the prime minister Peter Fraser, to the Minister of Justice, H.G.R. Mason, and to W.E. Perry, the Minster of Internal Affairs, about their anxiety to become New Zealand citizens. 'They want to feel that they belong somewhere. In allowing them to come to New Zealand they have been given freedom, but now they ask for equality, to allow those who had proved themselves worthy to become citizens of the country.'[23] When the wartime suspension of naturalisation was lifted, the Department of Internal Affairs was swamped with applications and with phone calls from aliens anxiously enquiring about the processing of their requests for naturalisation. Refugees were among those who applied to be naturalised as soon as they became eligible. By 1946 many of them had had their applications granted.[24]

During their first few years in New Zealand, refugee women were preoccupied with learning about their host society. For some, a sense of belonging was fostered at this time through friendships with local people at work, at university and in other associations based on common interests. For those who arrived as single women, marriage to a New Zealander helped to form strong local ties, despite the problems that resulted from cultural differences. Marrying a family, as well as an individual, was one way of integrating into a wider New Zealand community. Rose, for example, arrived here without 'a cousin, an uncle or an aunt'.

> My nearest relative was in America, which is a hell of a long way away. I think, if one is in a position where belonging to a family is really important, then one may marry a family rather than person. To build up a sense of belonging, there are decisions which one can make in a strange environment which are more survival decisions than self-enhancing ones.

For other refugee women, the birth of children and their involvement in Plunket, play groups and schools frequently provided contact with their local communities and allowed them to develop a sense of attachment to their new home. Esther believed that it was

> the effort of building our house that nailed me down to New Zealand ... it was such an effort physically and financially. Also we felt safe and secure here, with free doctors and hospitals. This gave us a good feeling with a growing family. With the Depression and the war over, there were plenty of jobs and everyone was optimistic about a better life that was being offered.

Making a home in Wellington for her husband and three children enabled Magda to put down new roots in a strange country. When asked about her sense of belonging, she replied: 'Where should I belong but in New Zealand? Certainly not in Austria.' Where should she belong but in the place that has been home for almost fifty years?

6
Letty Brown, Wahine Toa

Aroha Harris

Each [Maori woman's] story can be a model for those women who follow; each can be a place to rest and compare experiences and review their times. And each will testify that they have survived to carry on their way of being Maori and of being human.

– Irihapeti Ramsden[1]

As a topic for academic discussion, the rapid urbanisation of the Maori population in the 1950s and 1960s is as popular now as it was then. Common themes within such discussion have included adjustment to city life, the decline of traditional social controls and whanau values, government-driven policies to 'integrate' Maori into mainstream society and the transplanting of tikanga Maori into an urban setting.[2] Yet, when asked to contribute to this book, I thought not of a Maori world buckling under the stresses of modernity and the profound changes that urbanisation thrust upon it, but of a single Maori woman: Letty Brown – he wahine toa.[3] In a preliminary email discussion with the editors I very easily recited a list of Letty's achievements, all of which pointed to her keen commitment to Maori community development in the city. A mother of five, Letty was an advocate for Maori pre-schools in the 1960s, and founding member of a number of influential West Auckland groups, including the Hoani Waititi Marae fundraising committee, Te Atatu branch of the Maori Women's Welfare League and Te Atatu Maori Committee. I would have continued this list had I not paused to consider two wider realisations.

First, I realised that Letty was an important person with an important voice for reasons that are greater than the sum of her achievements. Her story is a richly textured narrative that values personal experience. She came to Auckland from Te Araroa at the peak of Maori urbanisation – that omnipresent phenomenon that seems to have framed understandings of the Maori experience since the end of the Second World War. There was something deliberate about this move that defies the notion of an urban 'drift'. Letty's approach to the urbanisation emphasises the continuation of those things she most valued from her East Coast upbringing. It is a story of her aspirations for her young family, and her ways of maintaining links to 'home' and including traditional values in her new life in the city. Adjusting to Auckland meant a great deal more to Letty than securing a good job and decent accommodation; it also meant shaping a future for generations to come.

My second realisation was that I was uncertain how or why or even when I had concluded that Letty's was a story to be valued and told. I did know Letty before I wrote this chapter and before I participated in the interviews on which it is based. I know her mainly through Te Amorangi, a Maori women's group based in central Auckland during the 1980s and part of the wider network known as the Maori Women's Movement. But I also knew about Letty well before we ever met. She features in the drawerful of newspaper clippings that my mother has collected since moving to West Auckland with her own young family in the mid-1960s. It would have been difficult to grow up Maori in that part of Auckland during that time without at least hearing of Letty Brown. In retrospect, I see Letty as practically a pioneer of Maori West Auckland, one of the many people who carved out the sociocultural space occupied by urban Maori. It is a space that is not tribal, or at least not consistently so, yet Letty is among those who had the foresight to pack the fundamental values and philosophies of 'the tribe' along with her material belongings when she first left Te Araroa. Such an approach is what makes Letty a natural community leader and, as such, a woman who has influenced and touched the lives of countless others, just as she was affected by an earlier generation of leaders. I think, then, that my interest in her life history comes from wanting to understand that kind of leadership and influence, to understand, for example, the whanau-like connections that Maori develop with people who are not, in the strictest sense, kin.

I interviewed Letty over a period of three days in late autumn 1998, and this chapter is based on those recordings.[4] Her korero travels the motu, pausing on particular places, events and lives. Often political, and sometimes revolutionary in a quiet, measured way, it is mostly anchored in a mother's aspirations for her family. She says herself that she is no radical and no feminist, but perhaps a 'strong Maori woman'. It has not been possible to fit in all of Letty's work or her multi-layered explanations and interpretations of how she has lived her life, so the chapter deliberately focuses on Letty alone and her experiences of the move to Auckland. It does not consider the numerous other leaders she mentioned frequently throughout her interviews, all of whom are implicitly acknowledged in this telling of her story.[5]

This is a great story, an empowering story, and yet one that cannot be conveyed fully in a written text. Delight in the eyes, laughter, the glow of success, moments of melancholy and remembrance, passion, determination, the flow of emotion and voice are absent. Nonetheless, the story here is Letty's. The analysis, on the other hand, is mine, and its intrusiveness is intended to be minimal. In this way I hope to address the double-dose of duty that can be the bane of the Maori academic: to honour the indigenous voice – which is what first attracted me to 'history' – *and* to meet the obligations of western academic frameworks, knowing full well that the two things are often incompatible. I hope also to be doing what Linda Smith says is vital for all indigenous peoples, that is, recovering our own stories, and 'reconciling and reprioritising what is really important about the past with what is important about the present'.[6]

Letty was born Ereti Taitua Bristowe on 9 July 1938 at her maternal grandmother's home at Te Kaha, in the heart of Te Whanau-a-Apanui. Letty's mother, Julia, was staying there while her husband, Eru, of Te Aitanga-a-Mahaki, was away managing a farm in Whakatane. Julia moved to Whakatane with one-year-old Letty, and the family stayed there for a couple of years before returning home to Te Araroa. It is important here to consider home: the rural tribal communities from whence Maori who opted for city life originated. The things left at home often became the things that motivated Letty and others like her in the activities they pursued in the city. Geographically at least, Letty's home was and is Te Araroa. Ideologically, home was the comfort and bosom of the whanau, linked, in Letty's experience, to many other parts of Te Tai Rawhiti, the East Coast. These qualities of home are evident in memories of her school years, characterised by whanau support and participation, an emphasis on educational achievement, and the influence and role modelling of strong Ngati Porou women.

Letty first attended school at Tikitiki, staying there with an aunty, Lena Goldsmith, because the family home at Te Araroa was too far from school. She stayed at Tikitiki until she was about seven, when she returned to Te Araroa to finish primary school. After two years at Gisborne Intermediate, during which time she stayed with a grand-uncle, Letty attended St Joseph's Maori Girls' College for three years. Her final year of school was spent back at Te Araroa at Rerekohu Maori District High. So, support for Letty's education came from outside the immediate family and moved her beyond Te Araroa, the physical bounds of home. As an aspect of her upbringing, though, education ran deeper than just getting to school. Letty remembers that education was important not only to her parents but to the whole community:

> [T]hat was the emphasis as long as I've known, ever since I was a child, was that we had to learn and get educated. I remember when I was a little girl having Apirana Ngata come round to our school and talk to us ... and also Tuini Ngawai come and teach us waiata-a-ringa and waiata. And also Apirana Ngata used to visit our home because he was a friend of my father's. So there was always that sort of influence around us with all our aunties and uncles.

Aunty Lena had been educated at St Joseph's, as had two of her daughters, and it was she who had insisted that Letty attend also. In fact, most of the mothers of Letty's contemporaries were old girls of St Joseph's, Queen Victoria or Hukarere, all well-respected Maori schools. The women who Letty knew as a child were 'strong Ngati Porou women', and the girls were expected to do just as well as the boys. Good teachers also had parts to play. In her year at Rerekohu High, senior students reaped the benefits of weekly after-school study sessions organised by one of the teachers. The outcome was that the college attained its highest rate of School Certificate passes that year. The results still show among Letty's peers: the girls she passed School Certificate with are now mothers and grandmothers as well as successful and skilled career women. Letty grew up knowing she 'had to be educated' and 'fortunate that good influences' surrounded the young people of Te Araroa.

Whanau participation and support and the guidance of elders featured not only in Letty's education but were also echoed in the security of the wider community:

> [I came from a] nice, secure kind of community ... where everybody helped each other, where my father would kill a beef or something like that and it would be shared [with] the whole community. Everybody shared, and that was the community. We stayed at each other's homes, and our parents never worried about us because they knew that we were at one of the relatives' homes. They had that nurturing for all the young people and children around. When we go to dances they'll all be there; all the elders will be there and they'll look after us at the dances. It didn't look so obvious, but when I think back that was the reason why they were there, they were just there to make sure we were all right and to protect us. And really they were the ones that organised all the dances, all the socials, everything for us.

It was this strong sense of community and belonging that Letty was loath to leave, yet her shift to Auckland about 1957 was itself a testament to the achievements that the home she loved could produce: Letty went to the city because she had been accepted at Auckland Teachers' Training College.

> Reluctantly, I must say reluctantly, I had to leave, because I didn't really want to leave ... I felt that I was really happy where I was in Te Araroa with all the whanau around and ... they had a little farewell party for me because I think they all knew that I didn't want to leave ... all my aunties decided to make it a big thing for [me] that night and then they'd push me onto the bus the next day and they did. They all had to help me get onto the bus, so I then made sure I came to Auckland. Looking back now, I think it was for a good reason because if I'd stayed there I probably wouldn't have achieved as much as I did. But I really didn't want to leave.

In Auckland, while overcoming initial culture shock, Letty also developed a stronger sense of the things about home that she missed. Ultimately, Auckland – specifically Te Atatu Peninsula in Waitakere City – evolved as her new home, and she worked at reproducing and cultivating the things she missed in a new suburban landscape. From this point of view, Letty Brown's story seems to match nicely the grand narrative that Ranginui Walker provides. Letty's dealing with the demands of a new life in the city could be seen as adjusting to the economic reality of the 'urban industrial complex', the first of two developmental tasks which, according to Walker, urbanising Maori faced in the 1950s and 1960s. The second task was to avert assimilation by relocating Maori culture (from home) into a modern urban environment. Letty may not have consciously aimed to avert assimilation, but she probably achieved it inadvertently as she re-created in Te Atatu the things she most valued about life in Te Araroa. In Walker's view, the success of this second task rested with such voluntary associations as Maori churches and church groups, culture, sport and family clubs, Maori committees, Maori wardens, Maori councils and the Maori Women's Welfare League. At the heart of such organisations is group membership and common goals, built around 'Maori identity, values and culture'.[7] These are the kinds of groups through which Letty displayed her particular brand of community leadership.

Although initially a reluctant urban Maori, Letty determined to make a success of things: 'I'm here now, I've got to do something with my life'. She did not, however, go directly to teachers' training college, deciding that she did not want to teach after all. Instead, she began work as a toll operator for the New Zealand Post Office, a job she secured through an uncle, Peter Awatere, then at the helm of the welfare division of the Department of Maori Affairs, Auckland. She lived at Seamer House in Remuera, a hostel for Maori girls run by the Methodist church. The hostel was 'huge and flash' compared with what she was used to at Te Araroa. She had to adjust to living with the Pakeha family who ran the hostel and, although they were good to all the girls, the culture shock lay in the everyday things. It took some time to get used to the traffic, catching the bus and getting to work in the morning. Homesick, she thought of Te Araroa constantly, 'wondering how everybody was' and ringing home often. She found the Pakeha she worked with had trouble understanding her English, which Letty says she could not speak properly. It could easily have been an alienating experience for any young Maori woman a long way from home and family, but the hostel environment fostered an active Maori social circle. The girls with whom Letty boarded were mostly from rural areas – many from 'North Auckland' and 'down the coast', but also from other districts. All the girls worked, so they would breakfast and commute to work together. They also met up with some of the boys at other hostels around Auckland, many of them whanaunga. The young Maori men and women would go to dances together at the Maori Community Centre and the Trades Hall – 'the places that Maori used to hang out'. Concerts, church services, indoor games like table tennis and other sports such as rugby were held at the community centre. No one had a car, so the young people would have to catch the last bus home at ten o'clock. If not, they were left with the option of either walking home or pooling their money to catch a taxi, which sometimes proved difficult as most were earning low incomes.

One of the things Letty longed for from home was the food: 'we hungered for the kai we missed'. Other interviews indicate that this was a common feature of city life for rural Maori, who developed a range of strategies to deal with it. Getting to know the Auckland beaches and their various supplies of seafood, such as the toheroa at Muriwai Beach, worked for a while. Often friends and relations would share the food they gathered, although it was rarely the same as 'getting it from home'. Kai from home could be brought back to Auckland after visiting the whanau for holidays and family events. Depending on the season and the location, this kai might include kumara, fish, kutai, toheroa, meat and cream.[8] The Maori Community Centre in central Auckland was also known for the kai it served, usually on Sundays after church. Another strategy for the newly urban Maori was to visit each other for meals. Letty had an aunty in Grey Lynn whom she would visit on Sundays for 'a good boil-up'. She also spent a lot of time with another aunt who was living in Newmarket. The food Letty shared with these aunties had a function beyond satiating an appetite: it was another means of activating the whanau network, and a pleasant, social way of gathering news from home. It suited Letty's approach to accepting city life.

To her pleasure, the guidance of the elders that Letty feared she would miss was already transplanted in Auckland, in the form of the many non-kin 'aunties and uncles' of the Maori Community Centre. Letty thinks that was one of the centre's main attractions:

> I think that's why we liked it, because there were old people there too. It was like being back home, down the coast. [There was] Aunty Sue Te Tai, the Stirlings [Amiria and Eruera], and Whina Cooper and ... We had all these old people that became part of our lives. ...They kept to their things Maori; they never lost it. [They] had that community sort of spirit; they kept everybody together; they looked after us ... just like down home, and we liked it. We were never allowed to wear jeans, we had to dress properly otherwise they wouldn't let us in the centre. All those different values that we left at home they still kept it up [in Auckland]. And we took to it. That's why I think they made it in the city because they never lost that community caring for the young people that came through. No matter who you were, no matter where you were from, they gave you a big kai on Sundays. Everybody went down there for pork-bones and dough-boys and puha and watercress. And at the same time they kept up jobs, they bought houses and that encouraged us to buy houses. All those people were always very much a part of our life in the city.

Somehow in this web of dealing with homesickness, adjusting to a new environment, remaining active in her existing whanau network, developing a newer 'city Maori' network and being young and social and Maori, Letty managed to settle into a routine. She developed a solid work ethic, learned to budget, paid her bills, provided for herself and saved. After a couple of years as a toll operator, Letty moved to a new position in the Post Office, in telephone accounts services, and it was about that time that she met the man who would become her husband: Hone Paraone from Otiria. At the behest of her father and her people, who wanted her 'to get married back home', Letty married Hone at Te Araroa in 1959, in the church where she had been christened. Back in Auckland, the newlyweds lived in a flat in Grey Lynn until they built their family home in Te Atatu North, where Letty still lives. They had their first two children while living in Grey Lynn, and the last three in Te Atatu.

No matter how alien city life had been, Letty was no youngster cast adrift in a foreign land. Rather, she lived deliberately, remaining firmly centred by and committed to the values of home. In Auckland she had accepted the embrace of an equally secure inner city Maori community, based around the Maori Community Centre, only to leave it again as the scene of her story shifted to West Auckland. Thereafter, while driven by what she felt were the needs of her growing family, she set about recreating the essence of her Te Araroa childhood in Te Atatu. In preparation for the task, the nucleus of kuia and kaumatua based around the community centre became an instructive and supportive foundation on which Letty could build.

> When I got married I never ever lost contact with all those people I met down at the Maori Centre. So they became real role models for us in the city. They'd made it in the city and we were just getting into it. They'd been here for years before we arrived ... so we sort of looked at how they handled the city life and we did the same ... Then our kids got to know them – Aunty Miria [Amiria Stirling] ... and Aunty Sue Te Tai [and others]. Even though we were surrounded by Pakeha, we were very much living in our own Maori world, and we never lost it.

It was to this Maori world in the city that Letty turned her attention in Te Atatu, in an attempt to mark out a Maori space within which she could raise a confident Maori family immersed in the cultural imperatives of her own tribal upbringing. The primacy of the family as motivator and anchor soon became apparent when Letty stepped into her first community leadership role. In 1961–1962, Letty decided it was time for her to 'do something' for her first two children, then aged about two and one: 'Everybody used to take their kids up to [Te Atatu] playcentre. I thought I'm sure this would be a good thing for my kids, for them to get to know everybody in the community, so I used to take them ... and I was about the only Maori mother there.'

Letty was sure there must have been more Maori mothers around, but in the meantime got used to playcentre as a 'Pakeha thing'. 'Playcentre [was] very much a community thing but a community according to the Pakeha way of doing things. And it was very Pakeha.'

Letty persevered with taking her girls to playcentre, often forgetting she was surrounded by Pakeha. She considered it an extension of looking after her children, and she began training to become a playcentre supervisor. Meeting other Maori mothers training to do the same at teachers' college, she discussed her concerns about the apparent reluctance of Maori parents to use playcentres. Then, when she passed her 'assistant's certificate', she went door-knocking to encourage the participation of Maori parents. She had seen Maori parents about the neighbourhood and worked out where they lived so she introduced herself and invited them to come along with their children. One by one parents and their children began attending, but few remained long term: 'a couple of weeks' seemed long enough for most. As parents dropped out, Letty would go back out into the neighbourhood and say something like, 'Oh, I didn't see you at playcentre the other day.' When she asked why, the responses would be about being too shy, too whakama. Some parents also made comments such as 'too many Pakehas' or 'can't stand Pakehas', which reminded Letty again of the Pakeha nature of playcentre, but she also understood the benefits of social interaction for children, through play and learning.

At the time Letty had nearly completed her supervisor's certificate, she called a meeting and asked the parents what they thought about setting up a Maori playcentre session. Letty took this action with a refreshing spontaneity and innocence. She had not broached the idea with playcentre staff, and had no intention of being provocative or radical or even political. 'All I was thinking about was the kids... they'd love to go up there and play in the hall... and run around and jigsaws and books and everything.' With the support of Maori parents, Letty asked the playcentre staff and parents how they felt about introducing a session for Maori children. She could see many of the parents were shocked, and she found herself having to explain why she would request such a thing: '... our [Maori] parents are very, very shy. They've all come up from the country, never mixed with Pakehas before, and all of a sudden I'm asking them to come into a Pakeha session with all the Pakehas, and they can't [get comfortable].'

From memory, it took Letty some three meetings before the Maori playcentre could go ahead. She had some training and experience under her belt and with the Maori parents, set up a committee. Again she found herself in Auckland in circumstances that were 'just like being back home'. 'We ended up getting thirty-five kids, per session ... with all the parents around, all wanting to fund raise, all wanting to participate. So we started fundraising ... we started the first housie in the West at the school... We made money, started a little culture group, and we called our play centre Waipareira Playcentre.' The funds raised were applied to the three Maori sessions that were held each week, the idea being to make enough to cover the costs of the children's fees. However, it was not an entirely smooth journey for the Waipareira Playcentre. Claims from education officials and local council members that the sessions were an unwanted example of apartheid shocked the Waipareira women. And even though the Maori Education Foundation had employed Lex Gray to help establish playcentres in rural areas for Maori mothers, it, too, preferred that city-based Maori mothers mixed more with Pakeha.

Fortunately, the Waipareira group was on good terms with the mayor of Waitemata, Jack Colvin, who gave them his support. On a personal level, Letty discovered her uncle Pita Awatere was 'so proud' of what she had done. Furthermore, Harry Dansey, then a journalist with the *Auckland Star*, wrote a very favourable article about the centre. In the face of some negative reactions, the strength of Te Atatu's Maori community, spearheaded by the group of women who emerged through the playcentre, became obvious. The women had set up a culture group, and a Maori language and arts programme, and other groups of Maori women in Auckland began to organise themselves along similar lines. It was no surprise that Letty's next community development – helping to found the Te Atatu branch of the Maori Women's Welfare League – grew from the kernel that had been sown at Waipareira.

Letty had been attending league meetings at the Arahina branch in the city. Along with her cousins, she had felt somewhat obliged to support this branch because an aunty, Maraea Te Kawa, was its president. Once again, what attracted Letty to the league were the social interactions and especially the 'old nannies' who were members. Eventually, Maraea encouraged Letty and a cousin, Ellen Wineti, to set up their own branch in their own area. The two younger women had learnt enough by attending the Arahina meetings and it was time for them to take a lead in their own community. Initially, Letty was reluctant:

> While I was there [at Arahina] I really liked it, I didn't want to go anywhere else ... it was an outlet for me because it gave me the opportunity to talk to other women about what I was doing in Te Atatu so it was kind of a support group for me ... They used to give me advice on certain things so I didn't want to set up a league of our own at that time.

But the task was not too difficult. The founding members of Te Atatu Maori Women's Welfare League were much the same women who were already involved in the playcentre: the branch is 'still going strong, very strong', with a junior branch (for girls) associated with it. The league became another organisation through which the mothers could structure their interactions and activities. It also pooled the skills of individual women into a collective. Letty did not focus at first on any specific kaupapa, such as education. Her view was that it would be best to build community cohesiveness before pursuing the range of interests in which she gradually became involved.

> I felt that for us in the community we had to get together first before we can do other things. I think we had to learn from scratch [alongside] the babies, and then our kids moved into the schools so we got involved in the programmes in the schools, in school committees ... and all that time, what we were doing, was involving Maori teachers into our schools so that our children would not be lost in the big schools, and teaching our Pakeha teachers ... I would put a 'turu' on their chair, and a 'tepu' on their table so the teachers would know that's a Maori name for a turu and a tepu.

Once more Letty's involvements were being driven by the changing needs and circumstances of her children. The league's *raison d'etre* – the health and welfare of women and children – neatly matched her aspirations for family and community. Connie Hanna, who was a welfare officer at the time, asserts that women joined the league to regain 'the sense of whanaungatanga which they felt they had lost' as a result of their urbanising experience. The league 'not only provided them with a forum, which offered support and friendship ... but also taught them new skills in parenting, budgeting homemaking etc'.[9] The Te Atatu branch busied itself working up its membership, teaching budgeting, and providing general mutual assistance among the families involved. One of the initiatives it supported was a series of community talks by Ranginui Walker, as a means of readying parents and teachers for the influx of Maori pupils and addressing any prejudices they harboured about their Maori neighbours. Letty explains:

> The schools weren't ready for [Maori children]. A lot of Pakeha that lived in Te Atatu had never ever come in contact with Maoris and it was real hard for them to learn ... So we brought in speakers like Rangi Walker to talk to these Pakeha parents about what it is to be Maori and how we operate and what we do and all the issues that we feel really strongly about. It's teaching, I suppose, our Pakeha friends and neighbours and people in Te Atatu about being Maori. I think that was the biggest job for us as the league, was actually being involved ... in a community that didn't know what being Maori was all about. They'd see [Maori] in the papers as drunks ... all these negative things ... in the papers, in the media.

Maori community development in Te Atatu gathered its own momentum, and soon Letty found herself involved in establishing the Te Atatu Maori Committee. First set up as tribal committees in 1942 as part of the Maori War Effort Organisation, in 1945 these committees were formalised under the Maori Social and Economic Advancement Act, and their work aligned with the welfare work of the Department of Maori Affairs. In 1962, the tribal committees became Maori committees, and a national umbrella was provided for them in the form of the New Zealand Maori Council. Although the committees were a reasonably common feature of tribal communities in the 1940s and 1950s, for urban Maori they were more a 1960s phenomenon.

Letty's decision to get behind establishing the Te Atatu committee was partly a way of claiming a space and authority for the local Maori community, and partly a reaction to complaints from Pakeha about the behaviour of some of their Maori neighbours. The 'Maori courts' – a type of marae justice system that operated through the committees – gave the committees authority to deal with minor misdemeanours among their community members. When some Te Atatu families were implicated in allegations to the Waipareira Maori Committee in Henderson about drunkenness and loud parties, Letty endeavoured to find out more about the committees and how to set one up. The resulting Te Atatu

Maori Committee was a timely development for the husbands of the women involved in the league. Letty saw it as a forum for the men to talk among themselves and consider the ways in which they could contribute to the community. Throughout the country the membership of these committees was typically all male, but in Te Atatu Letty was the secretary during its formative years.

In the background of Letty's narrative is the Department of Maori Affairs, arguably at its peak in both size and influence during the post-war period. Certainly, the department was the government's primary instrument of Maori affairs policy and a key distributor of resources to Maori communities. It had a clear agenda to infiltrate Maori communities and facilitate social change: 'the greater the change, the greater the need for the department's guidance'.[10] The work of the welfare officers focused on the tribal committees and the league, which were seen as the basic building blocks of Maori social organisation and the natural points of access into Maori communities.[11] Both of these building blocks existed throughout Auckland during the 1950s and 1960s, but were not dependent on state legislation or department sponsorship. Setting up a committee was not a prerequisite for communities to meet together. Letty's story is telling in this respect. Although she acknowledges the strong hand of the department, and individual welfare officers in particular, it is the energy of Te Atatu that comes to the fore in her interpretations of her various community roles. She says that, for the most part, the Te Atatu league and Maori committee had a healthy relationship with the department. It must have helped that Peter Awatere was both the head of the welfare division and a pivotal supporter of Waipareira/West Auckland's burgeoning Maori community. The league women knew that much of the work they did with individual families, such as assisting young people into accommodation and jobs, was rightly the work of the welfare officers. Ultimately, though, the community belonged to the people, and the people to it: 'If we want to help our community,' Letty says, 'we should do it [ourselves]'. Besides, 'a community that can do without government funds is a much happier community'.

Letty's various community involvements were recognised in 1968 when she was named Young Maori Woman of the Year. Sir Jack Butland of Auckland had established the award, inspired by the achievements of young Maori in recent years. At a ceremony to present the award, the Minister of Maori Affairs, J. Ralph Hanan, noted that many of the challenges facing the Maori people concerned the youth. At the same time, Maori had to depend on a younger age group for their leaders. At the time of receiving the award, Letty had had four of her five children. She was liason officer for the playcentres in her area, president of the local branch of the league and secretary of the Maori committee. She had been active in the Parent-Teachers' Association and was serving on a body known as Help, which co-ordinated the work of voluntary organisations in the area.[12] Still, she says, it 'was a real shock' to get the award as she did not feel she had the qualifications. Then the following year her branch of the league won the Te Puea Trophy for best community programmes, and went on to win it for four consecutive years.

These awards were more than well deserved; they were also an acknowledgement of the choices Letty and the league women generally had made for themselves, their families and the new Maori community in which they lived. They came at a time when more and more women were joining the league and thus expanding the range of skills on which the women could draw. Letty acknowledges the participation of June Mariu, for example. Another skilled and high-profile Maori West Aucklander, June has had a long history of community work in the area. She taught in a number of the primary schools before becoming a Maori language teacher at Rutherford High School in Te Atatu, and has been a prominent member of the league, including a former national president.[13]

This networking of skills and personalities bore an abundance of fruit throughout the remainder of the 1960s. Letty took part in discussions about setting up a West Auckland Maori culture group. In her view such a group would attract different people, perhaps those who might not want to attend league or committee meetings. It would become another group through which urban Maori could gather and express their Maoriness. The first meeting for the culture group was held at Matipo Road School in Te Atatu, and the obvious person to spearhead it was Peter Sharples, who had all the requisite skills. That culture group became the now popular and renowned Manutaki, and Peter Sharples is still at its helm.

About the same time that Manutaki got under way, people were also talking about the possibility of building a marae for West Auckland. Letty remembers Mavis Tuoro and Tuini Hakaraia asking her what she thought about the idea. By this time a steadfast, cohesive community of urban Maori had developed and was meeting regularly and organising around shared commitments. Even so, thinking about building a marae in suburban Auckland in the middle of the 1960s was something else altogether. But a marae did seem the natural focal point as a permanent centre for the many Maori voluntary groups that had grown up around West Auckland, and it would address the logistical difficulties that many families had faced when they needed to hold tangihanga. A marae, in Letty's words, would be 'the ultimate'.

Mavis Tuoro, a teacher and social worker and first president of the Waipareira branch of the league, says West Auckland needed a marae to 'help educate and motivate our people, a place we could bring manuhiri aboard and do things Maori'. Further: 'we were trying to create ... a sense of family and a sense of belonging when people were no longer able to readily access their whanau ties in the areas they were originally from ... We wanted to recreate whanau ties in the city. This is something that the League and the Maori Committees were trying to do as well.'[14]

The idea of whanau was already developing among many West Auckland Maori, and Letty had purposefully generated the idea with her own children: 'All the uncles [who my children] thought were 'real' uncles – they didn't realise they weren't real uncles until they were quite old ... But everybody was 'Uncle' and 'Aunty', and that was how I was brought up. They were my real uncles down there [Te Araroa], but I just wanted [my children] to feel that uncle and aunty kinship.'

For Letty, the marae was needed because it was becoming too difficult for the various Maori groups to meet – the numbers were too large for people's homes. The Te Atatu whanau was ready for a marae. It was probably Maori West Auckland's biggest project. By the end of 1967 a formal marae committee was busy fundraising, and the project marshalled the skills and resources of the 'cream' of Maori leadership.[15] Fundraising and project development occupied the remainder of the 1960s, all of the 1970s and much of the 1980s. The project peaked in April 1980 with the opening of Hoani Waititi Marae, and today the Maori education centre established there develops a tertiary arm.

Hoani Waititi Marae deserves its own history, but it enters this story as the pinnacle of Letty's community work, and a reminder of the longevity of the dedication to Maori community that built it. It is described as the 'prototype' of modern urban non-kin marae.[16] The importance of it, and other marae like it, ought to be understood not just in the context of the time in which they were built but also in the context of the time that had gone before. Hoani Waititi Marae is both the end result of decades of community development and the starting point of a whole new era for Maori West Auckland and urban Maori everywhere.

Letty's community work continued unabated throughout the following years as she involved herself with legal, justice and welfare services for Maori youth, and support for Maori girls living on inner-city streets. In the twenty-first century, Letty has come full circle. Forty years ago she planted a seed that gave Maori West Auckland a couple of sessions a week at a local playcentre. Now she runs Te Puna Reo o Manawanui, a kohanga reo in Te Atatu, the neighbourhood that has become home. There, surrounded by her own children and mokopuna, she teaches the children of children that she once knew at Waipareira Playcentre. In the beginning, Letty's shift to Auckland was reluctant, but it quickly became an empowering one for the new community that embraced her.

It would be easy to read Letty's narrative as a partial list of her various community involvements, but the juice is in the energy that underpins the groups of which she became a part, the spirit in which the various voluntary organisations conducted themselves. It was, according to Letty, a spirit of 'togetherness and evolving together' and, more to the point, it was 'just like how we were down home, the same sort of spirit'. This energy has been sustained over a period of decades, and the people's work has come in waves and layers. The early playcentres, branches of the league, Maori committees, Manutaki, Hoani Waititi Marae and all the triumphs and challenges that punctuated their journey, drew on the same pool of people, the same community spirit. It was a spirit that both attracted leaders and created leaders: Letty is one among many.

> There are a lot of people that have come and gone, there are a lot of people that have passed on that were very much involved in what was happening out in the West ... They were just ordinary people in their homes doing their ordinary things, who just wanted to be part of the community. Some got the limelight, well and good, that's their role ... other people just like to be the followers ... to be part of it but not out there in the limelight.

For Maori, adjustment to city life required community development – a Maori sense of belonging and connectedness that simultaneously drew on the cultural imperatives of the tribe *and* transcended tribal boundaries. Critical to Letty's recipe for a Maori life in an urban landscape were the primacy of the children and a re-creation of the Te Araroa she had loved as a child. 'I was totally involved in developing our people in West Auckland into a community very much like the community that I came from; that was my dream, to develop the same sort of community where all our children grew up [together]. I was really doing it for my kids and for everyone else's kids.'

7
Dissolving the Frontiers: Single Maori Women's Migrations, 1942–1969

Megan Woods

In the years during and immediately following the Second World War, Maori increasingly left their 'traditional' rural homes for lives in the cities, towns and boroughs of New Zealand, and in doing so radically disrupted the 'interior frontiers' of the colonial nation.[1] In only three decades, the Maori population transformed from predominantly rural (74%) in 1945 to predominantly urban based (77%) by 1976.[2] A cross-national study suggested that this may have been the quickest urban-ward movement of a national population anywhere, at least until the end of the 1960s.[3] For Maori, the geographic movement from country to town represented the most radical population movement since their arrival in these islands. As a result, Maori and Pakeha, geographically and socially separated for nearly a century, began to encounter each other in the 'contact zones' of the rapidly expanding post-war suburbs of New Zealand's towns and cities.[4] This change dissolved the fiction that New Zealand was a unitary and undifferentiated nation.

This chapter explores the migrations of young single Maori women to the cities in the decades following 1942. Despite their enormous impact on both Maori and Pakeha societies, the migrations of Maori to the cities have received very little attention in the history books. The examinations that we do have, both contemporary and historical, have focused largely on a universal and invariably male Maori urban migrant.[5] Maori women and their experiences of, and contributions to, post-war urbanisation have been obscured. This male focus has come about in spite of the gendered nature of the policies and practices of the population movement. Recently, however the urbanisation experiences of a group of Maori women are beginning to be recovered and revealed through examinations of the Maori Women's Welfare League.[6] Through these studies, the lives of, mainly, married women, and the importance of their domestic skills, have been illuminated. In this chapter, however, I cast the beam beyond married women and their homes, to illuminate the experiences of an additional group: young single Maori women.

In doing this, we will need to understand post-war urbanisation in a new way: not as a single population movement but, rather, a range of experiences. Although, for most Maori, the migration to the cities meant an encounter with the new world (Te Ao Hou), different groups and individual Maori experienced this new world in markedly different ways. It is crucial, however, not to replace the universalised male Maori migrant with a simple male/female dichotomy. To do this would obscure the multiplicity of stories and experiences of the migrations. Much work remains to be done in exploring the differences: How did the migrations differ according to iwi and hapu membership? How did the timing of the migration alter the experiences?

This essay looks to the years during and following the Second World War, a time when the tightly drawn demarcations between Maori and Pakeha homes were rapidly eroded. Following the New Zealand Wars (1845–72) most iwi and hapu withdrew into their rural communities and had very little to do with Pakeha.[7] By the 1920s, despite the continued place of rural New Zealand in the national psyche, Pakeha New Zealand was a predominantly urban society.[8] Maori, however, remained overwhelmingly rural.

Into the decades after 1945, Maori were seen as belonging to an ancient world peripheral to modern Pakeha cities. When many Maori migrated to the towns and cities, it was their first encounter with urban New Zealand, but the boundaries between the two worlds were not straightforward geographic divisions drawn on 'racial' lines. The reality, as it usually is, was far more complicated. Although an overwhelmingly rural people until the post-war period, some Maori had lived in urban areas since the nineteenth century. Likewise, particularly up to the 1920s, large numbers of Pakeha New Zealanders were rural dwellers. The interior frontiers of New Zealand were a complex tangle of class, 'race' and gender relations.

From the late 1870s, Maori began to leave their communities in search of work, a trend that began to intensify in the 1920s. Usually these migrations were to other rural areas where work was available, and were of a temporary nature. Overwhelmingly, these migrants were male. By the end of the 1930s, increasingly cities and towns became the destination of those seeking employment, and hostels were needed to house Maori workers in Auckland, Tuakau, Pukekohe, Tauranga, New Plymouth, Havelock, Nelson, and Bluff.[9] The Second World War stimulated the pace of urbanisation, and after 1945 this pace intensified.[10] Wartime and post-war Maori urbanisation differed from earlier migrations: it was largely permanent, and Maori women also began to make the transition.

Sometimes referred to as an 'urban drift' by contemporaries, the post-war migration of Maori from their rural communities to the cities was in fact highly organised and orchestrated. For the state, there was an 'inevitability' about the migrations, brought about by economic and social needs.[11] From the early 1940s, several factors collided to both pull and push Maori off their rural lands and into the towns and cities. Since coming to power in 1935, the first Labour government had been wedded to 'a kind of equality' between Maori and Pakeha.[12] After the war, a growing number of bureaucrats and politicians began to consider that the benefits of citizenship could most easily be bestowed on Maori in the cities. And from the late 1930s there had been growing official recognition that the land that remained in Maori ownership could only ever support a fraction of the population. The needs of the New Zealand economy also played a part. The wartime economy demanded Maori labour, and the state often directed Maori into employment that was located in urban areas. Following the war the thirst for Maori labour did not abate. From the late 1940s until 1967, the New Zealand economy boomed – these were the years of the 'golden weather' – and full employment was just one of the positive indicators that earned New Zealand the second highest standard of living in the world. Full employment, however, brought with it a labour shortage, and increasingly the New Zealand state eyed the rural Maori population as the solution to the problem. From the late 1940s, the Department of Labour argued for the utilisation of 'under-employed' Maori labour over assisted Central and Eastern European migration.[13] To many within the department, rural Maori constituted a 'reserve of industrial labour'.[14]

Despite the government's clear desire for migration of Maori from country to town, this is not simple tale of the Pakeha state's manipulation and exploitation of the Maori population. Young Maori, especially, migrated willingly with the dream of finding the 'big three factors of work, money, and pleasure' in the cities and towns.[15] Urban New Zealand was expanding, both economically and socially, and many young Maori wanted to be a part of it. Maori parents often actively encouraged their children to seek a better life for themselves in the cities.[16] Some, however were not as eager to try their luck in town, and for this group the government did turn to more coercive policies.

As Maori became an increasing presence in urban New Zealand, the state began to express a desire to integrate them more fully into Pakeha society.[17] From the late 1940s, this aim was discernible within government policy,[18] and by the 1960s government and the Department of Maori Affairs were explicitly articulating a policy of integration.[19] Much ink was spilt in an attempt to differentiate the policy from its nineteenth-century predecessor, assimilation, with integration being presented to the nation as the 'melding' together of Maori and Pakeha cultures.

Like many of the migrations of women into New Zealand, the mid-twentieth century internal migrations of Maori women within the country were driven by domesticity. Domestic work, either paid or unpaid, was a means to produce Maori women who conformed to Pakeha notions of femininity. Acquiring domestic competence not only equipped Maori women with the necessary and 'natural' womanly skills to be effective 'mothers of the race' but, in many cases, also coincided with the needs of the economy.[20] Since the nineteenth century, Maori male political leaders had concurred with Pakeha bureaucrats, churchmen and Pakeha women's voluntary organisations that the domestic education of Maori women was critical to the 'raising of the race'.[21] Domesticity, it was believed, not only made Maori women 'good wives and mothers' but, conforming to European notions of 'ideal womanhood', allowed for them to become 'influences for good among their own people'.[22] For this reason, domestic training had been the dominant aspect of Maori girls' education since the nineteenth century.[23] Into the mid-twentieth century, Maori women's domesticity became central to changing configurations of ideal Maori citizenship. In an equation that Maori women were acutely aware of, Maori achievement became inextricably linked to social worth.[24] Married Maori women migrants and their families could establish themselves in the cities and towns through acquiring and displaying the skills and qualities that constituted ideal European womanhood.

Domesticity also lurked at the core of official views about mid-twentieth-century young single Maori women migrants. Speaking in the House of Parliament in 1949, Terence McCombs, the Labour member for Lyttelton, argued that the government should encourage church schools to establish more hostels for the training of Maori girls. Maori girls should 'be given the opportunity to learn European standards of living, because they could do more to raise the standard of living of their people than the boys could'.[25] As with their older married counterparts, the young single migrants' citizenship was deeply entwined with domesticity. In the late 1940s, politicians argued that instruction in domesticity fitted Maori girls to 'undertake the highest responsibilities of citizenship'.[26] Initially, however, young single women were to use their domestic skills in the paid labour force, rather than as unpaid wives and mothers. Participation in the paid labour force, it was believed, actually equipped Maori women to become better wives and mothers. It was hoped and believed that Maori girls who had left their rural homes, earned an independent wage and 'lived and worked on equal terms with Europeans . . . would not be content to marry and live in squalid conditions with few of the materials comforts of the home'.[27] Their participation in both the wartime and post-war labour force was also critical to the expansion of the New Zealand economy. Urban migration and labour policy were intended to bolster the national economy and to produce Maori women who would want to become modern, urban housewives.

Employing Young, Single Maori Women Migrants

From the early 1940s, young, single Maori women began to migrate to the towns and cities. Although their migrations differed from those of either Maori men or older Maori women, with the exception of a handful of mentions and the fictional accounts of Noel Hilliard, their experiences have been relatively neglected in existing examinations of urbanisation.[28] The initial migration of young, single women, motivated by the needs of the wartime state, predated

Young Maori women were encouraged to the cities and towns of New Zealand through expanding domestic employment opportunities. The Auckland and Wellington Hospital Boards regularly placed advertisements in the Department of Maori Affairs periodical *Te Ao Hou* to attract these women to urban areas with promises of good pay, employment security, opportunities for advancement and the provision of accommodation. *(Source:* Te Ao Hou, *September 1965, no. 52, p. 12.)*

those of their older, married counterparts. In 1942, in an effort to combat a lack of labour and keep a lid on wages, the government introduced industrial conscription. Although there was no compulsion for Maori to join the military, the manpowering regulations applied equally to Maori and Pakeha. Although, according to Deborah Montgomerie, it largely 'went against the grain', industrial conscription also extended to women.[29] For many young Maori women, the Second World War and industrial conscription meant a shift from their rural homes to the cities.

Following the war, the seemingly insatiable appetite of the booming economy demanded even greater numbers of young Maori women workers in the cities. Initially, most young women migrants entered domestic employment. Although domestic training had been the dominant aspect of Maori girls' education since the nineteenth century,[30] and despite the ever present 'servant problem' in New Zealand, Maori women had not engaged in the work professionally in large numbers.[31] By 1945, domestic service as an occupation had largely 'collapsed'

Table 7.1 Occupations of residents of maori hostels in 1948.

Occupation	N	%
Attending schools and colleges	35	20
Attending training colleges	13	8
Attending universities	2	1
Employed in restaurants and domestic duties	47	27
Employed in factories	54	31
Employed in shops and offices	22	13
Total	173	100

Notes
1. All data obtained from AJHR, 1948, G–9, p. 10.
2. The figures do not distinguish between male and female residents.

in New Zealand, with the only increase in numbers occurring among Maori women.[32] But young Maori women were not moving into traditional 'live-in' positions in private houses.[33] Although desperate for domestic labour in their homes, Pakeha women did not seem to want Maori women in these jobs. A 1945 report from the New Zealand Council for Educational Research, on the question of vocations for Maori youths, recommended that any scheme to draft Maori girls into city homes 'as maids on the old pattern' should be discouraged. The report's author cited the fact that Pakeha would not tolerate such a scheme as the rationale for his recommendation.[34]

Instead, young Maori women moved into domestic positions in hotels and institutions. In 1948, over 27 per cent of all residents in urban Maori hostels were engaged in 'restaurant and domestic duties' (see Table 7.1). The figure for women, however, is much higher than this as the data supplied in the 1948 report were not broken down by gender. With women constituting 79 per cent of all Maori hostel residents in 1949, and assuming that no males were engaged in domestic work, the figure is more likely around 35 per cent, thus making it the largest employment category for young women in migrants in the late 1940s.

Into the 1960s, domestic work continued to be a large source of employment for young single Maori women. In 1964, Joan Metge suggested that around one-quarter of residents at Maori girls' hostels found employment in hospitals and hotels as domestics.[35] In 1962 Kia Riwai, the Maori welfare officer for Christchurch, reported placing 'many' girls in domestic positions.[36] Young Maori women who were contemplating moving to the cities were informed of the domestic employment opportunities that awaited them through the Department of Maori Affairs magazine, *Te Ao Hou* which, throughout the 1960s, sought to educate Maori about 'the new world'. It ran advertisements, on behalf of the Wellington and Auckland hospital boards, encouraging young Maori women into domestic positions.[37]

Single Maori Women's Migrations · 123

(Source: Te Ao Hou, March 1967, no. 58, p. 22.)

Unlike traditional domestic employment in private homes, hospitals and hotel work offered Maori women freedom and increased opportunities. In recent years, historians of New Zealand women have acknowledged the great need for research into why Maori women shunned domestic service.[38] Their consensus is that low social status ascribed to domestic servants discouraged young women accustomed to an autonomous and hierarchical society from seeking employment seeped in restrictions and servitude.[39] But the drive to recruit young Maori women migrants for post-war institutional domestic employment sought to avoid any of these connotations. Instead, the recruitment advertisements appearing in *Te Ao Hou* emphasised the good pay, cheap board and training that gave the employment a more professional veneer and, importantly, the opportunities for advancement that existed in such employment. Like their Pakeha counterparts, once they arrived in their new urban homes Maori had no desire to enter the restrictive life associated with private domestic service. Since the 1920s, more exciting, modern and glamorous employment opportunities had been developing for young, urban New Zealand women.[40]

Domestic and feminine skills also gave Maori women entry into the professions of nursing and teaching, with their emphasis on the traditionally female and maternal qualities of care and nurture. Like domestic employment, nursing and teaching were seen as natural extensions of the domestically focused high school curriculum, and a means of equipping young Maori women for their ultimate calling – as mothers of the race. Educationalists made no attempt to disguise their agenda: the 1946 report of a church-run Maori girls' college stated:

> The basic idea behind the organisation and development of the school is the necessity for inculcating the principles of healthy living in Maori girls, and the desire to give that training in household management essential for the future wives and mothers of the Maori race. Both from the point of view of economic security and to give incentive to the girls' studies, the immediate goal of the school is education of girls for admission to one of the professions whose basis is domestic training nursing or teaching.[41]

There was, too, a growing need for young women to become teachers and nurses. In the 1950s and 1960s a sustained recruitment campaign targeted school leavers, and later married women who had left the profession to use their maternal and feminine skills in motherhood.[42] Before the Second World War, nursing had been a predominantly Pakeha occupation in New Zealand, but the post-war recruitment campaign actively sought to recruit young Maori women.[43] Labour's 1938 Social Security Act had resulted in a massive expansion of hospitals and by 1950 it was apparent that this reform had produced a shortage of nurses.[44] In order to remedy the situation the Health Department and the New Zealand Hospital Boards Association mounted a campaign aimed to appeal to young single women, including Maori.

A REWARDING CAREER FOR YOU IN AUCKLAND

Because of the rapid expansion of its hospital services, the Auckland Hospital Board requires more household staff for wards and food service departments.

PAY IS GOOD — the minimum wage for a five day week averages £12/11/7 gross. This is increased considerably by special allowances and statutory holiday and overtime pay.

TRAINING — is given in hygiene, nutrition and housekeeping methods. Optional courses cover subjects such as cookery, menu planning, food buying and budgeting, anatomy and physiology, furniture and furnishings, laundry methods and supervision of staff. Food service staff are eligible for the basic cookery course at Technical Institute.

OPPORTUNITIES FOR PROMOTION ARE EXCELLENT. If you have the necessary aptitude and temperament and can accept responsibility, we can provide the training to fit you for advancement to supervisory positions paying over £22 per week.

VERY GOOD BOARD is available for £2/8/8 per week. Attractive uniforms are provided and laundered free, and there is an allowance for shoes and stockings.

For further details about the satisfying jobs and good prospects available in Hospital Housekeeping, write, phone or see:

THE PERSONNEL OFFICER,

AUCKLAND HOSPITAL BOARD,

WELLESLEY STREET EAST,

AUCKLAND. PHONE 32-690.

(Source: Te Ao Hou, *March 1967, no. 58, p. 12.)*

Throughout the 1950s and 1960s, *Te Ao Hou* encouraged young Maori women to enter nursing. In advertisements that depicted Pakeha women, hospitals attempted to lure young Maori women with promises similar to those used for institutional domestic service. Nursing was touted to perspective migrants as offering not only good pay, cheap board, increased opportunities and freedom but also as a 'natural' and honourable profession that offered opportunities for social advancement. A direct appeal was made to youth: young Maori women were targeted through appeals to 'girls' and there was an emphasis on the fact that training started in the teenage years. As well as general nursing, Maori women migrants were encouraged to enter the profession at the lower level of nursing aids and to enter psychiatric nursing. Historically, the latter had been a profession taken up by immigrant women in New Zealand. In noting British 'surplus women' entering the profession in the 1920s, Katie Pickles suggests that this may have been because New Zealand women eschewed such work (see chapter four). In the 1950s and 1960s, psychiatric nursing was once again targeted to migrants, only this time they were young, single Maori women.

Although the curriculum at exclusive church-run Maori girls' colleges explicitly aimed to ready their students for careers either as nurses or teachers, it soon became apparent that many young rural Maori women simply lacked the required criteria. In an attempt to remedy this, in 1952 the Auckland Hospital Board mooted the idea of a pre-training course in nursing for Maori girls, which would 'accustom the [Maori] girls to an entirely new way of living', concentrating on improving written and spoken English, the history of nursing and hospital management and hygiene.[45] Likewise, in 1969, recognising that many young Maori women lacked the School Certificate requirement, the Departments of Maori Affairs and Health, in association with the Wellington Polytechnic, began an 'Introductory Nursing Course'.[46]

Likewise, there was a courting of Maori women as teachers. Through the pages of *Te Ao Hou*, the Department of Maori Affairs outlined the advantages of kindergarten teaching to young Maori women and their parents.[47] Although perspective trainees were reassured that the job entailed 'more than child minding', the domestic nature of the job, and the training it provided for motherhood, made it ideal for Maori women. They were portrayed as 'being good with children', and as possessing a 'pleasant manner which instinctively draws children to them'.[48]

By virtue of their sex, and the qualities associated with it, young Maori women gained access to the professions in a way that was not open to their male counterparts. Between 1951 and 1956 there was a 69 per cent increase in the number of Maori employed in the professions, which was, the Department of Maori Affairs noted, 'largely due to the increase in the number of nurses and teachers'.[49] Throughout the 1950s and 1960s large numbers of young single Maori women continued to enter these professions. In a single year, 1958, the

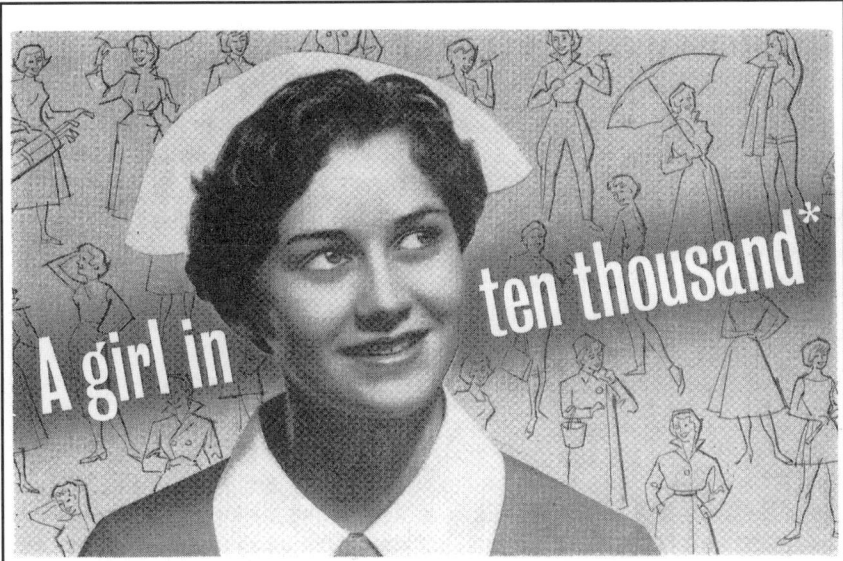

Young Maori women were targeted in nursing recruitment campaigns during the 1950s and 1960s with the message that this occupation offered a 'natural' application of their 'womanly skills' of care and nurture. *(Source:* Te Ao Hou, *October 1958, no. 24, p. 58.)*

Department of Maori Affairs assisted over one hundred women into nursing training.⁵⁰ Once trained, these young women found employment in the cities. In Christchurch alone, in 1959, Kia Riwai reported placing ten young women as nurses and four as dental nurses, and in 1962, twenty-nine young Maori women were placed as nurses and a further two as dental nurses.⁵¹

The needs of the flourishing economy demanded, however, the expansion of employment opportunities for young single Maori women migrants. Between the wars, young working-class Pakeha women had increasingly found employment in the burgeoning 'modernised' factories of New Zealand's cities and towns.⁵² But it was the needs of the wartime state and economy that had brought young Maori women onto the factory floor: from all over the country they found themselves manpowered into the munitions and food-producing industries.

Following the war, with the manufacturing sector enjoying a period of sustained growth, even more young, single Maori women were required to staff the factories. In order to encourage young Maori to take up urban employment, local businesses and schools organised tours to show boys and girls the opportunities that existed for them in the cities. In the late 1950s and 1960s Christchurch played host to a number of North Island Maori school children. In 1959, thirty-four Maori pupils from Bethlehem School, Tauranga, visited the city for five days on a tour organised by the Canterbury Public Relations Office. The visitors were entertained at the Civic Theatre with a concert party performance and were shown local factories, Canterbury Agricultural College and the Canterbury Museum.⁵³ In 1967, a similar tour was organised for a group of pupils from Queen Victoria Maori Girls' School. During their stay in the city, the young women visited the factory of Lane Walker Rudkin, a leading national clothing manufacturer.⁵⁴

School tours have recently been shown to have been an effective means of 'exhibiting' colonies to desired British migrants,⁵⁵ and these visits by Maori school children to New Zealand's cities need to be seen in a similar light. The Department of Maori Affairs was actively encouraging young Maori to migrate to Christchurch so the city was displayed to visitors from the North Island. These school tours were also critical in getting Pakeha to accept the intending migrants as both employees and residents of the city. Through reports of their activities, the Christchurch *Press* reassured the predominantly Pakeha population of Christchurch that the Maori children were sufficiently 'modern' to be made into 'ideal' citizens. In an article about the Tauranga children's visit to the Canterbury Museum, the *Press* reported they were far more interested in the reproduction of James Fitzgerald's cabin on the *Charlotte Jane* than in the Maori displays.⁵⁶ Christchurch residents were to be reassured and comforted by the fact that these potential Maori migrants had bypassed their own 'ancient' culture in favour of a display that epitomised colonisation and 'civilisation'.

The 'modernity' of the children was emphasised through reports of their enthusiastic responses to the epitome of the post-war era – the jet aircraft. Reportedly, the group was 'wide eyed' and 'excited' during their visit to Christchurch's new international airport. The *Press* emphasised that, for many of these North Island Maori children, this was 'the first time in their lives' they had seen an aircraft.[57]

In addition to school tours, the Departments of Maori Affairs and Labour assisted businesses in recruiting rural Maori women directly to their city factories. After an address by the Department of Labour's chief research officer, Noel Woods, to the Industrial and Development Conference on the 'surplus of Maori labour in rural areas', Amos, a soft goods manufacturing company, approached the Department of Labour wanting to recruit young Maori women for its Wellington factory. Collaboration between the Department of Labour, the Department of Maori Affairs and the company resulted in twelve 'suitable' young women being recruited from Wairoa on the East Coast of the North Island. The company stipulated that the girls must have 'good religious backgrounds' and that the Department of Maori Affairs must be involved in their welfare once they were in the city. For their part, the company paid not only their fares down to Wellington but also their first week's board. They also helped to find them accommodation either in hostels or in flats. Reports of this initiative appeared in both the *Labour and Employment Gazette* and *Te Ao Hou*, with the hope of encouraging more employers to recruit young Maori women into their workforces.[58]

The Department of Maori Affairs also actively sought opportunities to encourage more young Maori women to move to the cities. Noting the number of vacancies in the manufacturing sector, in April of 1961 the department offered the services of young North Island Maori women to the Canterbury Manufacturers Association. Although there were some apprehensions over the employment of Maori women, the general response was positive. One Christchurch manufacturer, C.H. Stockbridge, spoke of a Maori woman he had employed and advised his colleagues that they 'could do with more like her'.[59]

Office work also became an increasingly appealing employment option for young Maori women. In 1958, the state-owned New Zealand Post Office targeted young Maori women with a recruitment campaign featuring both a Maori model and a slogan in Maori. 'Girls with their clear young voices' were encouraged to become telephone exchange operators, with the slogan printed in both English and Maori: Mahia nga mahi kei tamariki ana – make the most of your time while you are young.' Good pay, a social environment and easy work were all emphasised as inducements to young Maori women to work in urban telephone exchanges.

> **Girls!**
>
> ## Join the Post Office Telephone Service !
>
> If you are looking for an interesting well paid job that provides plenty of congenial company—then join the staff of the Post Office as a telephone exchange operator. The work is easy to learn and applicants will be trained on the job and receive full pay during the training period. This is the sort of job specially suitable for girls with their clear young voices—so if you are interested get in touch with the Staff Officer at your nearest Post Office.
>
> **Mahia nga mahi kei tamariki ana**
>
> *(Make the most of your time while you are young)*
>
> ISSUED BY THE NEW ZEALAND POST OFFICE

During the post-war era the expanding public sector provided good employment opportunities for women. Advertisements placed in *Te Ao Hou* **by the New Zealand Post Office Telephone Service explicitly targeted young Maori women through appeals to their youth.** *(Source:* Te Ao Hou, *October 1958, no. 24, p. 4.)*

Protecting Young, Single Female Migrants

Following the war, the arrival of even greater numbers of unsupervised Maori women in the cities provided a source of anxiety for the National Council of Women, an organisation that had historically been concerned about the welfare of women. With this in mind, in June 1947, Mrs E.J. Chesswas, the dominion secretary, wrote to Peter Fraser in his capacity as Minister of Native Affairs, requesting that the government provide hostels for Maori girls in the large centres. These would be administered along the lines of the girls' hostels operated during the war years.[60] In turn, Peter Fraser, via the Native Department under-secretary, reassured the Pakeha women's organisation that the state was also concerned about the issue and had already established hostels for Maori girls in both Wellington and Auckland.[61]

A change to a National government in 1949 did not abate the state's desire to offer protection via hostels to the growing number of young, single Maori female migrants: in fact, into the 1950s, National increased funding for the provision for urban hostels. Although, in 1950, the government had rejected the United Council of Churches' offer of assistance in running and controlling the hostels,[62] there was a growing realisation that the state alone could not 'take upon itself the burden' of providing all the hostels that were needed.[63] In May 1951, with an eye to reducing state expenditure, cabinet approved a pound-for-pound subsidy scheme under which religious and welfare organisations wanting to establish hostels for young Maori women or men were eligible to for up to 50 per cent of their establishment costs.[64] In announcing the scheme, Ernest Corbett firmly expressed the link between the need for hostels and the need for young Maori workers in the city.[65] A series of conditions was attached to the funding, and the government succeeded in securing church financial support for Maori hostels and, at the same time, managing to maintain control of many aspects of the scheme.

Maori communities also became concerned about the lack of protection and supervision for their young women in the cities and joined the state and voluntary organisations in the immediate post-war drive to offer shelter to the migrants. During the war years, Tainui elders had expressed alarm about the temptations that Hamilton, and particularly the American servicemen, presented to its young women. Eager to provide a refuge in the city, the iwi, and Princess Te Puea Herangi in concert with the Methodist church, opened Te Rahui Wahine, a Maori girls' hostel in Hamilton in 1945.[66] Likewise, in Christchurch Rehua Maori Girls' Hostel was opened in 1952. Run jointly by the Department of Maori Affairs and the Methodist church, Rehua had received its impetus from individuals within Ngai Tahu. In June of 1951, the superintendent of the Christchurch Central Mission, Reverend Falkingham, D.V. Ayres, a member of the mission's social services committee, and Joe Moss, a Ngai Tahu man and honorary Maori Welfare officer in Christchurch, met Ernest Corbett to request funding assistance to establish a Maori girls' hostel in the city. The trio explained that young women were living 'in undesirable conditions', and some were being sent back to their rural homes owing to a lack of suitable accommodation.[67]

Throughout the post-war period, however, the desire to protect young Maori women gave way to the desire to house and supervise young Maori male apprentices and trade trainees in the cities. In the twenty-year period between 1948 and 1968, the total number of places in Maori hostels increased from 173 to 1129 (see Figure 7.1). This meant that, in 1968, there were six-and-a-half times more spaces available than there had been in 1948. Although the total number of spaces for girls grew, the relative number of spaces declined markedly: the spaces for Maori boys increased by a massive twenty times, but those for girls increased by little under three-fold (2.85). On the advice of the Department of Maori Affairs, hostels that had previously housed young Maori women, such as Rehua in Christchurch, were converted into hostels for young Maori male workers and apprentices.

Despite the dwindling hostel accommodation available, many young Maori women continued to migrate to the cities, sometimes in larger numbers than

Figure 7.1 Total and relative number of hostel places provided for Maori boys and girls, 1948–68

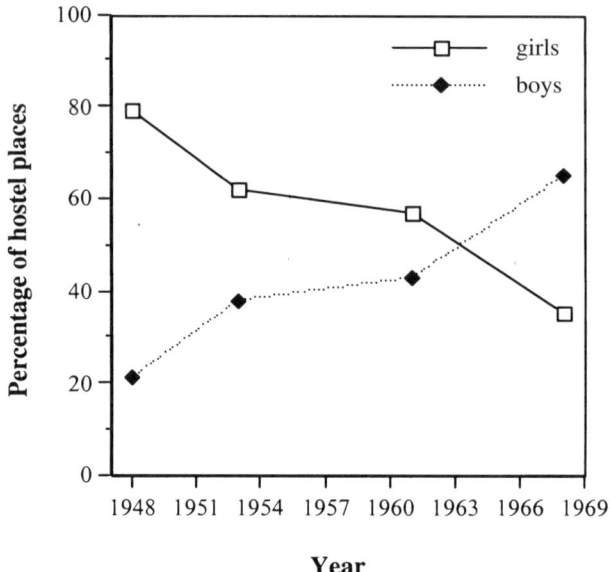

Source: AJHR, 1948, G-9, p.10, *Appendices to the Journals of the House of Representatives*, 1953, G-9, pp.10–11; Draft Report, September 1953, AAMK 869, 37/1, Vol.3, box 1116a, National Archives, Wellington; L.M. Kenworthy, T.B. Martindale, and S.M. Sadaraka. *Some Aspects of the Hunn Report: A Measure of Progress*, Wellington, School of Political Science and Public Administration, Victoria University of Wellington, 1968.

their male counterparts. For the years 1960–66, young women aged between fifteen and twenty-four constituted the largest Maori migrant group to Auckland city. Throughout the 1950s and 1960s, hundreds of young Maori women migrated to Christchurch and were placed in employment after the Motueka fruit-picking season. For the five-year period between 1958 and 1962, the Christchurch office of the Department of Maori Affairs aided eighty-nine young migrant women into apprenticeships in the city.[68] Clearly, young single women constituted a major component of the post-war Maori population movement, so why did the availability of hostel accommodation for them grow so slowly compared with that for males?

The answer can be found in the Department of Maori Affairs' belief that young Maori women were more able to cope in urban environments than their male counterparts, and were therefore in less need of hostel accommodation. Girls, the bureaucrats believed, matured faster than boys, and were thus 'more able to fend for themselves'.[69] This maturity and independence, it was argued, led girls to bypass hostels in favour of more independent lives in flats. In the early 1960s, the acting secretary of Maori Affairs, Jack Hunn, argued that Maori girls regarded hostels as 'transit places', useful for the initial stages of the move to the city; however, according to Hunn, once they had adjusted to urban life and had found friends, they soon abandoned the hostels in favour of flats and other accommodation.[70] The bureaucrats also saw the girls as being more able to support themselves financially than male apprentices.[71]

But the state also believed that hostels were not crucial in transforming young Maori women into ideal citizens. It was thought that, even without hostel accommodation, young Maori women (unlike young men) would become integrated into Pakeha society. Separate and dedicated Maori hostels were no longer deemed necessary for Maori girls, who were seen as 'good mixers' and 'able to adjust themselves fairly easily to European Hostels'.[72] With the number of Maori hostels needed, and fiscal constraints operating, the provision of Maori girls' hostels was no longer deemed necessary.

By 1960, with many Maori boys' hostels established, the Department of Maori Affairs, under mounting pressure from employers of young, single Maori women, again turned its attention to the provision of urban accommodation. This time, though, the bureaucrats favoured traditional hostels. Women living in small groups were responsible for their own living expenses, and did their own cooking and laundry, using shared facilities. Although the young women all had door keys, the presence of a master and matron regulated and confined the freedom of the residents. Although they were referred to as 'bachelor' flats, it was clearly understood and intended that this arrangement was solely for young Maori women. Their male counterparts, the department maintained, 'needed the closer supervision of a traditional hostel'.[73] Also operating was a deeply ingrained belief in the relative domestic roles and capabilities of men and women. Whereas the flatting arrangement allowed young women to hone the skills that would make them modern, and therefore ideal, housewives, the young male residents needed 'domestic assistance in maintaining their rooms and preparing their meals'.[74] Even when young Maori women were employed in occupations such as factory work, their domestic skills were still deemed necessary for their survival in the cities.

Conclusion

The migration of young, single Maori women to the cities and towns of New Zealand in the period between 1942 and 1969 complicates and fractures our understanding of the post-war Maori population movement. Their migrations reveal a complex and entangled web of labour requirements, state race relations policy and rural Maori's desire for lives in the cities and towns. State and Pakeha societal beliefs about the 'success' of their migrations made the women's experiences very different from those of their young male counterparts. Definitions of a successful migrant turned on the perceived ability to assimilate or integrate into Pakeha culture, and young single women were deemed to fulfil this criterion. Deeply held gender beliefs also played an essential role: although home was not the primary place for the integration of young, single Maori women migrants, nevertheless domesticity was a powerful undercurrent in their move to city life.

8
Emele-Moa Teo Fairbairn

⚘

Peggy Fairbairn-Dunlop

When we were young we thought we owned Mulinuu. We didn't know that was government. Our house was there, we swam and fished in the sea with our cousins and attended the pastors' school. We even helped our father plant the coconut trees that today surround the Fosno buildings. Life was good. When my father died in December 1919, our lives really changed. We moved to our mother's village, and for a long time it was like we didn't belong anywhere. We even stopped going to the Sa Petaia lotu, until my sister Faavevela had a dream in which my father was asking why we weren't going. That made us strong again. The lotu o le aiga has been our strength.

I was born at Mulinuu on 6 May 1908. My name is Emele, but my father nicknamed me Moa, because he said that every time he came home from work I was feeding the chickens. I have been known as Moa most of my life. My father was Teo Tuvale, born at Faleasiu, Aana on 26 August 1855. He was the son of Vaaelua Petaia who was the pastor at Faleasiu at the time. Petaia's first marriage was to the daughter of Le'auanae of Iva, and they had one child, Le-Mamea Faletoese. My father's mother, Saniie Vinepa, was Petaia's second wife. They had six sons and two daughters, my father being number six in this line. Vaaelua Petaia was one of the early Samoan converts to the London Missionary Society (LMS) and one of the first students at Malua Theological College when it was founded in 1844.[1] Vaaelua was one of the five Samoans who helped LMS missionaries translate the Bible into the Samoan language. His name is printed on the plaque on the monument stone at Avao, Matautu, Savaii, which commerorates this achievement.

This marks the beginning of the aiga Sa Petaia. Petaia taught his children to serve – the church, the country and the aiga. And this is what our family has done. Most of my father's brothers and sisters, and now their children, have been pastors and pastors' wives, or worked in the government like my father. Vaaelua believed so strongly that family must stay together that he started the family lotu (religious observance), which met twice every year at Leufisa, then at Fasitoo. The family meetings were the place where aiga must welcome new members and get to know each other better. These meetings o le aiga continue today; in fact, we celebrated one hundred years in 1991. Looking back, the family lotu was what I missed most when we moved to New Zealand in 1943. One of the proudest moments of my life was when we started the Sa Petaia meetings in Wellington in the 1970s.

To get back to my father, Teo Tuvale. We didn't really know much about Teo's early life, as we were still young when he died. But I know he was well educated because he could speak English, German and some Fijian and he was also well travelled. Teo spent time in Fiji in the 1880s and was a friend of Ratu Cakobau, the Fijian paramount chief. I'm not sure how he got to Fiji or who paid the passage: it may have been the missionaries or the government. Teo also travelled to Germany as part of an official delegation, and Kaiser Wilhelm gave him an engraved gold watch, which we still have. It was on this trip to Germany that Teo met my mother, Naitua. This picture is how I remember my father. He looks very stern in his uniform, but he was really very kind and patient.

Teo enjoyed recording events; writing was his talent. Teo wrote *A History of Old Samoa*, the original manuscript of which is held at the Mitchell Library in Sydney.[2] This has been translated into palagi (English). Teo also helped compile the *Tusi Faalupega*, the list of the ceremonial addresses of Samoa. Teo's older brother Le Mamea began this task, and Teo and their younger brother Faletoese completed this. This book was gifted to the LMS church to print and sell for the benefit of the church.

I didn't know Teo had been a teacher until I read his papers. These show Teo attended Malua in 1875, then became a teacher there in 1877. He moved to work for the government in 1878 on the recommendation of his brother Le Mamea. Le Mamea was Secretary of the Interior at the time, and had to go to the United States to participate in treaty negotiations with that country: this was the period when Germany, America and Britain were vying to have Samoa as a colony. Before he went, Le Mamea placed Teo in the job of chief clerk. From that time until he passed away Teo worked for the government, and our family lived at Mulinuu, the seat of government.

In the early years Samoa was ruled by the Taimua and Faipule. When the government of the Taimuas and Faipules was driven away to Aana in May 1878, and it was decided to select a ruling town in each district, my father became secretary of Vaialua, the ruling town of Aana district. In 1891 Malietoa Laupepe appointed him native clerk of the inquiry conducted by the commissioners of the three nations regarding the Samoa Lands, a position which he held through to 1897, when he was appointed chief justice and chief secretary to government. Teo continued in this post during the German administration, then became clerk in the Samoan Affairs Department during the years of the New Zealand military occupation, until he passed away in 1919.

Teo's papers are full of stories of the kingship battles between the Malietoa and Mataafa supporters. One incident we don't like to think about, but it's there in the papers, happened in 1899. Teo writes that on 22 March the Samoan forces 'burned all the villages from Faleata to Satapuala, and from Laulii to Eastern Fagaloa, also Safotulafai, Savaii from Vaimaunga to Tuasivi'. These were the ways opposing factions were suppressed in those days. The Samoan forces at that time comprised 160 men, selected and commanded by Lieutenant Guy Gaunt, an Englishman. Teo was chief Samoan commander of the forces.

One incident that Teo did take great pride in telling us about happened in 1899. Some of the Malietoans had been betrayed at Mulivai near the Catholic Mission yards, and had been taken as prisoners of war to Mulinuu with the people of Iva village, who had their fortress in front of the Marist Brothers. When the road was empty, Mataafa's men had immediately charged and scattered the troops who guarded Malietoa outside Tuiletufuga's house at Apia. My father asked Malietoa to accompany him to the Tivoli Hotel where Malietoa would be safe. When they arrived at the Tivoli, the other division of Mataafa's troop passed between Apia Church and the hotel. Teo asked Herr Partsch, the German proprietor, if there was a vacant room for Malietoa. Partsch said, 'There is a room, go and see Mrs Annie Partsch.' So Malietoa, the Salelesi and my father went upstairs to the room and remained there, Teo leaning against the door with his gun, guarding Malietoa. Then, according to Teo, there was a knock on the door. It was Mrs Partsch, who asked, 'I say, Teo, will you open the door and let the British consul and Captain Sturdee of the man-of-war see Malietoa?' The British consul wanted to take Malietoa to the LMS yards so that the soldiers could guard him there. Malietoa's reply was that he'd rather remain at the hotel. Next, the British consul came upstairs and told Malietoa not to be afraid. At that, Malietoa left. The battle went on into the night. Teo sat down and wrote an application from the Malietoa troops to the consuls of the three nations asking them to proclaim peace and for all weapons to be handed over to them. This request was accepted, and all the Malietoans were taken to the man-of-war that night. Teo and some other chiefs and troops remained in the LMS house at Apia.

We found a letter about the events in the papers at the Mitchell Library, Sydney. Samoan historian Malama Meleisea provides the context for the letter:

> 1989–99 was a very crucial period in the history of Samoa. The last civil war was fought between Mataafa Iosefo and his Samoan supporters (backed by the Germans) on one hand, and Malietoa tanumafili I and Tupua Tamasese Lealofi and their Samoan supporters (backed by the British and the Americans) on the other, to determine who would be King (Tupu) of Samoa.
>
> The letter was written at the time (March 1899) when there was a kind of stalemate. Malietoa manumafili I and Tupua Tamasese Lealofi were declared by

the Chief Justice as King and Vice King respectively but Mataafa and his forces, annoyed by the decision, successfully attacked Malietoa and Tupua Tamasese's forces and they (Malietoa and Tupua Tamasese, the Chief Justice and some officials) took refuge on the Porpoise. From there they tried to solicit support from their traditional allies throughout the whole country (including the islands of Tutuila), with British and American support clearly behind them (mainly because they didn't want the Germans to become prominent).

Tamasese was clearly on shore at the time Teo Tuvale's letter was written, soliciting manpower support, guns and ammunition for their side.

Falealili had been a very strong supporter of Malietoa and the letter from Falealili referred to in Teo Tuvale's letter may have been an expression of support for Malietoa or a letter complaining about the way in which the Mataafa forces had intimidated all the known and active supporters of Malietoa and Tupua.[3]

I remember my father as a very kind and patient man, always busy on government business, carefully listening to people, and writing. I think of Teo's trip to Germany, the gold watch from Kaiser Wilhelm and Teo meeting my mother Naitua. As my mother told it, Teo was supposed to marry a girl from Papauta Girls' School.[4] Around that time it was decided that a Samoan cultural group would accompany the official delegation to Germany, and taupou (village ceremonial virgin) from certain villages were selected to make up this group. Naitua was the taupou from Tanugamanono: she was the sole daughter of Atoa Soonanofo, and her mother was Tapasu from the Tofaeono Aiga at Siumu. Naitua was sixteen at the time of this trip to Germany, and my father in his forties: so he was much older. Naitua had never been on such a long sea trip before and she suffered from seasickness for most of the journey. My father looked after her, and that's how they became friends and eventually husband and wife. I don't know what happened to the girl from Papauta.

My mother always talked about that trip to Germany with such pride. It had been an honour to be chosen. Recently I saw pictures of the group taken in Germany, and it looked very much like they were on show, like in a zoo. That made me wonder if this had been such a wonderful trip after all. But Naitua did meet my father.

My mother was a midwife and healer. She learned this knowledge from her mother and, in turn, passed these skills to my sister Faavevela. Naitua delivered all her own children, sometimes with the help of my father. Seven children survived in our family: our older sister Talisala, me, brothers Sepelini, Taulalo and Tuvale, then sisters Faavevela and baby Sina. Two children died in childbirth; they were Fene and Feneliko, and I was responsible for the death of another. On that day, I was looking after Mafuie, the baby, as my mother wasn't well. Mafuie was so hot that I took her to bathe in the sea, to cool her down. I didn't know what else to do. Mafuie caught a chill and died of pneumonia. She probably had the measles.

When it came time for my sister Talisala to enrol at Papauta, as the second sister I became responsible for my younger brothers and sisters, a responsibility which is still mine. We were very proud that Talisala was a Papauta girl – she was to be our 'pastor's wife', our gift back to God. I still remember the song the Papauta girls used to sing:

Teine Papauta, sei gasolo mai,
Fai lau ula, fai lou sei,
Sulu lou titi, fai lou palepua,
Tausi teu teu faaSamoa
Aua nei a faagaloina
Nei malo, mai tu faa-Europa.

Papauta girls come by,
Wear your necklaces, and your flower,
Wrap your skirt, and put on your flower wreath,
Always follow the Samoan ways.
Don't ever forget these
Or else the European ways will take over.

A little piece of me used to envy the Papauta girls, even when I saw them out cutting the grass with bush knives or walking down to Mulinuu on a Saturday afternoon to do their fishing for the Sunday toonai (lunch after church, feasting). I would have liked to have been a Papauta girl. As it turned out, Talisala didn't marry a pastor, but her grandson Niu Sila is now the pastor at Vailima in Samoa. Instead of Papauta, I attended the Malifa Government School with my brothers. I loved school, especially history and geography, which I was good at because I had sat and listened to Teo and other chiefs talking at Mulinuu ever since I was young. I also loved maths. We were lucky our English was good because Teo often brought palagi soldiers home to Mulinuu, especially the New Zealand troops when they were stationed at Vaimea. In the beginning we'd run away from the palagi, but we grew used to them, and started to enjoy talking to them.

Our childhood at Mulinuu was very happy. We went to school, came home, did our tasks, then went to the pastor's school. My main job after school was to mind my younger brothers and sisters. Our father worked very long hours, but when he was home he always made time to be with us. He always took me with him if he could.

The last job I remember Teo doing was to supervise the burial of the dead during the epidemic.[5] Teo would come home at night totally exhausted. He'd shake his head and talk about the waste, and how the soldiers were working overtime to close up the contaminated houses, dig the mass graves and bury the dead. Way into the night he talked about the awful sights he had witnessed. My mother would plead, 'Stop and rest', but Teo never did. He said there was so much to do.

Teo died straight after the epidemic. I think he died of exhaustion and sadness at what he had seen. Looking back, Teo knew he was going to die. That Sunday morning, he woke early and with my brother Taulalo walked all the way from Mulinuu to Faleasiu, where his brother Faletoese was pastor. He wanted to ask Faletoese to take care of Naitua and us children: that was my father's last duty. I can remember begging Teo that day to let me go with him, as I always did. But that time Teo said no, Taulalo must go with him. Teo's walk to Faleasiu is recorded in the newspaper of that day. Teo tried to borrow a car from our aiga, the Currys, but Curry was using his car, so they walked. When they passed Malua, the missionaries sitting under the trees there called out, 'Teo, where are you walking in the heat? Come and sit with us for a while.' Teo thanked them for their kindness, but said he had to keep going. When Teo arrived at Faleasiu he talked with Faletoese but it was clear that he was quite ill. The aiga did everything they could for him, but Teo died the following day.

Teo was buried with his father and other Sa Petaia at Asofana, Faleasiu: the flags flew at half-mast on that day and Malietoa sent one of finest mats we had ever seen to honour my father. The Sa Petaia burial plots are still at Faleasiu. When the airport road was being widened in the 1970s the engineers wanted to run the highway right through these burial grounds. My brother Atoa Teo Tuvale, who was interpreter with the government at the time, successfully petitioned to preserve the graves: so the airport road still circles them. Today there are volleyball and netball courts across the front of the graves and the old Faleasiu church where we worshipped has been knocked down and replaced. That is the way of progress.

Our lives really changed when Teo died. It was as if we didn't belong anywhere. We even stopped going to the Sa Petaia lotu, until Faavevela dreamt my father was asking why we weren't going. As in the faaSamoa, my brothers and sisters and our mother returned to our mother's village of Tanugamanono, back to the care of her father and her brothers. Tanugamanono was quite a wealthy village with the Atoa lands reaching right up into the hills of Vailima and Letava. Even the land where Avele College stands today is Atoa land. My grandfather Atoa Soonanofo had a taavale (a four-wheeled cart) to carry foodstuffs down from the plantation, and he also had cows. One of my jobs was to take the cows down to the river. I really hated that job. The cows would look at me as I pushed and pulled them. I was still scared of cows when I came to New Zealand.

When we arrived at Tanugamanono, Atoa Soonanofo told Naitua to make our home at Matamoana at the back of the village, so we children would be safe from the traffic on the cross-island track. We still have our Teo malae there today, just above the river, next to the electric power station. There is one space of land for each child of Naitua and Teo. We have our family house. Even if my children live in New Zealand, or any other part of the world, they will always have a place to stand, a place where they belong in Tanugamanono.

Naitua wasn't very well for some time after Teo died as she had just given birth to our youngest sister Sina. So, again, I was in charge of my brothers and sisters. One day as I was watching my mother's brothers working in the plantation, I could see that looking after us was making extra work for them. I went away and thought about it.

It's funny the way things happen, but soon after that our teacher told the class some new palagi teachers were coming and they would need a house girl, but it must be someone with good English. So, thinking about my uncles and knowing that my mother had trouble getting money for school fees, I put up my hand. I got the job. My mother was very angry. She said that Teo had always wanted us to be well educated. But my mind was set. So that was the end of my proper schooling. I remember going with the palagi teachers to Savaii as they did the school inspections. I was only eleven or twelve at the time, and sometimes I got so tired that the boys in the group had to carry me. We slept at the pastors' houses. I was very homesick.

Me taking this job meant my brothers could keep going to Malifa. Taulalo later went to Malua to train as a pastor, but he didn't finish, which was a great sadness to my mother; Tupuola Sepelini worked for the Electric Power Corporation (EPC) for many years and Atoa Teo Tuvale worked at the radio station then was chief interpreter/translator with the Samoan government, following Luafatasaga Kalapu.

If you tell someone today that you were a house girl, or a children's nanny as I eventually became, people think that's a very low-class job. In those days, being a house girl for a palagi family was one of the only ways of making money. Also, I learnt so many things: how to look after children, how to embroider and sew and make puddings and cakes and hams and chutneys. In fact, my children used to joke that I'd preserve anything I could get my hands on! And I still do! Sometimes nannies were not very well treated; it all depended on the family.

I was nanny to Dr Mail's children. Dr Mail was a New Zealand doctor working at the National Hospital. I went to New Zealand with this family twice, but I didn't really see much; I just worked. I can remember, though, that we got off the boat at Auckland and went by car to Wellington. When we stopped at Taupo for some food, Dr Mail said something to the lady at the shop, and she went out the back and came back with a Maori girl. The doctor put the Maori girl's arm next to mine and said, 'See, Maoris are brown just like you.'

The baby I remember most was Pearl West, a beautiful baby with golden bouncing curls. Her parents called her 'Pearl of the Pacific'. Pearl looked up our family in Wellington in the 1970s and when she visited Samoa in 1986 she brought her scrapbook of pictures to try and find the house where she had been born. Pearl now lives in Queensland.

Because of my job I had to live in with the families I worked for. Often there wasn't enough time to get back to the Tanugamanono church in the weekends, and so I started attending the Apia Protestant Church along with many of the other young girls working as house girls or nannies. I enjoyed APC. Most of the Afakasi went to APC because APC had the best Sunday school and Bible class and they always had a palagi minister sent by the London Missionary Society. They say that Robert Louis Stevenson went to APC. I saw my first game of tennis on the APC tennis court at the manse behind the church.

Just after I started working, the Saleimoa Choir visited the Tanugamanono church. I remember this vividly because one of the choir members was Moenoa, who was the nephew of the Tanugamanono pastor. Soon after this event Moenoa became my mother's second husband. This brought big changes to our lives again. Naitua moved to live in the village of Saleimoa with Moenoa but Sina, the baby, stayed at Tanugamanono with our grandfather Soonanofo, as did our brothers so they could continue their schooling. Faavevela went with my mother to Saleimoa, but she ran away so many times to our aiga at Fasitoo that Naitua agreed that Faavevela should stay with the Fasitoo aiga. While I kept working in town, every weekend I bussed to Saleimoa to take my wages to Moenoa. I guess the reasons we didn't like living in Saleimoa was because this was not our village and Moenoa was a very strict man. Over the next years my mother and Moenoa had three children: Aiga now lives in Los Angeles, Leitufa is in Porirua, New Zealand, and Oa is still in Saleimoa.

Then Moenoa died and, just as happened with Teo, my mother came back to her home village of Tanugamanono with Leitufa, Aiga and Oa. Naitua lived at Tanugamanono until she passed away in 1958. She is buried at Alaoa, where all the Atoas are buried.

I had found living in town was quite a strange life. Luckily, my cousin Mautuli and her husband McIntosh ran a boarding house at Tauese next to the old Tivoli theatre and they were good company. Their house was the meeting place for all the Scottish people living in Apia. Mautuli and McIntosh also had a trading shop in Salailua, Savaii which they ran for O.F. Nelson. Mautuli used to drive all around Savaii in this old, very loud truck collecting supplies and copra to put on the vaa kerosene to take to Apia for export. As you can imagine, a Samoan woman driving a truck was very unusual in those days, but Mautuli didn't mind!

I met Jim Fairbairn, or Jock as he was known, at the McIntoshs', although I had seen him before at the Apia race course. Jim had migrated to New Zealand from Govan, Glasgow, and had joined the New Zealand troops coming to Samoa. That's another interesting story. According to Jim, the Fono o Matai (meeting of a village's chiefs) complained to the League of Nations about having 'troops' in command in Samoa. So, almost overnight, all the New Zealand troops were designated 'policemen': same uniform, same duties, but policemen! When the

New Zealand unit left, Jim stayed on in the Samoa police force for nearly twenty years, serving in various offices.

Jim used to tell very funny stories about what happened at the police station, the boxing matches and the weight-lifting competitions. The late member of parliament Alfonso Philipp featured in many of these stories. It is strange that Alfonso came to visit us only once in New Zealand: that was in September 1973, the day after Jim passed away. Alfonso was minister of education at the time. We asked Alfonso, 'What made you come now?' He said, 'I just felt I had to come.' We sat with Alfonso and looked at all the parade photos Jim had kept of the Samoa police. I wish we had taken the time to label these pictures properly.

Jim was good looking and very kind, like all the palagi soldiers. At the time the New Zealand administration didn't like palagi policemen going with the local women. Funny thing was my family didn't want me to go with a palagi either, or to marry a palagi. I was the only one of my brothers and sisters, or my aiga, to marry a palagi. Over the years, though, my aiga did come to appreciate and to depend on the generosity of my palagi husband. My stepfather, for example, found out that some government land at Saleimoa was going to be sold, so he told my mother, 'Tell Moa to get the money from the palagi.' I asked Jim to give the money because I was scared of what my stepfather might do to my mother. Moenoa's family still have that land at Saleimoa.

Our first child, Mabel, was born in Suva. Jim had been sent to Fiji to relieve the chief warden of the Suva jail who was going on home leave. Jim stayed at the jail, and Mabel and I stayed with some of my aiga, who were wardens at the Suva asylum. There were quite a few Samoans working at the asylum at the time, mainly because Fijians didn't like that job. Our aiga told us so many stories about the asylum that we hardly slept, especially when we heard the wailing and cries in the night. I don't remember that much about Fiji except that I was glad to get back to Samoa.

When we returned to Samoa, Jim started looking for some freehold land to build a house. He said the Tanugamanono land would never really be ours, and he wanted our family to be secure. Jim purchased 16 acres (6.5 hectares) of Vailima land, which had been part of the German estate. This land was right in the middle of the bush. Everyone, but especially my aiga, said we were crazy to live up there: what about the aitu (spirits)? But we made Vailima our home. We still have the receipt for the small wooden house Jim bought and transferred there. Soon after we settled, my good friend Tuliomanu with her husband Eti Eves (chief inspector of schools at the time) came to live and raise their family on the next block. Our sons, Ian, Jimmy, Rex and Alfred, were born at Vailima, and we had a daughter, Margaret, who died at birth. Margaret is buried at Alaoa, close to Naitua. My mother helped deliver our babies: I never wanted to go to hospital for this. I always link hospitals with dying. I still have a fear of hospitals.

Jim often had to stay overnight at the Apia police station, and so he brought home a huge police guard dog called Flea to look after us. We used to laugh, because the police cook, a Chinese, often gave Jim a big meat bone for Flea. Instead, we used that for our soup! The kids would say, 'Poor Flea!' I'm sure the cook knew what we were doing. If Jim was stationed at outlying police stations for any length of time, such as Poutasi, my mother or my sister Faavevela would come and stay and keep us company.

At Vailima I made a big garden, and today you can still see where my planting blocks were. I planted guava, pasio (passion fruit), peanuts, coffee and cocoa, and kapok which I sold to the hospital for mattresses and pillows. I also exported bananas to New Zealand under my cousins' quota. My children still growl at me for planting what I thought was a very pretty pink bush that I had picked on the Avele College grounds. It turned out to be Hawaiian rose, a very noxious weed.

We always wanted our children to be well educated. Jim had prizes he had won at school in Scotland but, like me, he had had to leave school early. He was always reading: Stevenson, Hardy, Burns, all the classics. Right up until he died he read. He brought the children up on the stories and poems of his fellow Scotsman, Robert Louis Stevenson. For schooling, Mabel, Ian and Jimmy rode their horses down the cross-island track to Leififi Government School with the Eves' children from next door, tying their horses up behind the police station during the day. Sometimes, prisoners working the road gangs called out to them as they rode by – they knew they were Jim's children. Although that scared the kids, we had no troubles. As I recall, Ian and Jimmy started school at Mulivai Marist first, but moved to Leififi as soon as there was room, because the Catholic school had too many holidays.

In the 1940s Jim started thinking about going to New Zealand so that the kids could go on to college. We made our plans. On one of his furloughs, Jim found a job at Island Affairs in Wellington, processing the visas for Samoan migrants. He journeyed ahead of us, started work, got a loan and bought a little house in Kilbirnie, high on a bush-covered hill with a view of the sea, very like Vailima. Then we followed in 1943.

Our migration photo was taken by Tattersals. Rex, the baby, is the only one who has never returned to Samoa, but his son was a pilot for Polynesian Airlines.

In Kilbirnie, we learned to live with windows and cold. We also learned the enormous kindness of New Zealand women, particularly those we met at church. It was really hard finding a church. One night when I was shopping in Kilbirnie, I heard a band playing hymns, and so I went to watch. It was the Salvation Army band having an open air-meeting. One of the women walked right over to me and the children and asked if we'd like to come to church. That's how we began going to the Salvation Army. It was just like the Samoa lotu – no smoking, no drinking, no gambling; the only difference was the uniform. Even when the

LMS church opened on Kent Terrace and the Pacific Island Congregational Church began in Newtown, we still went to the Salvation Army. That little hall in Kilbirnie was our home. I still thank the Lord for sending that woman to talk to me. Apart from the church, we raised the children very strictly according to the faaSamoa. We had our family lotu in the evening using the Samoan hymn book and Bible. I didn't care if there were ten people at home, or just me. Every night there had to be a lotu. I talked Samoan to the children most of the time, but mostly they answered in English. English was important because we wanted them to do well in the palagi school. Their Samoan isn't as good as it could be: in fact, that's the thing I think I really failed in.

We were the only Samoans in Kilbirnie, and for many years it seemed like we knew every Samoan in Wellington, and in New Zealand. Not like today. In the early years so many of our aiga and friends started their New Zealand life at our little place on the hill that Jim built a large shed at the back of our house to fit all the people, which my daughter describes in her story 'How many people live in your house'. Jim became very well known at places like Hannahs, the hospital laundry, the Atlas Shovel Company, the wharf and the freezing works, because he was always trying to find work for our aiga coming from Samoa. In those days people had to have jobs as well as places to stay if they wanted permits to come to New Zealand.

We were honoured by the visit of Mataafa Faumuina, our aiga on scholarship including Fetaui, Suia, Eni and Moana Matatumua, Saisalui Ieriko and George Schuster. I remember how Jim used to close his eyes and shake his head with wonder at the hardcase antics of Alice Godinet (Ore), Mina McIntosh (Young), Hermione and Lavinia Langton, Elsie Schuster (Betham) and Lydia Betham (Groves) as, together with Mabel, they boogied through the little house and experimented with the latest palagi fashions. Even my mother Naitua came for a visit in the 1950s and went home with her first pair of reading spectacles.

Some of our aiga couldn't cope with life in New Zealand – the cold, the homesickness, parties and drink. My brother Tupuola Sepelini returned to Samoa, but my sister Sina lived out her life in Wanganui, and my brother Leitufa still lives in Porirua. Like others, our family saved and saved for trips back home, and sent money home for fares for aiga to come to New Zealand, to build churches and houses, for school fees, and what seemed like many, many church clocks. Jim used to joke that he worked for the children, and I worked for my family back in Samoa. That was true.

Our last two daughters, Barbara and Peggy, were born at that house on the hill. When Peggy was almost five, I got a job winding amatures at the Electrolux Factory in Kilbirnie. I did that for over thirty years, taking all the overtime I could get. Only six married women worked in the factory at that time, and a few single women. In my children's classes, I was the only mother who worked. Later a Maori family moved behind us, and their mother came to work at the factory as well. I started work at eight o'clock, then ran home at lunchtime to see if there were any letters from Samoa and make sure the children had a good lunch (they always came home for lunch even though it was twenty-minute walk, because we couldn't afford lunch papers or fancy sandwich fillings). On Wednesdays I'd put a leg of mutton in the oven at lunchtime, and the kids would add the potatoes and vegetables when they got home from school. After lunch, I'd run back to work again until five o'clock. Often, Barbara and Peggy would wait for me after work on the zigzag path, and I'd save the afternoon tea biscuits for them. The factory always gave out two biscuits with the afternoon cup of tea. We always made sure that there were proper meat and vegetables for every meal, but our family never had things like Weetbix, chocolate, biscuits or Ovaltine.

Everyone had their home jobs, just like in Samoa. All the boys had paper runs, they delivered groceries, they mowed lawns and sometimes they helped the milkman. The boys worked honestly and often palagi gave them tips. They gave us the 'pay' for the family, and they kept the tips and saved these to buy special things, like Weetbix, and their bikes. In the morning before school the boys walked the beach with their father collecting firewood to light the copper. They made this a game, trying to get more firewood than the other palagi combing the beaches each morning. I learnt all about layby and time payment. We can all remember the exact days we got a washing machine, a fridge, a telephone. These were all big events.

The children usually wore second-hand clothes passed on from the church women. One day the boys got into a fight when a classmate called them 'patchy pants'. The palagi never did that again, because my nephews, Sonny Schuster and Soo Teo (who were living with us) were both particularly good boxers. Sonny, especially, always protected our boys from bullying. But our boys never fought this way again because their father was so angry. Our children came straight home after school and stayed together at the house so that they wouldn't get into trouble. They did the house jobs first, then they played. They put cricket balls in my nylon stockings and tied these to the clothesline so they could practise their strokes, made a cricket wicket on the clay patch next door, lifted weights and practised all the latest body-building poses, played the guitar, studied, and went to cubs, scouts, Sunday school and church. Every Saturday I gave them ten pence: six pence to get into the pictures at the Kinema theatre and four pence to spend. We were a very tight group up on the hill. Our children had to be very strong. I know they were called niggers.

The children did quite well educationally. Jim sent them to the Wellington Technical College because he wanted them to have good steady jobs as builders, electricians, and plumbers and secretaries. Mabel's college days were cut short by the polio epidemic. She got so annoyed by the school closing, reopening and closing that she found herself a job and wouldn't go back to school! Mabel worked in photography, colouring black and white prints. The photo her boss, Robert Smith, took of Mabel posed as 'the' Polynesian beauty won the national competition and was featured at the Wellington Railway Station for many years.

When the time came for Ian to leave school, one of his teachers, Max Riske, came to visit us. We were a little scared, because we thought it was trouble. That was our first experience with a caring teacher. Mr Riske said Ian should go to university. We hadn't even thought about that – university was a place for the very well-off, not for Afakasi (persons of mixed descent) from Samoa – but Max Riske was very persuasive. We followed his advice, and Ian went to Victoria University, then on scholarships to Seattle and later to Canberra, which meant that we didn't see him for a long time. In fact, Ian never came back home until he had a Ph.D. Ian set a pattern for our children, and for many other Samoans who came to New Zealand as well.

Our children studied hard at school, they were in all the sports teams, they were prefects, they sang in school plays and church groups. They had part-time jobs during the school year and worked all the holidays for money for their fees and uniforms. In all those years I never watched my children play sport – I didn't have the time. But we went to school prizegivings. I framed and put the children's graduation pictures on the wall, and these were soon followed by their wedding photos: to three New Zealanders, one Austrian, three English and one Maori. Now our grandchildren's graduating pictures are pinned up, underneath their parents.

As I said, a highlight in my life was when the Sa Petaia family lotu started in Wellington. Our cousins Auelua from Lepa, Afele Atoa from Leufisa and my brother Atoa Teo Tuvale from Tanugamanono came for this event. The Sa Petaia lotu also started in Sydney in 1989, when my daughter was there. Aiga lotu are important to keep the family strong. At these meetings we always call out the branch names, and each branch stands up to be counted. Our Teo branch often 'wins'! The hundred-year lotu of the Sa Petaia was held at Leufisa just after Cyclone Val (Christmas 1991). The family falesa (church building) at Leufisa was opened at the same time. My sister Faavevela, our cousins Afele Atoa and Afamasaga Maua and Mili Afamasaga and I had been talking about this centenary for many years, just waiting for hundred 100 years. Those four passed away soon after this event. Then my younger sister Sina passed away in Wanganui. Now it's just me left in the second generation of the Sa Petaia.

A second highlight was when our son Ian was chosen to be the Teo after my brother Atoa Teo passed away in 1981. I can still remember the saofai (ceremony in which a matai title is bestowed and in which the chiefs of the village and often the district formally welcome the new chief into the position), my pride in remembering my father, my brothers, and now my son holding the family title. The Teo family is secure in Teo Ieni.

I've been in New Zealand almost fifty years. Jim passed away in 1973 soon after he retired. In 1980 my daughter Peggy and her family went back to live in Tanugamanono. They are now playing my part, serving the family there. I am happy to know that one of us is in Tanugamanono again. When Peggy's girls finished at Samoa College, one by one they came to stay with me in New Zealand while they did further studies, and we family in New Zealand looked after them here. That's our job. It's like the whole circle is starting again. Every one of us has our part to play for the family.

What of the return home? I go back to Samoa every year, but I'm not as strong as I used to be. Like many others, I have found that I can't live in Samoa now as I find the heat too much. When my sister Faavevela passed away at Tanugamanono in 1993, I really didn't feel like going back again. Unfortunately for others in Samoa, my memory is too long. I can recall the background of many cases that people would rather forget. That is another penalty of old age.

A few years ago an *Evening Post* reporter interviewed me for an article about early migrants to Wellington. I never really thought about my life until he started asking me questions. I just worked. I worked all day, and usually there was some church activity in the night. In the weekends, it was time to clean the house, to do the washing and ironing. Then church all day Sunday and back to work on Monday. My joy was in serving the family and the church. Each of my children has had a good education, they serve the church, and they know who they are. That is what matters. But when I read the article the reporter wrote about me, I wondered, had my life in New Zealand been as lonely as he described?

9

Redefining Chinese Female Migration: From Exclusion to Transnationalism

Manying Ip

The subject of Chinese female migration often conjures up exotic myths and images of 'mail-order brides', 'paper daughters' and 'hurry-up weddings' in villages where young women were quickly married off to migrant men on the eve of their departure from China, so that extra links were created to ensure their regular remittances and eventual return.[1] In recent decades, Chinese females who came to New Zealand as part of the so-called 'New Asian Wave' are often depicted as privileged middle-class wives leading leisurely lives in oversized houses, waiting for their husbands' periodic visits while they clock up time in order to gain citizenship status.[2] In this chapter, I want to explore the many facets of Chinese female migration in New Zealand, and examine the grounds on which some of these popular truisms have flourished.

Chinese women already featured in New Zealand's first census of 1867: there were six Chinese females and a total of 1217 Chinese males. Early migrant communities everywhere are commonly known for their gender imbalance, with males far outnumbering the females, but the gender-ratio of the New Zealand Chinese community remained severely unbalanced until very recent times. It was not until 1991 that the Chinese gender-ratio achieved a balance of ninety-nine males to one hundred females. The 124 years that took the New Zealand Chinese community to attain gender-ratio normalcy remain a powerful reminder of the long struggles that the Chinese faced. Both the exceptionally lengthy process and the severity of the imbalance were the result of New Zealand's discriminatory immigration policies, on the one hand, and, on the other, of China's traditional cultural practices, born out of harsh economic necessities.

Migration is commonly recognised as a means of bettering one's own circumstances. Historically, migrants to New Zealand have largely been voluntary, people who made their decisions by choice, after weighing up the pros and cons and deliberately taking the plunge, leaving the comparative security of the homeland and venturing into a new, less rigid and conservative world. Many female migrants, especially single women from Britain, chose to come to New Zealand largely because they saw opportunities of advancement in a less constrained society.

No Place for 'Asiatics' in 'New Britain'

The ideal of building a 'better Britain in the South Seas' necessitated large-scale migration from Britain.[3] The rationale of keeping New Zealand white and British was seen not as racist or self-serving but rather as a lofty mission of the utmost consequence to the world's civilisation. Premier Sir George Grey's 1879 memo to Parliament was at once grandiose, extravagant and highly self-righteous:

> The first migrants to New Zealand were selected with extraordinary care ... the future of the islands of the Pacific Ocean depends upon the inhabitants of New Zealand being true to themselves and preserving uninjured and unmixed that Anglo-Saxon population which now inhabits it ... This can only be accomplished by New Zealand possessing a population of a superior character ... a people manifestly capable of exercising that vast influence ... which appears to be the inheritance appointed for them by Providence.[4]

The presence of the Chinese was seen as an aberration to this ideal, pre-ordained New Zealand future. They were loathed and feared not just as Chinese people *per se*, but more for their debasing influence on New Zealand's British immigrants. 'The presence in this country of a large population of Chinese ... would exercise a deteriorating effect upon its civilization.'[5] The pioneers' vision of nation building was purist and exclusive: it simply had no place for the Chinese, who were seen as heathen, backward and 'Asiatic'. Malcolm McKinnon succinctly contrasts the nation-building ideal of New Zealand with that of the United States, which, theoretically at least, welcomed the huddled masses: 'New Zealand was not a New World, but a new Britain'.[6]

Chinese Female Migration Patterns

Chinese female migration stands apart from mainstream migration history in several ways. First, Chinese women migrants came as wives or, much more rarely, as daughters of Chinese men who were already naturalised New Zealand citizens. Early migration records show no instances of Chinese migrating together as a family, and there is no record of any Chinese female travelling to New Zealand on her own, as a pioneer migrant.[7] In other words, Chinese females ventured here only as a result of male migration; there was no independent female migration to speak of. This was in direct contrast to female migration from Britain and Ireland, when independent women were recruited as domestic helpers or simply welcomed to bolster the female population of the new land.[8]

Second, the Chinese were designated 'undesirable immigrants' by the New Zealand government. Even when their frequently cited virtues of industriousness, inoffensiveness and docility were counted, they were deemed to be 'too different' to become good settlers. The words of a parliamentarian in 1880 were typical: 'The Chinaman, however docile, however imitative, and however industrious he might be, in so far as he knew nothing about free government, were [sic] unfitted to take any part in the government of a free country'.[9] The logic of rejecting the Chinese on the grounds that they were simply 'different' was never questioned. John Ballance, the M.P. for Wanganui, said in 1888 during another parliamentary debate, 'They [the Chinese] will always live apart, their ideas are not ours, their modes of life are not ours ... it would be an extremely undesirable addition to our population'.[10]

From the very beginning, the Chinese were tolerated rather than welcomed, even when their labour was found to be useful in the goldmines. They were treated as itinerant workers rather than would-be settlers. In fact, they were invited into New Zealand in the first instance by the Otago Provincial Government to rework the abandoned goldfields precisely because it was assumed that none of them would want to stay in New Zealand.[11] This expectation was clearly stated in 1871, when a parliamentary committee recommended that the Chinese be tolerated because they were harmless, and they would not like to stay. The committee stated in the conclusion that 'as a rule, they return to China as soon as they have amassed a net sum from 100 pounds upwards ... no considerable number of them are at any time likely to become permanent settlers in the country'.[12]

ATTACHMENT TO CHINA ACCENTUATED

The view that the Chinese would not want to settle overseas was widely held. It has long been asserted that the Chinese people were singularly attached to their homeland. They seemed to believe in the infinitely superior culture of China and would always return to their homeland, even after decades of hard work overseas, after making it rich in such host countries as the United States, Canada, Australia or New Zealand. Such widely quoted sayings as 'Like fallen leaves returning to the ground' or 'Going back to the Tang Mountain' supposedly encapsulated the Chinese psyche. Allegedly they never wanted to settle down in foreign lands. Even those who died overseas would wish to have their bodies repatriated. Dying men who knew there could be no speedy repatriation would leave instructions for their bones to be disinterred and eventually sent back to China.

Such practices were regarded, variously, as Chinese eccentricity or superstition, and often cited as proof of Chinese sense of separateness, and their lack of commitment to their host country. The sad episode of the 1902 *Ventnor* shipwreck, during which the coffins and exhumed bones of some 490 Chinese were lost off the coast of Hokianga, was featured on New Zealand television in the 1990s as a bizarre footnote to the country's early history.[13] No one asked why the Chinese went to such lengths to repatriate their dead. The answer is simple and mundane: without their wives and children here, there was no one to tend their graves. If they had no families in New Zealand, there could be no real sense of belonging. A group of 'married bachelors', with their wives left behind in China, could not constitute a real and sustainable community.

It is no doubt true that the Chinese were attached to their homeland, but was their connection any greater than that of the Irish to Ireland, or that of the Jews to Israel? The fact that the Chinese remained a largely floating itinerant group in New Zealand for about a century before sinking roots was due as much to discriminatory immigration restrictions as to Chinese cultural practices.

The Chinese had always been reluctant migrants, but in Southeast Asia, in the kingdom of Hawaii and in many Pacific Islands they also had long histories of very successful settlement. In these countries, the comparative lack of restrictive legislation gave the Chinese the opportunity of moving in large numbers and, most importantly, of intermarrying with the local people, thus giving rise to sizeable Chinese communities. Migration, settlement and intermarriage are the necessary steps for any migrant community to become embedded and integrated into the adopted country.

At the same time, sojourning was a time-honoured necessity and a survival strategy.

> Sojourning is a concept well served by the Chinese lexicon, which possesses many terms to express the ideas of roving, lodging and being away from home temporarily … The simple fact is that aside from the peasantry large numbers of men in traditional China pursued their occupational calling away from home; they were sojourners, and where they sojourned were typically more urban … exporting local skills and occupational specialties, or just supplying labour.'[14]

In this scenario, the Chinese female's position was to serve as an anchor at home, and also as a magnet to ensure that the sojourner would eventually return. Chinese women must wait patiently for their men's return visits to the home village. If they were lucky, they would become pregnant in the process and sons would be born. It was then their duty to raise these children dutifully to preserve the patriarchal lineage. At the same time, they would also serve their husbands' parents obediently and respectfully. It was a life of 'live-widowhood', as portrayed by a mournful 'Gold Mountain Song':

> Do not marry your daughter to a Gold Mountain man
> He would not be home in one full year out of ten.
> Spiders webs would cover half of her bed
> While dust covers fully one side.[15]

More prosperous and successful Chinese merchants would sometimes take secondary wives, usually local women, at their ports of call. In New Zealand, some Chinese men married European or Maori women. Others, who could afford the poll tax and whose wives would brave the English test on their arrival, might send for their women when they accumulated enough wealth. In New Zealand, largely because of legislative restrictions and particularly their gendered effects, it was extremely rare to see Chinese women arriving in New Zealand.

Although most Europeans felt that the Chinese would only be itinerant sojourners and not permanent settlers, the New Zealand government found it necessary to introduce restrictive legislation to ensure that not too many would come in, even temporarily. The first piece of legislation, passed in 1881, was plainly called the Chinese Immigrants Act. It imposed a ten-pound poll tax on all Chinese arrivals and introduced a tonnage-to-passenger ratio of one to ten.[16] Further restrictions followed in 1896, when the poll tax was raised to a hundred pounds.[17]

Gendered Effects of New Zealand Immigration Legislation

Although the New Zealand government's restrictive laws were directed against all Chinese, in effect they made Chinese women's migration more difficult. When a Chinese immigrant could afford the poll tax to send for a family member, he often preferred to send for a son, a brother, a nephew or a male cousin rather than his own wife or daughter. In the poll tax receipt books stored in Archives New Zealand in Wellington, there are about three thousand names of Chinese who entered New Zealand between 1888 and 1930: only forty-seven of them are women.[18] It made better economic sense to bring in somebody who could work – in the goldmine, in the orchard or market garden, or in the laundry – in order to justify the huge capital outlay of a hundred pounds. Very often, families and clans pooled resources together to send a young man overseas, and it was a joint investment. The capital outlay could not be justified for women, who were not regarded as being useful economically.

It was against this background that the phenomenon of 'picture brides' and 'hurry-up weddings' flourished in the home villages. Young men of marriageable age would get married before migrating. Their families often recognised the value of wives as extra bonds to ensure regular remittances. If a man were not rich enough to support a wife, he could wait until he accumulated some wealth overseas and then get a matchmaker to arrange a picture bride, who would wait for her husband to return home for a formal wedding ceremony. The practice of Chinese men returning to their home villages to seek brides was reinforced by the difficulty of meeting European women as social equals, and also by the very low number of Chinese girls overseas. After marriage, the wives were routinely left behind in China while their husbands would re-emigrate. It was the duty of the men to seek a living and send their money home; the women were expected to hold the fort at home, serve their aging parents-in-law and raise any children they had. Usually the men would not be able to make conjugal visits to China more frequently than once every five or ten years. Within the home villages, people could always tell how many return trips the husbands could afford by the age gaps between his children. Quite often, the fathers would send (and pay the poll tax) for their sons when the latter reached their early teens. These boys would enjoy a few years of schooling, then start helping their fathers in shops, laundries or market gardens.

CHINESE WOMEN IN THE EYES OF NEW ZEALAND POLICYMAKERS

Although there were no specific laws against Chinese women's immigration, archival records clearly show that women were regarded by the New Zealand authorities as potentially more menacing than their men – because they could procreate. In 1907, during the debate on the Chinese Immigrants Amendment Bill, the arrival of thirteen females, referred to as 'the largest number of Chinese women arriving ... in the country's history' led to openly discriminatory public pronouncements: 'The result of this is that we are having New Zealand-born Chinese children, who are, unfortunately, brought up to live according to the habits of Chinese'.[19]

Chinese women seem to have been regarded as being a problem for two reasons. First, they could produce New Zealand-born Chinese children and thus increase a population that the government wished would disappear. Second, as upholders of the heritage and as home-educators, they would bring up these children in the Chinese way. It is clear that 'the habits of the Chinese' were regarded as evil and undesirable, and that ethnic Chinese children, even when born in New Zealand, were not good enough to be considered New Zealand citizens.

The same 1907 debate went on, 'There are in New Zealand at the present time fifty-five Chinese women. I think these figures alone will go to prove conclusively that it is about time something is done to deal with this matter.' It should be noted that these fifty-five Chinese women lived in a community with over 2500 Chinese men, and that the numbers of both were in rapid decline.[20]

The same year saw the introduction of the reading test that empowered customs officers at the port of entry to pick 'one hundred English words at random' to test Asiatic immigrants.[21] Chinese women of the time seldom saw or spoke to any men outside their own families, even in China. The prospect of being orally examined by a white man in a foreign language must have been extremely daunting. The hurdles put in the women's way in an attempt to prevent them from joining their husbands made many of them apprehensive and marginalised long after their arrival. Some would refuse to speak English altogether. All were condemned to very lonely existences with little social support – there were simply too few Chinese women in New Zealand.[22]

Repatriation of Local-born Chinese Girls

Another reason for the very low numbers of Chinese females in New Zealand (26 listed in the 1896 census, and 32 in 1901, 11 of them under 14 years old) was that young girls were often sent back to China.[23] This phenomenon has seldom been explored. It is well known that many local-born Chinese boys were sent home for 'proper Chinese education'. The incentive for sending the girls home seemed to be rooted in the desire for them to find proper marriage partners. Local-born Chinese girls were often disparagingly referred to as 'jook-sing', literally bamboo pole, meaning that they were empty (of Chinese culture), uncouth and unrefined. Lily Doo, a Canadian-born woman whose mother was also born in Canada, explained why she herself was sent back to China. (With the help of a matchmaker, Lily subsequently married a New Zealand merchant's son.) According to Lily,

> Chinese men in Canada preferred to make trips back to China to select their wives there, whereas European men would seldom marry Chinese girls. There was a surplus of Canadian-Chinese girls. Anyway, their families would rather they became concubines of Chinese men than marry westerners. On the other hand, westerners looked down on Chinese women and would not marry them.'[24] Lily's own mother became the fourth concubine of a man twenty years her senior.

Many New Zealand-Chinese girls ended up marrying New Zealand-Chinese men, with their matches made back in their home villages.

The Doors Closed: 1920s

By 1920, the permit system meant that New Zealand's doors were closed tightly against coloured immigration. All prospective immigrants had to have an entry permit, which the Minister of Customs had the right to grant or decline. No criteria for selection was given and when cases were declined there was no explanation. No appeal was possible. The system had no overt racial clause and was designed to be inscrutable. In reality it was an extremely powerful instrument to keep 'aliens' out and to keep New Zealand white.[25]

A quota was in force, according to a special negotiation between the New Zealand government and the Chinese consulate: one hundred permanent entry permits per annum would be issued to the Chinese from 1921 onwards. By 1925, women were excluded from the quota. In the words of a confidential internal Customs Department memorandum, 'This was presumably adopted as another means of preventing the Chinese population from increasing'.[26] This lasted until 1935, when the concession of ten permits for the wives of Chinese born in New Zealand was introduced. Permanent Chinese-born residents were not permitted to send for their wives at all.

Only one other immigration channel existed for Chinese people: to enter New Zealand on student permits. This began in 1930 and ran for twenty years until 1950. Chinese residents could apply to bring in their children for education on temporary six-month permits, which were renewable on condition that the children were doing well. Once more, the number of boys far outnumbered the girls. The entire Gisborne district file, which is the most complete one I have seen, includes only two Chinese girls.[27]

The absence of Chinese females ensured that the Chinese community remained a 'broken-stem' society of bachelor males, with no roots and no anchor in the host country. The men would therefore be obliged to leave, or to die out.

The Second World War and Refugee Families

The policy of restriction and segregation, based on the hope that the Chinese would diminish by attrition, did not really change until the eve of the Second World War. China was under Japanese attack a full decade before the 1941 attack on Pearl Harbour. Japan attacked northeast China in 1931 and established a puppet regime under the last Manchu emperor Puyi in 1933, calling it Manchukuo. Beijing (called Peiping at that time) was occupied in 1937, and the advancing Japanese armies rapidly overran important coastal cities. Canton and its surrounding villages, the homes of the New Zealand Chinese, were threatened in 1938. The escalation of the Sino-Japanese War in south China led to the temporary opening of New Zealand to the wives and minor children (under sixteen years of age) of Chinese men who already had permanent resident status. It was a special, one-off, temporary permit concession, approved by cabinet as a humanitarian gesture in February 1939. Originally designed as a short-term measure offering the women and children refuge for only two years, and carefully supplemented by various provisions to ensure that all these refugees would eventually be repatriated, the 1939 concession was to become a milestone in the history of Chinese settlement in New Zealand: an unintentional outcome of a hesitant open-door policy.

The period for this temporary permit application was also very short-lived. The first permits were granted in June 1939, and the concession was withdrawn in early 1940 'following complaints that Chinese fruiterers were employing their wives and children in their shops while their assistants were starting their own businesses, in some cases taking over shops vacated by European fruiterers who had joined the forces'.[28]

The remarkable speed with which the Chinese applied for their families to join them belies the popular perception that all Chinese wished to return home.

By 31 December 1939 permits had been issued for the temporary admission of 240 wives and 244 children. Considering that the resident Chinese population in New Zealand was only around 2500 at the time of the 1936 census, every one eligible to apply probably did so. The stringent and expensive conditions of the concession was not a deterrent. Each application required the following:

1. A deed of covenant executed by the husband and two other sureties that all cost on any public institution would be paid.
2. A bond for £500 guaranteeing that the wife would take all children born to her in this country way from New Zealand, and that the husband would 'give all necessary consents for this'.[29]

If the application were successful, the permit would be issued only under the condition that 'on arrival, the sum of 200 pounds was deposited with the Collector of Customs, together with a deed to the effect that the deposit would be forfeited if the conditions of the permit were not complied with'.[30]

Ensuring that the Chinese Would not Multiply

The 1939 concession was not designed as an open door to the Chinese, and the extraordinary precautions the New Zealand government undertook are worth examining. To enforce the eventual repatriation of the refugee women and any babies who would be born in New Zealand, the legal status of these infants had to be limited. There seemed to be no legal means of forcing a child born in New Zealand to alien parents to leave the country, and hence the large bond was imposed.

Even more problematic was the prospect that children born during the two-year concession period would insist on returning to New Zealand some time in future, even if they were repatriated initially. All ethnic Chinese, including local-born and naturalised citizens, were required to have certificates of registration (commonly known as re-entry permits) in order to return to New Zealand. So, in May 1939 the regulations were amended, stipulating that only people aged fifteen or over could obtain a certificate of registration. A confidential Customs Department memo explained the reasons behind such a move:

> It has recently been decided to grant permission in approved cases for the wives and minor children of Chinese residents of the Dominion to enter New Zealand for a period of two years, but before doing so it has been considered advisable for the Minister of Customs to be vested with power to refuse to grant Certificates of Registration authorising the re-admission ... of children who are born in New Zealand to Chinese women visiting their husbands in this country under the above-mentioned concession'.[31]

Subsequent history and world events would render this precautionary regulation change superfluous, but the New Zealand government's meticulous planning to keep the Chinese out and limit their numbers was evident even in the 1939 concession – so far the most generous and tolerant policy towards Chinese women and children. Once more, the potential menace of the Chinese females was highlighted by the extraordinary measures the government took to exclude their babies who might be born in New Zealand.

FEMALES IN A MYTHICAL 'MODEL MINORITY'

The decision of the Chinese to make the best of any opportunities was evident in the manner and speed with which the tiny community grew and prospered. The educational advancement of the young Chinese in the 1950s, new migrants and local born included, was particularly impressive. James Ng, himself a refugee child, checked through university graduation lists of the 1940s and reported that, 'In one remarkable bound, 92 of them, including about one third of the refugee children, graduated from University between 1945 and 1961'.[32]

This highly visible success of the Chinese children was backed up and actively nurtured by their parents, who rightly saw academic success as the single most effective ladder to enable their families to elevate themselves socially and economically. Bickleen Fong Ng, the first Chinese woman to attain a master's degree in New Zealand, recalls, 'I can't remember Mother saying anything about wanting me to study, but she must have endorsed it heartily. Because ... I had very little time to help her with her chores ... Father didn't finish his own college education, so he wanted me to fulfil his lost ambition.'[33] It was not uncommon for all the children of Chinese families to undertake tertiary education, supported by the hard work of their parents in fruit shops and market gardens. Their academic excellence enabled them to rise professionally. Within one generation, the Chinese in New Zealand moved from being market gardeners to becoming doctors, lawyers and architects, although their habitual humility kept them low-profile and invisible. They were widely praised for their frugality, inoffensiveness and modesty. Few mainstream New Zealanders would admit it, but the Chinese were liked because they knew their place and were not too assertive or demanding. Hardly any Chinese featured in the negative statistics of crime, alcoholism or unemployment. They were patronisingly called 'the model minority'.

The right of naturalisation, denied to the Chinese since 1908, was finally restored in 1951. Unfortunately, this important legislative move coincided with the period of the Cold War and McCarthyism. The fear that the ethnic Chinese in any western country might be a potential Communist fifth column was widespread. The allegiance of the New Zealand Chinese was under extra scrutiny. The criteria for Chinese naturalisation were so stringent, and the process so cumbersome, that the first naturalisation did not take place until 1952.[34] Mabel Sang of Napier, who arrived as a young girl, was the only one who qualified that year. There were ten more naturalisations in 1953, followed by another ten in 1954 – all of men.

In a small and marginalised community, where the males had long been relegated to menial service industries such as market gardening, fruit shops and laundries, most of the Chinese females worked within the confines of their home and family businesses. Typically, these businesses were labour intensive, required low capital and demanded long working hours. New Zealand-born Chinese women were generally well educated but, like their men, they kept a low profile and a polite distance from the mainstream community.

Growing up in their parents' shops was an experience widely shared by many local-born Chinese New Zealanders and most Chinese businesses required input from all family members.[35] Violet Leong, who was raised in Lower Hutt in the 1950s, expressed her strong feelings about growing up in a family shop, where all children were expected to serve customers, and where the golden rule of 'the customer is always right' was invariably enforced. 'From an early age, I was taught to smile to customers, to be polite … I knew I was Chinese, and so I had to always bite my tongue. I could never be honestly open … Business-wise, we had always to be courteous, and put our head down and never be rude.'[36]

The women's chores, such as cooking, washing and cleaning, were often carried out in the shops as well, and this blurring of private and public spheres further accentuated the modesty and compliance of many Chinese females. Kirsten Wong probably spoke for many when she lamented, 'How we have stunted ourselves! How we could not escape curbing our lives and ideas about ourselves because we have been in a minority … Racism has convinced us that it is a virtue to be passive. We even define ourselves negatively … we are not criminals, we're not lazy, we're no longer market-gardeners, we don't work in laundries now.'[37]

THE 1990s NEW FEMALE IMMIGRANTS

Nineteen eighty-seven marked a significant turning point for the Chinese community in New Zealand. In line with general economic deregulation and the opening of the country to the rest of the world, the fourth Labour government established a new immigration policy based on personal merit irrespective of racial or national origin. It was not intended to be revolutionary, but what followed not only changed the components of the longstanding Chinese community but also profoundly altered the ethnic composition of New Zealand, especially in the big cities.[38]

Many of the new Chinese immigrants arrived from countries outside China: Taiwan, Hong Kong, Singapore, as well as other parts of Southeast Asia, and even from South Africa and Australia.[39] From the late 1990s, however, the biggest source country of New Zealand's ethnic Chinese immigrants has been the People's Republic of China. Since 1991, the number of Chinese females has exceeded that of Chinese males. The 2001 census figures give the number of Chinese females as around 55,000 (and Chinese males as around 50,000), making the total number of ethnic Chinese just over 105,000.[40]

The new immigration policy recognises personal merit, measurable by youth, educational qualifications, professional experience, business track record as well as settlement capital: most of the new Chinese immigrants are middle-class professionals or business people. Media attention has tended to focus on the moneyed class who have built 'ostentatious houses' in sought-after school zones, and absentee parents who fly back and forth to their Asian origin countries leaving their children to take advantage of New Zealand's free education system. The anti-Asian backlash, which reached a height in the 1996 election campaign of the xenophobic New Zealand First Party, was largely fuelled by strong public resentment against the highly visible behaviour of the so-called 'astronaut parents' and their 'parachute kids'.[41] These aeronautical terms vividly capture the family arrangements of some new migrants within this post-1990s cohort. Often the chief breadwinner of the family, usually the man, would fly back to his wife and children left at the new destination periodically, but he would continue with his business in Asia. Sometimes, it was alleged, the children were like air-dropped paratroopers, left behind on their own in the new destination.

Academic studies of this phenomenon generally agree that it has its roots in the new migrants' desire to have the best of both worlds, and that frequent commuting is routinely practised by migrants of all ethnic groups, not just the Chinese.[42] However, the specially noticeable large-scale, short-term commuting to and from destination countries (seen not just in New Zealand but also in Canada and Australia) was popular among Hong Kong people before 1997. The fear and uncertainty of what might happen when the British colony became part of Communist China propelled worried middle-class Hong Kongers to leave the prosperous metropolis in search of a safe haven elsewhere. They were the 'reluctant exiles' whose sole reason for leaving was '[to fulfil] ... the residence requirement for a foreign passport, which was sought as an insurance policy against things going wrong after 1997'.[43] Since many of the females in this particular cohort had no intention to stay, they were merely 'clocking time in a strange land, with their hearts divided between their old homes and their children in New Zealand'.[44]

Differences among Women in Sub-ethnic Communities

Some significant differences marked the composition and settlement patterns of the new Chinese migrants according to their country of origin. Generally, research carried out to coincide with the 1996 census found that migrants from Hong Kong were older and many came as business migrants,[45] one of the reasons why more of their women tended to live as 'astronaut' wives in New Zealand. Many looked upon foreign citizenship as insurance against the volatility of Communist China's policies towards Hong Kong after 1997. The widespread conviction that Hong Kong was the best place to make quick money meant that comparatively fewer Hong Kong people wanted to remain in New Zealand.

Multi-local families were also common among the Taiwanese, but the decisive push factor was somewhat different from that of the Hong Kong arrivals and the fear of younger than their Hong Kong counterparts, and the women were more highly educated: like the men, many had had professional careers in Taiwan.[46] The majority of the Taiwanese immigrants to New Zealand qualified under the 'general skills' category, and therefore found the high rate of skills wastage after migration particularly galling.[47] Since Taiwanese qualifications are usually not recognised in New Zealand, many of the men also took to long-distance commuting, leaving their families behind. Judging from the number of Taiwanese choirs, women's associations and the dominance in many parent-teachers' associations as well as religious groups, Taiwanese women seem to be among the most philanthropic and socially active groups in New Zealand.[48]

Among the Chinese immigrants from the People's Republic, absentee parenting is comparatively rare.[49] Both parents usually live with the children, and grandparents are often present as well. Most of the working-age females in this cohort are actively engaged in various aspects of New Zealand life, either in employment or seeking further qualifications.[50] Like their Hong Kong and Taiwan sisters, many do not work in their specialised or qualified fields, but the People's Republic females seem to be the group most determined to strive for a better future in New Zealand by further studies or sheer hard work.

PROFILE OF THE NEW CHINESE FEMALES

The most accurate measure of the stability of settlement, the well-being and economic status of any ethnic group is their profile yielded by the national census. Before 1996, however, it was difficult to glean much meaningful information from the census statistics on the Chinese in general, and on Chinese women in particular. The very positive statistics of the established Chinese New Zealanders in education, income, professions and employment tended to obscure the dire situation in which many of the new Chinese migrants found themselves. In 1999, Statistics New Zealand subdivided the Chinese population into three groups: the New Zealand-born, the 'established' who had been in New Zealand ten or more years, and the 'new' Chinese who had arrived within the decade before the 1996 census.[51]

The crucial indicator of successful settlement is the labour market measure. The present author stressed this particular point at the nation's historic population conference in 1997:

> probably there is no better gauge to measure a migrant community's successful settlement than by looking at its employment status profile. When a new arrival finds a job or starts a business, it marks the crucial milestone of sinking roots, the beginning of the long process of social and economic integration by which the immigrant will derive steady income as well as acquire a circle of work mates and friends.[52]

Since the sub-ethnic group data of the 2001 census are not yet available, the following analysis of various aspects of the Chinese female population is based on the 1996 census results. The 32,835 Chinese females nationwide were significantly underemployed. Thomson characterised the nation's Chinese women as having 'fewer employed, more not in the labour force, and their patterns dominated by recent immigrants'.[53] A closer analysis of the working-age 'new Chinese' females (a total of about 20,000) shows that a high percentage (63%) were 'not in the labour force', and 20 per cent of these officially unemployed. Among new Chinese females who had work, 13 per cent were employers themselves and an additional 5 per cent were self-employed with no employees.[54] The failure of these new Chinese women to find work, and their high percentage of self-employment, are both tell-tale signs that inherent hindrances in the job market existed, preventing them from finding suitable employment in spite of the successful pre-migration track record many of them possessed.

The new Chinese females are very well educated: 25 per cent had completed tertiary education. The percentage of university graduates stood at 14 per cent, exactly twice the New Zealand proportion of similarly qualified females. This comes as no surprise, mainly because the new immigration policy targets the highly skilled and the highly educated. However, the occupational profile was less satisfactory. Although the percentage of managers was high (consistent with their self-employed status), the percentage of restaurant and hotel workers was higher than the national average, and 17 per cent of the new Chinese females worked as machine operators and in textile/apparel.

Corresponding to the bleak employment picture and the comparatively humble occupations in which the new Chinese females found themselves, their income level was 'well below the New Zealand average'.[55] About 19 per cent reported nil or loss income in 1996, and many reported very low incomes.

The willingness of the new Chinese to come to New Zealand, in spite of the comparatively unsuccessful economic outcome, underlines the fallacy of the established theory that migration is motivated primarily by economic considerations. The theory just cannot be applied to present-day migrants who are well educated, highly skilled and also comparatively wealthy. When asked the major reason for migrating to New Zealand, the most common response of the new Chinese was that they came in order to give their children improved education and better futures. Chinese parents clearly made significant monetary sacrifices to migrate. The mothers, in particular, interrupted their professional careers, gave up an extensive family support network and opted for a much less stimulating home life.[56] If their husbands were frequent commuters, these women also had to cope with all the challenges of settling into a new land as sole parents.

MULTI-LOCALITY STRATEGY:
WOMEN IN DIASPORIC FAMILIES

In a country where the very history of nation building is based on the settlement of British migrants, the frequent circulatory movements of the Chinese are understandably conspicuous and baffling. But migration has never been a single-direction movement. The migration and settlement patterns of the Chinese need to be understood within the wider context of New Zealand social and economic development. The impact of globalisation is significant, both in generating and accelerating the movement as well as in complicating the pattern of the integration of the Chinese community into New Zealand life.

The new immigrants' extra-local orientation comes from the fact that many of them have found the business environment and employment situation uninviting compared with the familiar, vibrant and high-growth economies of East Asia. Scholars studying the new migrant communities of Canada and Australia generally agree that the strength of the Asian economies, which created the Asian middle class with its venturesome migrants, also put powerful strings on these same people, pulling them back to Asia.[57] Even during the 'Asian 'flu' period of the late 1990s, during which the region's economy slowed down considerably, many business people continued to see more opportunities in Asia than in their host countries. It is this unwillingness to relinquish a lucrative and familiar markets, coupled with the belief that there might be new openings for linkages between their homelands and adopted countries, which has given rise to substantial increases in migrant international travel.

To some less fortunate new immigrants whose new business ventures have never taken root in New Zealand, and for those whose vocational skills have not been recognised, transnationalism has also become a necessity. Faced with the threat of prolonged unemployment and nil income, many new Chinese migrants feel that they have no option but to become 'returnees'. Shuttling across the Pacific is less an active choice than a survival strategy. The income earners go back to their countries of origin to pick up their former business or to engage in ventures in a familiar economic climate, and to support their families left in New Zealand with overseas funds.[58]

At the dawn of the new millennium, all indicators point to the tendency of new Chinese immigrants, both male and female, to develop into 'transnationals' for whom commuting is the norm. It is highly likely that they will remain bi-local or multi-local, never forfeiting the option of maintaining frequent contact with both their country of origin and their country of adoption. Migration to a particular host country is very often the beginning of step migration to a third country. On the other hand, return migration is not so much a permanent re-settlement in the county of origin, but in many cases involves periodic visits for the purpose of maintaining a diasporic network.

Furthermore, any apparent attachment to the place of former residence (People's Republic of China, Taiwan, Hong Kong or other overseas Chinese centres) may not be based on any lingering patriotism. The convenience of modern jet travel and telecommunication advancements have made trans-Pacific ties much easier to maintain, allowing both former business networks and family ties to be nurtured and built on.

The radically changing behaviour of Chinese migrants to Pacific Rim countries has gone hand in hand with the changing role of women. At the turn of the nineteenth century, entire villages in the Pearl River Delta were kept prosperous by remittances from the goldfields of the New World, New Zealand included. In these first years of the twenty-first century, we witness the reverse phenomenon of Chinese men working in Asia where the economy is expanding faster and where jobs are more plentiful, to support their families in Vancouver, Sydney or Auckland.

Developing simultaneously with this shuttling between the homeland and the new country of adoption is the building up of multi-locality networks among members of the extended family of the migrants. Contrary to the expectation of chain-migration theorists, the new Chinese New Zealanders survey reveals that comparatively few new Chinese immigrants have siblings and parents staying in New Zealand with them.[59] Instead, many have siblings and parents in their country of origin or in various Pacific Rim countries. For example, respondents to the survey have more of their siblings located in Australia and Canada than in New Zealand. This phenomenon is highly significant and has far-reaching implications for the future of the diasporic network. Many of the new Chinese New Zealanders have spatially extended families, with members scattered around the cities of the Pacific Rim.

Superwomen or Incidental Transnationals?

An optimistic view is that the long-term future of the many new Chinese diasporic centres, New Zealand among them, could develop into linkage points of the overseas Chinese network through which the Chinese conduct their trade and technology transfer. In this scenario, Chinese women would be superwomen:

highly skilled, adaptable and driven to build better futures for themselves and their children. They would instill an international outlook and global perspective within their communities. As individuals, mothers and wives, their successful coping strategies would help to bring stability to the twin processes of sinking roots and establishing diasporic networks.

A high percentage of Chinese parents came to New Zealand mainly for the future of their children. Therefore, it would be useful to look at the children's intentions. In a 2001 study of how Asian teenagers view their future employment opportunities, the researchers found that a significant percentage of the young migrants feel that their career opportunities are best fulfilled in either their country of origin or a third country, rather than in New Zealand.[60] There is a common perception among these teenagers that they might meet with discrimination from their prospective New Zealand employers, or that they might be passed over because of perceived language deficiencies.

Since these children of the new Chinese are highly mobile, not unlike their mainstream New Zealander compatriots who regard overseas experience as an essential part of growing up, their mothers may have additional incentives to be frequent travellers as well. However, transnational movements themselves do not necessarily engender economic activities and lucrative linkages. The New Zealand situation has so far shown the readiness of new Chinese migrants to invest in the future of their children by choosing a destination that is politically and socially stable, a country with a superior lifestyle and clean environment.[61] There is little evidence of persistent international business network building, and trends point to a mode of behaviour that is transnationalism more by default than by intent.

In the section entitled 'Patterns of Migration', in the seminal work *The Encyclopaedia of the Chinese Overseas,* Lyn Pan wrote 'Emigration has been both necessity and advantage, both exile and opportunity ... incorporating both onward relocation and repatriation'.[62] The new Chinese will most probably maintain multi-national residence and linkages, and also acquire bi-citizenship wherever possible. Transnationalism has by now become a long-term strategy, rather than a temporary expediency. Chinese females will be active participants in this process, bravely and innovatively building their futures, at once coping with the challenges of frequent commuting and looking after the changing needs of their families as opportunities unfold.

10

Gendering German Migration Experiences in The 1980s and 1990s

Brigitte Bönisch-Brednich

'Men', said Bea very firmly, 'have quite different experiences'.

Post-war migration to New Zealand has not only increased and positively enriched the country's population but also created a huge pool of cross-cultural memories reaching out to the Pacific, Asia, South Africa, continental Europe and in a renewed form to Britain. Many single men and women, and also families from all over the world, came to settle in the Antipodes. Early research concentrated on statistical figures and immigration politics, in order to show the diversity of immigration to New Zealand, and its impact on the country: the work of K.W. Thomson, A.D. Trlin and P. Spoonley created an important background and a foundation for a number of interview and other fieldwork studies focusing on personal experiences and immigrant (auto)biographies.[1]

Research on migration, certainly projects done during the past ten years, uses gender as both a methodological and an analytical framework. Both women and men are usually included in interview and questionnaire samples, as well as in the historical sources, although sometimes a single sex is exclusively chosen for a detailed analysis.[2] As a rule, in recent studies based on oral history men and women are interviewed in equal proportions. It seems somewhat surprising, therefore, that there are few specific attempts to compare female and male migration experiences.[3]

This chapter will give a short overview of the issues German women and men have raised in interviews with the author, and of the different ways they referred to their immigration experience. The basis for this analysis is a comprehensive research project on the oral history of German immigration to New Zealand. The primary sources are interviews with 102 immigrants (forty-two men and sixty women) who came to New Zealand between 1936 and 1996. The fieldwork was done in 1996–98 and the average duration of the interviews was ninety minutes. Ninety per cent of the interviews were conducted in German, so most of the quotations given in this article are translations into English.[4] The project was designed as part of a long-term ethnographic field study, comprising participant observation, a field diary and interviews with focus groups, as well as interviews with couples, families and single people.[5]

Although the material of the long-term project covers six different phases and periods of immigration, in order to concentrate on significant points of gender-related migration experience, this chapter concentrates on immigrants from the 1980s and the 1990s.[6] The main questions discussed are the differences between men and women with regard to the decision to emigrate and the way in which these decisions are explained and justified. How are the stories of integration told, and what memories – particularly those that constitute the turning points – are considered important? What are the key stories in male and female narratives? And how do women and men see the impact of migration on their own personality, personal growth and so on?

Who Decides?

A very important aspect of assessing emigration experience is the decision-making phase, when the new country is chosen and the entire future of the individual and perhaps his/her family is determined. Generally there is a huge difference between people migrating on their own and family groups of migrants. For example, backpackers, yachties and other types of globetrotters often arrived haphazardly, happened to stay on for a period and finally decided to remain indefinitely. For individuals the decision to leave Germany, then, quite often meant leaving for an unspecified period of time, not necessarily with the intention to migrate permanently to a specific country. In contrast, most families made conscious decisions to leave and planned their migration carefully, going through the usual procedures of deciding, applying, packing up, farewelling the family and the old life, and finally arriving in the chosen country.

Where family migration took place, a collectively used 'we' in the interviews makes it difficult to work out how the decision was made. Frequently, in fact, the crucial discussion inside the family group or the couple is covered up in a joint 'we decided', 'we went', 'we expected'. Although it is not possible to make a thorough analysis it is possible to express doubts about the reality of this 'we'. In most cases, certain phrases point towards the man as the main motivator. Women sometimes provide a clue, saying something like 'And then Werner came home and said …', 'Gert said he could no longer live here, something had to happen'. Men, too, often went on exploratory forays into New Zealand, leaving the women at home to run the family. Men talk about their initiatives in finding a job in New Zealand, including through preliminary enquiries, and of having presented job offers as surprises to the families. In general the men were frequently the driving force in the migration enterprise, and the women seem to have permitted themselves to be infected with their enthusiasm. The family 'contract' often made before leaving was that, after a period of two or so years, the decision would be reconsidered by every single family member. But this contract often no longer applied after a short time in New Zealand. Meanwhile, it was usually the women who had the greatest adjustment problems, with men and children adapting faster and easier to the new living conditions, especially through work and school.

Within families, women felt unable to assert their wish to go back. This did not usually result in open conflict within the family, but rather, was frequently described as a silent process of withdrawal. The husband was happy, the children were content and the women 'couldn't make the demand on the others to go back only for my sake!' The women had often given up their jobs in Germany before migrating (if not before, for example, to care for their children). They were often of the opinion that they should not work immediately in New Zealand, but take care of the family and provide a secure background at home.

From a feminist perspective, therefore, migration often became counterproductive, leading women into isolation and financial dependency during the first years after arrival. Most women who came with their families did not start jobs until three to five years later. This point was frequently described as the turning point in their immigrant biography. A job would open up new social networks and improve their English skills, thereby making them more confident and content. In retrospect, however, about half of the interviewed women were glad to have had the 'home-alone' experience: they expressed the belief that having survived such hard and lonely times had improved their lives by giving them the opportunity to discover hidden strength in their characters. The other half said that although they were now happy and could laugh about their early years and tears, they would not be prepared to go through such a hard experience again.

Since the 1980s, increasing numbers of young women have travelled on their own, and a sizable number have decided to migrate to New Zealand. The way that single women remember their migration, and how they dealt with their arrival and settling in period, is completely different from that of family women. They made some very firm statements about their reasons for coming to New Zealand in the first place, and in some cases their determination to emigrate officially.

> *Ingrid:* I travelled for three years and the conclusion of those three years, when I was on a journey around the world, was New Zealand. I was travelling by myself. And the country simply fascinated me ... And then I went back, actually with the idea that I would save some money and then come back here as quickly as possible. And then I met Rolf and made it clear to him from the beginning that I was going to go to New Zealand and if there had been no interest of any kind in that I would not have gone into a relationship. Oh well, New Zealand was more important than a relationship with a man who was not interested in New Zealand.

Explaining Decisions

Although on the surface many women made confident decisions about migration, after their arrival they seemed to think longer and harder than men about why they decided to migrate. Certainly, equal numbers of men and women gave an overall set of reasons for migrating in the 1980s and 1990s: for example, the nuclear danger in Europe and environmental pollution, overpopulation and everyday racism. But women quite often also had decision-making stories of another kind that reflected the workings of fate or supernatural powers in their lives.

These uniquely female reasons are connected to 'alternative' lifestyles and to the removal of women's lives from the traditional ties of Kinder, Küche, Kirche (children, cooking, church). Women who migrated on their own were nearly always linked to alternative lifestyles. As well as outlining a critical attitude to Germany and an enthusiasm for New Zealand, like the men, many women interviewees added a second dimension to the discussion: that of a pre-determined destiny. For some, migration was 'preordained' during childhood or puberty; others had an inner feeling of spiritual arrival when they first reached New Zealand.

Many women said they had had the feeling they must leave Germany even when they were children. Either New Zealand played an important part in these prophetic childhood episodes from the very beginning, or else they simply expressed a feeling that they had to go away. In particular the phrase 'wanting to leave Germany' was often used in this connection. (Interestingly, men and women were asked the same questions; women offered these reasons in response to general enquiries.)

> *Annegret:* I always wanted to go away. Even as a child. I always wanted to go away. Funnily enough I could always see myself in South America in a big house at the seaside. ... The funny thing was that when my son Oliver, my youngest son, came to visit me here, for the first time here in New Zealand ... he said: 'Listen, Mum, you have made your dream come true here, haven't you?'
>
> *Inge:* I wanted, from childhood on, to see the other side of the world. I just had this idea. My father was always talking about the antipodes and that sort of thing. And as a child I always thought: so what is an antipodean? And I thought about the way their feet pointed up towards ours and I had all sorts of fantasies. And it never left me, this urge to find out what's going on on the other side of the world.

For other women, dreams of discovering the world came during puberty.

> Rachel: When I was —how old was I then? – when I was about fifteen or sixteen we did something about New Zealand at school. And also I had a friend back then, a girl called Martina, and I had a talk with her once. About men, the way you do when you're young, and then we talked about who we wanted to marry, and then I said to her back then: 'One day I'm going to marry someone who comes from America or New Zealand.' And I was fifteen then. And of course she thought that was silly and said, 'Oh, rubbish,' and I said 'Ah, you'll see.'

The moment of arrival in New Zealand was of great significance to many women, a spiritual and a physical event. Some simply described this as an intense sensation of having come home:

> *Inge:* And when I came to New Zealand and was sitting in the bus from Auckland to Tauranga and saw the green hills with the little white dots on them: there I was in the bus and I knew that I was at home. And that was it, and it has never left me: the feeling that I belong here. And now when New Zealanders ask me 'How did you come to end up here?' I simply say, 'The stork lost its way [laughs], it flew in the wrong direction and delivered me in Northern Germany, and I should really have come to New Zealand; somehow it got its wires crossed … I thought that was funny, and I thought I would have to find reasons for it or something like that. Sometimes I say that this is my spiritual home. This is the country that made it possible for me to grow up in my soul and that still makes it possible for me to develop my strengths. But those are just some kind of justification. All I know really is that I belong here: enough, stop, end, cut! [laughs]

Some young mothers felt that they *had* to come here so that their child could be born or grow up in the 'right' country. Characteristically, however, this reasoning did not refer to the Pakeha world, but to the world of the Maori, to Aotearoa rather than to New Zealand. This does not necessarily mean that these women have a very strong connection to Maori culture or even Maori friends. It seems to be rather a romantic view about the indigenous culture, connected to notions of fate.

> *Sina:* I always say we were meant to come here so that we could have our daughter. She wanted to be born here. She's a real Kiwi; she belongs here. I think she was some kind of Maori warrior or something in her last life. So she had to come back here. [laughs]

> *Corinna:* Anna always gets so amazingly brown and it's also the language and this [natural adaptation to the] culture group; that's so natural for her that I think: she has to be a reborn Maori. It really could be true. It's really strange! She's so completely involved with iwi.

Different types of 'spiritual' assurance have been especially important for women in the most recent period of immigration. Since it was their own decision (even if in conjunction with a partner) to stay or migrate to New Zealand, there seems to be a need to find added justification later for this decision. This justification takes place not only on a logical but also on a spiritual and emotional level.

Men, on the other hand, did little more than carefully present their decision to migrate in rational terms, generally using the set of explanations mentioned above. They may have had an overall wish for a new challenge, often feeling that their life in Germany seemed to have slowed and staled. As we have noted, they often drove the decision to migrate: women's 'spiritual' reasons may be reactions to this.

Narratives of Integration

In general, well-known gender-specific patterns can be detected in stories about the familiarisation phase. Women tell stories very subjectively, offering their feelings and personal experiences (including those of the family); men tend rather to emphasise their specific reasons for migrating, and talk about their professional careers, as well as reflecting on political, historical and general topics. For women the most important topics are homesickness, problems with integration, the health of ageing parents at home, the progress of their children and assessments, in hindsight, of their own development. Weaknesses and mistakes (misinterpreting 'ladies a plate' or 'bring a plate' as a request to bring an *empty* plate to a function[7]) are detailed and discussed. Exemplary stories often reflect a symbolic meaning for a person's life.[8] Married women and/or those who did not take up work at once, tend to stress the successful organisation of daily life in quite practical ways, more like the men.

Men, on the other hand, construct their immigration narratives more as *success* stories. Homesickness is not one of their topics, and bonds with Germany are often made objective rather than personal by emphasising such matters as *responsibility* for ageing parents. Any expression of an inner desire to go back is immediately blocked off by reference to the fact that it is financially impossible to do so. They focus on ongoing integration, especially in the form of the various steps in their career or of their own social progress. Initial difficulties in the workplace are usually described as closely associated with language problems and a lack of professional discipline among their New Zealand colleagues.[9] At the same time, their reporting is often peppered with humorous remarks, suggesting that now they can smile about it all and that these problems are things of the past.

Men measure the success of their own integration in terms of whether they can explain, without emotion, certain problems and differences. In general men speak more about their career and their 'success', while women who have migrated with a family speak of both homesickness (often referring to 'absent things') and overcoming it. Women who came alone talk about gaining strength and the development of their personality. These three variants are now presented in more detail.

Masculine Success Stories

In contrast to many women, men give only limited space to describing problems, doubts and homesickness. It cannot be assumed, however, that homesickness is a women's topic: men also talk about problems and express self-doubts, but indirectly. In their descriptions of the arrival and familiarisation phases, however, they use fundamentally different narrative techniques. The impression is that they had fewer problems and 'had the matter in hand' fairly quickly. Their first years in New Zealand are seen more in relation to their first jobs and their wages and to the subsequent steps in their careers; in some cases this employment-related range of subjects is extended to other spheres, such as political or club activities. Initial difficulties with such matters as language, lower wages and the casual attitude of their new colleagues serve especially to emphasise their subsequent improvement in English language skills, raises in wages and adaptation to the new world.

> *Wulf:* The language was the biggest problem. My first job was for a consultancy company and I had been working there for two weeks when they put me into a firm and I was sitting there at a big board meeting where they were all telling me what they wanted to do and I didn't understand anything at all about what they wanted me to do. But they were paying a hundred dollars an hour for me. And I sat there and the third time I asked a question I thought, I just can't go on; I can't ask four times, no. It was an absolute nightmare. That was not good.

When men tell stories about first jobs they try to record the subjective side of the experience by using objectively measurable statements. Since a hundred dollars an hour were being paid for Wulf, it is perfectly credible that he was suffering from some kind of pressure; no doubt, this is what he was trying to get across without saying so. From the men there is often the suggestion that feelings are acceptable only in relation to the facts of earnings, hours and time management:

> *Norbert:* Oh yes, financially, measured by the fact that I halved my German earnings by a factor of two, on the other hand we paid only $140,000 or about the same in marks for our house. My income went down from about 90,000 to about 30,000, but during the years I spent in New Zealand I pushed that up to roughly 80,000, which was very good in New Zealand terms. There is no doubt at all that that step was really difficult and that I made it and was also successful from the firm's point of view.

Men often spend a lot of time describing such matters as the founding of a firm or the various stages of a career, with only a few brief remarks about states of mind or personal development. For example, one interviewee, between descriptions of two different contracts with companies, mentions in passing that his marriage to the woman who had migrated with him had split up at around the same time. Indeed, questions about personal development are very often answered with stories about work. This does not necessarily mean that interviewees wish to evade such questions, but rather that working for a living plays a fundamental role in their emotional life and that self-assessment depends a great deal on one's job.

Even if men deliberately push working for a living to the margins in their interviews, the narrative techniques remain similar. So-called 'dropouts' with alternative lifestyles talk of *successfully* dropping out and of *successful* personal development. Even here, feelings or detailed descriptions of crises do not take up much space, and we have to be content with short remarks in the course of detailed descriptions. Overwhelmingly, the success of migration, and therefore of dropping out, is measured in contrast to the people who 'changed countries but not jobs' by how little money one really needs to live on and a focus on the things that are really important in life:

> *Arne:* And that's a matter of fate, where you happen to be. Things can't go on in Germany the way they are now, because the country changes you. The main thing is that it changes you into having more freedom. You suddenly discover, we could do that too and you don't need that at all. There are all the things you no longer have to do, that you have to do when you're in Germany. You don't need any insurance policies, for example. I haven't got a single insurance policy! You don't have to. I just live. I have very few extra costs.

Often, in fact, specific problems can be detected only between the lines. For example, Arne comments that it is indeed the fulfilment of a dream to own a house on the hill with a view of the ocean, but he adds that in the lonely region where he now lives there is a lack of intellectual stimulation.

> *Arne:* The landscape is such an incredibly powerful presence here, and such a source of strength, and every day, every day I am on my 'rebounder' out there. I always make a hop and look out [laughs], do my exercises, because at my age I have to do them slowly, and then I always tell myself how happy I am that I can afford to do that, to live here. Really, you just have to do that, it can get dead boring if you don't create that in your consciousness every day afresh. What else can one do here?

Although men and women use different narrative techniques, this does not mean that it is impossible to tell whether a man is happy, unhappy or mixed about his migration. It is just that the messages are packed in masculine narrative codes. To decode them, at least for me as a female listener, it is necessary to go through the entire conversation again and again, listening very carefully. Women, on the other hand, generally make very clear and meaningful statements about their personal feelings and their emotional development. This makes it difficult to reconstruct a conventional curriculum vitae from the interviews with women: for example, one can only indirectly discover anything about their financial situation. But it is personal life, of course, that is central to such a fundamental experience as migration – and one can grasp this far better from women's interviews than from men's.

FEMALE HOMESICKNESS STORIES

The most problematic aspect of migration is *homesickness*. I listened to narrations of homesickness not only in the interviews but also in many informal conversations, and it occurs in most female group discussions. Suffering from homesickness is closely related to the intensity of bonds with Germany, and the *real* extent to which the decision to migrate was shared by the women in partnerships. When families migrate the pre-existing traditional gender roles are often reconstituted or reinforced in the new country. In the families who migrated during the 1980s and 1990s, especially, the children were often still infants or were just reaching primary-school age. In such cases the women had already given up their professional careers in Germany, or they no longer practised their professions when they reached New Zealand. As a rule, then, migration meant concentrating on finding a position for the man or helping him settle happily into prearranged work. The woman, meanwhile, took over the tasks of finding a suitable flat or house, unpacking the container and looking after the children. This led to rapid and profound isolation in surroundings where the woman neither understood the language nor felt familiar with cultural codes. In addition, for mothers it was often a shock to find that, unlike Germany, New Zealand schools ran all day, so there was not the same need to care for children so intensively. In Germany, schools are run for half of the day, and with limited arrangements for childcare it is often necessary for one parent to stay at home or work part time.

> *Bea:* And here in New Zealand, from the very beginning the children were away from nine or half-past eight until half-past three, if you include their way to and from school, and I was by myself all day! And then, when the container arrived I first had a bit of time to unpack and decorate the rooms and so on, and when I had done that, I thought, what now? Nothing. ... Get a bit angry, cry a bit, and things like that. That was just unavoidable, really ... I was feeling very homesick.

Other women speak of intense attacks of homesickness before and after the birth of a child, often the first child. At that time they felt the absence of their own mother, or of a sister or close friend, as a heavy burden. Homesickness, many said, is not concerned with an abstract idea of Germany; rather, it is the absence of something very concrete: familiar social networks and the comfort of close family. Birth, for example, often represents the high point in feelings of loneliness, compounded by language problems arising in the meetings with doctors or midwives. As a result, some women spoke of an inner determination to fly home for the second pregnancy, or at least to take a trip home after their next birth.

Women often talk at length of their feelings of despair, homesickness and tearfulness, and their attempts to hide this from their children, and sometimes from their partners as well. These descriptions are often followed by an account of the moment when their destiny took a turn for the better:

> *Edith:* Well, and then we arrived here and ... and it was as if we had taken a step ... backwards in time. Oh, that was terrible. Oh, how I cried, how I cried! Terrible, that's what it was! And I was homesick, HOMESICK! HOMESICK! So alone. I didn't know anyone. I had two children. Yes, I could speak English, but Andy was at work all day and I mean we arrived in New Zealand and we had nothing. ... And then Andy went to an auction and bought some furniture. [laughs in anticipation because everyone knows about Andy] And when I saw it I burst into tears. The furniture looked as if it had come here with Captain Cook. ...[10]

The disappearance of homesickness is usually coupled with taking up work. Although this was often just an ordinary job, sometimes it was training for a new career. Some kind of unpaid activity also helped to cure homesickness: finding any kind of meaningful task strengthened the woman's self-esteem, led to a rapid improvement in English language skills and to new acquaintances, and ultimately meant faster integration into the new way of life. Even so, work activities constituted only one strand in their migration narratives: others included their circle of friends, the lives and development of their children, and (again and again) their own state of mind – culminating in contentment, and even happiness.

Finally, talking about homesickness, and about the earliest years and their associated trials, emphasises the success of migration. Describing homesickness by narrating, remembering and recapitulating pain is extremely important: it is not only part of one's own life story, but, above all, a part that has been *mastered*, and so although it constitutes a stark contrast with present life it is also the foundation for current happiness. Almost all women interviewees feel that in the end they have profited from migrating, even if their paths were considerably harder than that of their husbands and children; and even if half of them would not want to go through such difficulty again, however happy the ending.

Stories of Personal Growth and Cathartic Experience

One of the final prepared questions in the interviews was 'Would you do it again?' The interviewees themselves had often already raised the topic, in reflecting the impact of migration has on their personality and personal growth. Indeed, most interviewees of the 1980s and 1990s put it in exactly such terms. This topic is often closely combined with a reflection on the (sometimes former) partner with whom migration was planned and carried out. Many women feel that their migration story – whether happy or otherwise – is very relevant or even central to their personal development and their general biography. If they migrated by themselves, homesickness usually has no great role to play in their narrations. Rather, the emphasis is on opportunities for personal development and getting to know one's own strengths. These are described not so much in terms of a professional career as in terms of cognitive processes, extending horizons and the conviction that life in New Zealand has been better than it would have been in Germany.

Often, in hindsight, certain memories take on the role of key experiences. This might be, for example, the separation from a partner they migrated with but who turned out to be an emotional burden. Also often reflected on are the development of a new relationship and crises following migration. For both men and women migration is by no means a good way of reviving a relationship. On the contrary, it often imposes a considerable burden on a dysfunctional relationship. This *can* in the end lead to a sturdier partnership, but separation, and subsequent new beginnings, also play an important role in the memories of female emigrants. Women often describe such separation as the equivalent of a leap in personal development and a feeling that a new life has started. For these reasons the description of the failure of a relationship is often viewed as equally important as the migration itself. In such cases, the ex-partner often comes to stand for patterns of behaviour and styles of life brought from Germany and found to be intolerable in New Zealand. These stories of separation often take the form of a short digression that is consciously given a humorous structure, but at the same time makes an effective point:

> *Annegret:* And at some point, I don't know, I got into a panic. I thought: 'I can't go on living like this.' He was so pessimistic! He was so unbelievably negative! That I was always busy thinking about suicide. And some time I had just had enough. And then he went to Germany for six months for a holiday. And I thought, 'Now or never!' And so I ordered a container. And I sent his stuff on the journey after him. [laughs]

Such stories of separation, then, can often relate to the migration itself, to the liberation from life in Germany. In a kind of intensive comparison of outcomes, the German life story is cut off like fetters and newly achieved personal freedoms emerge. New Zealand then stands for a new 'I'; migration represents the chance to get rid of bad memories, compulsions, traumatic family relationships and long-held fears. In these stories migration becomes a kind of metamorphosis, after which the real, previously unknown personality is revealed.

> *Sina:* For me it was like this: Because I was so much alone here and so dependent on myself, you just have to do it somehow, you are driven to your own limits. And then I noticed, 'Hey, action I can really do that', you know? And that gives you so much strength, you know, I'm a completely different person here from the one I was in Germany. You know: much, much stronger.

In spite of their more restrained narrative style, a number of men also suggest that they have been through development processes of this kind, although these are not told so personally or with the same enthusiasm as that of women. One such statement might be, for example, that 'migration can be recommended to others because of the quality of experience it brings with it'. In this way, personal experiences are generalised and such a rhetorical trick neutralises the individual's experiences so that they can be expressed in a covert way.

A frequently occurring issue is whether the migrant would recommend migration to others. Women tend not to make any explicit recommendations. They point out that it was important for them in a very personal way, but that this experience cannot be generalised: everyone has to make an individual decision and perhaps put it to the test. Men, on the other hand, often use the formula of recommendation as a 'safe' way of expressing their own feelings; they have fewer inhibitions about uttering such recommendations, based on their own experiences (which are generally, initially happy). Thus, a recommendation expressed by a woman interviewee can sound rather vague, and that by a man can be emphatic. In this comparison, the man emphasises his recommendation loudly and with laughter while the woman is tentative in her presentation:

> *Werner:* You fall on your face now and then, it's true. But it's a really great space for personal growth. I can only recommend it: [laughs] New Zealand!

> *Birgit:* Oh, yes. Well, I'm very pleased, really. Even if we go back I am pleased that we have done this. In fact I think it is really a total enrichment. I can only recommend it. Yes I can.

Conclusion

After analysing a number of autobiographical stories it is clear that both men and women regard their migration enterprises as successful, enriching and of great value for their lives. But the *way* in which the two sexes describe this overall achievement is very different.

Men tell their stories in terms of their work experiences and professional successes, mentioning their emotional experiences in passing; they tend to present their accounts as more or less linear narratives, emphasising good, funny and success stories. Women who migrated with their families often describe the time of arrival and integration as a period of (passive) endurance, dealing with sadness and feelings of loss. But all of them contrast this period with their current happiness and confidence and the emergence of new, strong sides to their personalities. Women who migrated alone also describe initial feelings of loneliness and hardship, although this period passed relatively quickly and was soon interpreted as a positive and enriching experience.

Recounting their own migration experiences is a crucial part of the everyday life of German immigrants to New Zealand. It is vital for their happiness and their confidence that their decision to migrate is seen as positive. Moreover, positive migration stories enable them not only to get a firm grounding in New Zealand but also to develop a healthy attitude towards the Germany they left behind. All interviews used for this chapter were conducted with migrants of the last twenty years, and this timeframe adds an extra factor to the positive view of migration. For migration is considered to be a vital and desirable part of *modern* life; part of a globalised, easily travelled, interconnected world. Nevertheless, interviewing such migrants reveals that the process of changing countries is also full of difficulty and anxiety, and requires a lot of emotional energy and hard work.

Telling stories about one's migration experience, then, is vital for gaining emotional security and happiness, but women approach the task quite differently from men. Although, in this case, both genders have come to the same (positive) conclusion, migration is and will probably remain a different story for men and women.

About the Authors

Ann Beaglehole's research has focused on the experiences of immigrants and refugees and on aspects of women's history. Two of her books (*A Small Price to Pay* and *Facing the Past*) are about Jewish refugees who came to New Zealand from Central Europe in the years before and after the Second World War. *Eastbourne, A History of the Eastern Bays of Wellington Harbour* (by Ann Beaglehole with Alison Carew) was published by the Eastbourne Historical Society in December 2001.

Brigitte Bönisch-Brednich works as a Cultural Anthropologist at the Georg-August University of Goettingen (Germany) and at the Stout Centre for New Zealand Studies at Victoria University in Wellington. Currently, she is the New Zealand National Library Fellow. Her special fields of interest are migration, the history of traveling and tourism, and the anthropology of politics. She has published four books and numerous articles.

Peggy Fairbairn-Dunlop has published widely on Pacific development issues, including the documentation of women's stories as in *Tamaitai Samoa: Their Stories*, Suva and Carson City, 1996. She holds a Masters Degree from Victoria University, Wellington, and a PhD from Macquarie University in Sydney. Peggy is the daughter of Emele Moa: she and her husband, Jim, and their family have lived in Samoa since 1980 and represent the ripple of migrant children returning to Samoa to live.

Lyndon Fraser lectures in the Department of Sociology and Anthropology at the University of Canterbury. His first book, *To Tara via Holyhead: Irish Catholic Immigrants in Nineteenth-Century Christchurch*, Auckland, 1997, won the inaugural Keith Sinclair History Prize. He is the editor of *A Distant Shore: Irish Migration and New Zealand Settlement*, Dunedin, 2000.

Aroha Harris (Ngapuhi, Te Rarawa) is currently completing her PhD in history at the University of Auckland, where she also lectures part-time in New Zealand history. She is also managing partner of Te Uira Associates, a Maori research group.

David Hastings is an Auckland journalist with a long-standing interest in history. In 1998 he completed an MA thesis at the University of Auckland that examined everyday life on the migrant ships coming to New Zealand in the 1870s. In his spare time, he is working on a book about the same subject. David, who is the deputy editor of the *New Zealand Herald*, is married with three children.

Manying Ip is Associate Professor in the School of Asian Studies at the University of Auckland. She has written two critically acclaimed books on Chinese New Zealanders – *Home Away From Home* (1990) and *Dragons on the Long White Cloud* (1996) – and has been a highly respected advocate for Chinese communities in this country. In recognition of her work, she was awarded a Suffrage Centennial Medal in 1993 and an ONZM (Officer of New Zealand Order of Merit) in 1996.

Katie Pickles was born in the United Kingdom and moved to New Zealand in 1976 when she was seven. She is a senior lecturer in the Department of History at the University of Canterbury, author of *Female Imperialism and National Identity: Imperial Order of the Daughters of the Empire (IODE)*, Manchester, 2002, and editor of *Hall of Fame: Life Stories of New Zealand Women*, Christchurch, 1998. She is currently writing a book about memory, colonial identity and the martyrdom of Nurse Edith Cavell.

Angela Wanhalla is of Ngai Tahu descent, affiliated with the Taumutu and Otakou runanga. She is a PhD candidate in the Department of History at the University of Canterbury, researching 'A History of the Ngai Tahu Families of Taieri Mouth, 1830s–1920s'.

Megan Woods is a PhD candidate in the Department of History at the University of Canterbury. She is currently completing a thesis that examines Maori post-war urbanisation, and particularly the ways in which policies, practices and processes were gendered.

Notes

Introduction

1. Patricia Grimshaw, *Women's Suffrage in New Zealand*, Auckland, 1982, 1987; Raewyn Dalziel, 'The Colonial Helpmeet', *NZJH*, 11, 2, 1977, pp. 112-123; Judith Devaliant, *Kate Sheppard: A Biography*, Auckland, 1992; Margaret Lovell-Smith, *The Woman Question: Writings by the Women Who Won the Vote*, Auckland, 1992; *The Suffragists: Women Who Worked For the Vote: Essays from The Dictionary of New Zealand Biography*, introduction by Dorothy Page, Wellington, 1993; Margaret Lovell-Smith, *How Women Won the Vote: A Canterbury Perspective*, Christchurch, 1993; Caroline Daley and Melanie Nolan, eds, *Suffrage and Beyond: International Feminist Perspectives*, Auckland and Annandale NSW, 1994.
2. For some examples see Angela Ballara, 'Wahine Rangatira: Maori Women of Rank and their Role in the Women's Kotahitanga Movement of the 1890s', *NZJH*, 27, 2, 1993, pp. 127-139; Judith Fyfe and Gaylene Preston, eds, *War Stories Our Mothers Never Told Us*, Auckland, 1995; Frances Porter, Charlotte Macdonald and Tui MacDonald, eds, *'My Hand Will Write What My Heart Dictates': The Unsettled Lives of Women in Nineteenth-Century New Zealand as Revealed to Sisters, Family and Friends*, Auckland, 1996; Deborah Montgomerie, *The Women's War: New Zealand Women 1939–45*, Auckland; Dianne Bardsley, *The Land Girls: In a Man's World, 1939–1946*, Dunedin, 2000.
3. See Barbara Brookes, Charlotte Macdonald and Margaret Tennant, eds, *Women in History: Essays on European Women in New Zealand*, Wellington, 1986; Barbara Brookes, Charlotte Macdonald and Margaret Tennant, eds, *Women in History 2: Essays on Women in New Zealand*, Wellington, 1992; Sandra Coney, ed., *Standing in the Sunshine: A History of New Zealand Women Since They Won the Vote*, Auckland, 1993. More specifically see Ruth Fry, *It's Different For Daughters: A History of the Curriculum for Girls in New Zealand Schools, 1900–1975*, Wellington, 1985; Philippa Mein Smith, *Maternity in Dispute, New Zealand, 1920–1939*, Wellington, 1986; Margaret Tennant, *Children's Health, The Nation's Wealth: A History of Children's Health Camps*, Wellington, 1994; Bronwyn Dalley, *Family Matters: Child Welfare in Twentieth Century New Zealand*, Auckland, 1998; Melanie Nolan, *Breadwinning: New Zealand Women and the State*, Christchurch, 2000.
4. Anne Else, ed., *Women Together: A History of Women's Organisations in New Zealand*, Wellington, 1993; Charlotte Macdonald, *The Vote, The Pill and the Demon*

Drink: A History of Feminist Writing in New Zealand, 1869–1993, Wellington, 1993; Roberta Nicholls, The Women's Parliament: The National Council of Women of New Zealand 1896–1920, Wellington, 1996; Dorothy Page, The National Council of Women: A Centennial History, Auckland, 1996.

5   Charlotte Macdonald, Merimeri Penfold and Bridget Williams, eds, The Book of New Zealand Women Ko Kui Ma Te Kaupapa, Wellington, 1991, Dictionary of New Zealand Biography, vols 1–5, Wellington, 1992–99.

6   Maureen Molloy, Those Who Speak to the Heart: The Nova Scotian Scots at Waipu, 1854-1920, Palmerston North, 1991; Anna Rogers, A Lucky Landing; The Story of the Irish in New Zealand, Auckland, 1996; Lyndon Fraser, To Tara Via Holyhead: Irish Catholic Immigrants in Nineteenth-Century Christchurch, Auckland, 1997; Tony Simpson, The Immigrants: The Great Migration from Britain to New Zealand, 1830–1890, Auckland, 1997; Tom Brooking and Jennifer Coleman, eds, Scottish Migration and the Settlement of New Zealand, Dunedin, 2002; Megan Hutching, A Long Journey for Sevenpence: An Oral History of Assisted Immigration to New Zealand from the United Kingdom, 1947–1975, Wellington, 1999; Lyndon Fraser, ed., A Distant Shore: Irish Migration and New Zealand Settlement, Dunedin, 2000. See also S. Greif, Immigration and National Identity in New Zealand: one people, two peoples, many peoples?, Palmerston North, 1995.

7   Charlotte Macdonald, A Woman of Good Character: Single Women as Immigrant Settlers in Nineteenth-Century New Zealand, Wellington, 1990; Manying Ip, Home Away from Home: Life Stories of Chinese Women in New Zealand, Auckland, 1990; Manying Ip, Innovators and Cultural Guardians: How Far Forward New Zealand Chinese Women? Auckland, 1993; Manying Ip, Dragons on the Long White Cloud: The Making of Chinese New Zealanders, North Shore City, 1996; Val Wood, War Brides: They Followed their Hearts to New Zealand, Auckland, 1991; Angela McCarthy, '"In Prospect of a Happier Future": Private Letters and Irish Women's Migration to New Zealand, 1840–1925', in Lyndon Fraser, ed., 2000, pp. 105-16; Angela McCarthy, ' "A Good Idea of Colonial Life": Personal Letters and Irish Migration to New Zealand', NZJH, 35, 1, 2001, pp. 1-21; Wendy Larner, 'Labour Migration and Female Labour: Samoan Women in New Zealand', Australia and New Zealand Journal of Sociology, 27, 1, 1991, 19-33; Ann Beaglehole and Hal Levine, Far From the Promised Land? Being Jewish in New Zealand, Wellington, 1995; Ann Beaglehole, A Small Price to Pay: Refugees from Hitler in New Zealand: 1936–46, Wellington, 1988; Ann Beaglehole, Facing the Past: Looking Back at Refugee Childhood in New Zealand, 1940s–1960s, Wellington, 1990; Rosalind McClean, 'Gender and National Identity: Revisiting Scotland's Emigratory Traditions', paper presented at Connections: From Local to Global, New Zealand Historical Association Conference, 1–3 December 2001, University of Canterbury.

8   For some key work see Rita James Simon and Caroline B. Brettel, eds, International Migration: The Female Experience, Totowa, NJ, 1986; Donna Gabaccia, 'Immigrant Women: Nowhere at Home?', Journal of American Ethnic History, 10, 1991, pp. 61-87; Silvia Pedraza, 'Women and Migration: the Social Consequences of Gender', American Review of Sociology 17, 1991, pp. 303-25; Pamela Sharpe, ed., Women, Gender and Labour Migration: Historical and Global Perspectives, London and New York, 2001.

9   Adrienne Jansen, ed., I Have In My Arms Both Ways: stories by ten immigrant women, Wellington, 1990.

10 Caroline Daley and Deborah Montgomerie, eds, *The Gendered Kiwi*, Auckland, 1999; Barbara Brookes, ed., *At Home in New Zealand: History, Houses, People*, Wellington, 2000; and Bronwyn Dalley Bronwyn Labrum, eds, *Fragments: New Zealand Social and Cultural History*, Auckland, 2000.
11 Denise Riley, *'Am I That Name?': Feminism and the Category of 'Women' in History*, Minneapolis, 1988, Vron Ware, *Beyond the Pale: White Women, Racism and History*, London and New York, 1992; Anne McClintock, *Imperial Leather: Race, Gender and Sexuality in the Colonial Contest*, London and New York, 1995; Antoinette Burton, ed., *Gender, Sexuality and Colonial Modernities*, London and New York, 1999; Katie Pickles, *Female Imperialism and National Identity: Imperial Order Daughters of the Empire (IODE)*, Manchester, 2002.
12 See James Belich, *Paradise Reforged: A History of the New Zealanders From the 1880s to the Year 2000*, Auckland, 2001; Michael King and Merle Van de Klundert, *God's Farthest Outpost: A History of Catholics in New Zealand*, Auckland, 1997.
13 James Clifford, 'Diasporas', *Cultural Anthropology*, 9, 1994, pp. 302-38.

Chapter 1

1 Rawiri Taonui, 'Waka Traditions – Some Post-Fleet Considerations', in Hans-Dieter Bader and Peter McCurdy, eds, *Proceedings of the Waka Moana Symposium 1996: Voyages From the Past to the Future*, Auckland, 1996, pp. 87-94, p. 87.
2 M.P.K. Sorrenson, *Maori Origins and Migrations: The Genesis of Some Pakeha Myths and Legends*, Auckland, 1979, p 84.
3 Margaret Orbell, 'The Religious Significance of Maori Migration Traditions', *Journal of the Polynesian Society*, 84 (1975), p. 346.
4 Taonui, p. 92.
5 Ibid., p. 93.
6 Elsdon Best, *Tuhoe, the Children of the Mist: A Sketch of the Origin, History, Myths, and Beliefs of the Tuhoe tribe of the Maori of New Zealand; With Some Account of Other Early Tribes of the Bay of Plenty District*, Auckland, reprinted 1996. John Grace, *Tuwharetoa: The History of the Maori People of the Taupo District*, Auckland, 1992; John H. Mitchell, *Takitimu: A History of the Ngati Kahungunu People*, Papakura, 1990; and Don Stafford, *Landmarks of Te Arawa*, Auckland, 1994–96.
7 Orbell, 1975, p. 341.
8 Andrew Sharp, *Ancient Voyagers in the Pacific*, Harmondsworth, 1957.
9 D.R. Simmons, *The Great New Zealand Myth: A Study of the Discovery and Origin Traditions of the Maori*, Wellington, 1976.
10 Sorrenson, p. 44.
11 Jeff Evans, *The Discovery of Aotearoa*, Auckland, 1998, p. 10.
12 Jane McRae, 'Maori oral tradition meets the book', in Penny Griffith, Peter Hughes and Alan Loney, eds, *A Book in the Hand: Essays on the History of the Book in New Zealand*, Auckland, 2000, pp. 1-16, p. 7.
13 'The Maori Canoe', *New Zealand School Journal*, June 1907, pp. 23-4.
14 See 'The Fairy Canoe: A South Sea Island Legend', *New Zealand School Journal*, June 1908, pp. 72-5; 'The Coming of the Maoris', *New Zealand School Journal*, February 1916, pp. 10-16; 'The Coming of the Maoris', *New Zealand School Journal*, March 1916, pp. 26-32; 'The Fairy Canoe', *New Zealand School Journal*,

September 1919, pp. 109-112; 'Rata's Canoe', *New Zealand School Journal*, June 1945, pp. 76-80.
15 A.W. Reed, *Treasury of Maori Exploration: Legends Relating to the First Polynesian Explorers of New Zealand*, Wellington, 1977, p. xii.
16 Gavin McLean, *Captain's Log: New Zealand's Maritime History*, Auckland, 2001.
17 Rawiri Te Maire Tau, 'Nga Pikituroa o Ngai Tahu: The Oral Traditions of Ngai Tahu', PhD, University of Canterbury, 1997, p. 7.
18 Sorrenson, pp. 37, 50.
19 James Cowan, *Legends of the Maori*, Auckland, 1987, p. 29.
20 *Ibid.*, p. 29.
21 Tipene O'Regan, 'Ngai Tahu and the Crown: Partnership Promised', in Garth Cant and Russell Kirkpatrick, eds, *Rural Canterbury: Celebrating its History*, Lincoln, 2001, pp. 1-20, p. 1.
22 Janet Davidson, *The Prehistory of New Zealand*, Auckland, 1984, p. 26.
23 Rosalind Murray McIntosh, p. 26.
24 Lloyd Ashton, 'Where did we come from?', *Mana*, 33, 2000, p. 5.
25 For discussion of Maori as a 'dying race' see M.P.K. Sorrenson and Raeburn Lange, *May the People Live: A History of Maori Health Development 1900–1920*, Auckland, 1999.
26 Leonard Bell, *The Maori in European Art: A Survey of the Representation of the Maori by European Artists from the Time of Captain Cook to the Present Day*, Wellington, 1980, p. 92.
27 *Ibid.*, p. 100.
28 O'Regan, p. 9.
29 Jock Phillips, *A Man's Country? The Image of the Pakeha Male – A History*, Auckland, 1987; James Belich, *Making Peoples: A History of the New Zealanders from Polynesian Settlement to the End of the Nineteenth Century*, Auckland, 1996.
30 See Jeff Evans, *Waka Taua: The Maori War Canoe*, Auckland, 2000.
31 Kuini Jenkins, 'Reflections on the Status of Maori Women', *Te Pua*, 1, 1992, p. 37.
32 *Ibid.*, p. 38.
33 *Ibid.*, p. 43.
34 *Ibid.*, p. 43.
35 Margaret Orbell, 'Maori Mythology', in Carolyne Larrington, ed., *The Feminist Companion to Mythology*, London, 1992, pp. 288-304, p. 302.
36 *Ibid.*, p. 290.
37 *Ibid.*, p. 300.
38 See Stacy Aliamo, *Undomesticated Ground: Recasting Nature as Feminist Space*, Ithaca, 2000, p. 9. Examples of ecofeminism include Mary Mellor, *Feminism and Ecology*, New York, 1997; Carolyn Merchant, *The Death of Nature: Women, Ecology, and the Scientific Revolution,* New York, 1980; Irene Diamond and Gloria Feman Orenstein, eds, *Reweaving the World: The Emergence of Ecofeminism*, San Francisco, 1990.
39 For examples of the way the ocean is gendered in Maori traditions see Margaret Orbell, *The Illustrated Encyclopedia of Maori Myth and Legend*, Christchurch, 1995.
40 *Ibid.*, p. 29.
41 Orbell, 1992, p. 297.
42 Ngahuia Te Awekotuku, *Mana Wahine Maori: Selected Writings on Maori Women's Art, Culture and Politics,* Auckland, 1991, p. 75.

43 Orbell, 1995, pp. 27-8.
44 *Ibid.*, p. 244.
45 *Ibid.*, p. 244.
46 *Ibid.*, p. 109.
47 Margaret Orbell, *Hawaiki: A New Approach to Maori Tradition*, Christchurch, 1985, p. 38.
48 Te Awekotuku, p. 45.
49 Antony Alpers, *Maori Myths and Tribal Legends*, Auckland, 1989, pp. 179-80.
50 Jennifer Garlick, *Maori Language Publishing: Some Issues*, Wellington, 1998, p. 20.
51 Orbell, 1995, pp. 170-71.
52 Betty Gilderdale, 'Children's Literature', in Terry Sturm, ed., *The Oxford History of New Zealand Literature in English*, Auckland, 1998, pp. 525-574, pp. 529, 567.
53 Orbell, 1992, p. 303.
54 Te Awekotuku, p. 45.
55 Anne Nelson, *Maori Canoes: Nga Waka Maori*, Auckland, 1991, p. 11.
56 Alpers, p. 141.
57 Orbell, 1985, p. 29.
58 Alpers, p. 147.
59 Orbell, 1985, p. 40.
60 Rosemary Madden, *Dynamic and Different: Mana Wahine*, Palmerston North, 1997, p. 6.
61 Aroha Mead, 'Maori Leadership', *Te Pua*, 3 (1994), p. 17.
62 Francis Pound, 'The Land, the Light, and Nationalist Myth in New Zealand Art', in Jock Phillips, ed., *The Land and the People,* Wellington, 1987, pp. 48-60, p. 48.
63 Claudia Bell, *Inventing New Zealand: Everyday Myths of Pakeha Identity,* Auckland, 1996, p. 5.
64 Keith Sinclair, *A Destiny Apart: New Zealand's Search for National Identity*, Wellington, 1986; Miles Fairburn, *The Ideal Society and Its Enemies: The Foundations of Modern New Zealand Society, 1850–1900*, Auckland, 1989.
65 Giselle Byrnes, 'Surveying Space: Constructing the Colonial Landscape', in Bronwyn Dalley and Bronwyn Labrum, eds, *Fragments: New Zealand Social and Cultural History*, Auckland, 2000, pp. 54-75, p. 55.
66 See, for example, Neville Peat, *Land Aspiring: The Story of Mount Aspiring National Park*, Dunedin, 1994; Craig Potton, *National Parks of New Zealand*, Nelson, 1998; David Thom, *Heritage: The Parks of the People*, Auckland, 1987.
67 Linda McDowell, *Gender, Identity and Place: Understanding Feminist Geographies*, Oxford, 1999, p. 1.
68 *Ibid.*, p. 2.
69 Ngahuia Dixon, 'The Power of Place in the Maori Psyche', Paper presented to the New Zealand Historical Association, University of Canterbury, Christchurch, 1–3 December 2001.
70 Te Aue Davis, Tipene O'Regan and John Wilson, *Nga Tohu Pumahara. The Survey Pegs of the Past: Understanding Maori Placenames*, Wellington, 1990, p. 5; *He Korero Purakau mo nga taunahanahatanga a nga tupuna: Place Names of the Ancestors, a Maori Oral History Atlas,* Wellington, 1990.
71 Davis *et al*, p. 5.
72 *Ibid.*, p. 5.

73 O'Regan, pp. 1-3.
74 Te Awekotuku, p. 107.
75 Orbell, 1985, p. 36.

Chapter 2

1   Emilie Letts diary, 12 July 1883, MS 964, AIML.
2   John and Emma Fowler diary, 30 September 1879, MS papers 0986, ATL.
3   J.D. Ormond to Colonial Secretary, 24 April 1873, *AJHR*, 1873, D–1, p. 87.
4   Elizabeth Brough diary, 13 June 1874, MS papers 2043, ATL.
5   Catherine Parnell diary, 15 December 1870, MS 89/193, AIML; Thomas Ashton diary, 2 February 1883, NZMSS 835, APL; Enis Priestley diary, 1 October 1879, 85/136, AIML.
6   Dr William Hosking evidence to Royal Commission on the *Scimitar*, March, 1874, IM 5/4/13, No 127, p. 12, NA–W.
7   Report of *Scimitar* Royal Commission, March 1874, *AJHR*, 1874, D–1A, p. 10; report of Berar RC, 8 March 1875, *AJHR*, 1875, D–3, p. 53.
8   William Gray diary, 13 May 1875, MS 1297 84/64, AIML; Bertha and Mary Dobie, 3 November 1877; in Margaret Drake-Brockman, ed., *The Voyage of the May Queen*, Braunton, 1992, p. 43.
9   Letts dairy, 5, 8 August 1883.
10 Commissioners' report on the *Cartvale*, 29 October 1874, *AJHR*, 1875, D–3, p. 30.
11 Parnell diary, 2, 3 February 1871.
12 Christina Macdonald diary, 18 September 1879, Misc MS 731, Hocken Library.
13 Letts diary, 5 September 1883.
14 Parnell diary, 25 February 1871.
15 Report of the court of inquiry into the *Cospatrick* disaster, 11 February 1875, *AJHR* 1875, D–2, pp. 86 ff; Neil Hanson, *The Custom of the Sea*, London, 1999, pp.131-3; Belich, 1996, p. 286.
16 Jan Findlayson diary, 24 November 1876, MS papers 1678, ATL.
17 Sydney D. Waters, *Shaw Savill Line: One Hundred Years of Trading*, Christchurch, 1961, pp. 42-3.
18 William Gray diary, 7 May 1875.
19 Millen Coughtrey, medical journal on the *Chile*, 1873, IM 5/4/6, No 37, NA–W.
20 Letts diary, 12 July 1883.
21 Joseph Bayes diary, 28 November, 1882, NZMSS 83, APL.
22 J.H. Hillary diary 19 January 1880, published as *Westland: Journal of John Hillary, Emigrant to New Zealand*, Fakenham, 1979; Dobie diary, 9, 10 October 1877.
23 James Pirie diary, NZMSS 427, APL; Parnell diary, 14 December 1870.
24 Pirie diary, p. 4.
25 Pirie diary, p. 8; Letts diary, 19 July 1883.
26 Dobie diary, 18 October 1877.
27 George Fearnley diary, 19 December 1879, NZMSS 782, APL.
28 Dobie diary, 17 November 1877.
29 Pirie diary, p. 38.
30 Instructions to surgeon-superintendents of emigrant ships, August 1873, IM 5/4/9 No. 86, NA–W; Instructions to matrons of emigrant ships, June 1874, MS papers 3657, ATL.

31 Order in council, regulations, August 1873; Instructions to surgeons, August 1873; Instructions to captains, August 1873; Instructions to matrons, June 1874.
32 Findlayson diary, 4 October 1876.
33 Coughtrey diary, 29 August, 5 September, 9 September, 22 October 1873; Coughtrey journal, 20 October 1873.
34 *Evening Post*, 24 March 1875; Commissioners' report on the *Adamant*, 14 December 1875, *AJHR*, 1876, D–3, pp. 27-8.
35 Macdonald, 1990, pp. 73-4.
36 Walter E. Houghton, *The Victorian Frame of Mind, 1830–1870*, Yale, 1995, pp. 364-72.
37 Immigration officer, Dunedin to W.H. Reynolds, 7 May 1874; Julius Vogel to agent-general, 3 June 1874, *AJHR*, 1874, D–2, pp. 60-1; Report by Henry Meadows, surgeon-superintendent of the *Woodlark*, 25 March 1874; H.J.H. Elliott, immigration officer to Wellington superintendent, 13 April 1874; Sub immigration officer Orbell to Elliott, 14 April, 1874; Vogel to agent-general, 7 May 1874 in *AJHR* 1874, D–2. pp. 44-9.
38 Letts diary, 12 September 1883.
39 Coughtrey diary, 28 September 1873.
40 Inquiry on board the *Chile*, 2 October 1873, pp. 1–9, IM 5/4/6, No 37, NA–W.
41 Coughtrey diary, 2 October 1873.
42 Alfred Knight diary, 5 June 1883, MS 1165, AIML.
43 Fowler diary, 18 October 1885.
44 Gray diary, 20 May 1875; John Cowie diary, 13 August 1883, NZMSS 818, APL.
45 Gray diary, 28, 29 May 1875; Priestly diary, 21 October 1879; Cowie diary, 13 August 1883; Hillary diary 8 December 1879; Findlayson diary, ATL, 8 October 1876; Henry Herringshaw diary, 11 July 1874, MS papers 4355 C254; Ebenezer Johnson diary, 16 September 1875, in Rex Johnson, *The Johnson Line: Ebenezer and Ellen*, Wellington, 1992.
46 Alfred Lawrence diary, 11 April 1874, published as *Alfred's Diary*, Christchurch 1974.
47 Elizabeth Fairbairn diary, 21 December 1877, qms 0709, ATL.
48 Gray diary, 8 July 1879.
49 Eric Hobsbawm, *The Age of Capital 1848–75*, London, 1997, p. 271.
50 Gray diary 14 June 1879; John Stone diary, 4 November 1883, NZMSS 495, APL; Johnson diary, 20 December 1881; Cowie diary, 11,12, 13 August, 1883; Hillary diary, 25 November, 25 December, 28 December 1879, 1 January 1880; Lawrence diary, 11, 28 April 1874.
51 David Fitzpatrick, 'Ireland since 1870', in R.F. Foster, ed., *The Oxford History of Ireland*, Oxford, 1992, p. 179.
52 E.P. Thompson, *The Making of the English Working Class*, London, 1991, pp. 246, 321, 343, 348, 471-2, 480; Arthur Bryant, *English Saga 1840–1940*, London, 1961, pp. 75-6, 122-7.
53 Letts diary, 4 October 1883.
54 Johnson diary, 16 September 1875.
55 William Hosking, general observations on the voyage of the *Dallam Tower*, 12 March 1875, IM 5/4/16 No. 164, NA.
56 Surgeon's report on *Agnes Muir*, 1872, *AJHR*, 1873, D–1, p. 33.
57 Commissioners' report on the *Aldergrove*, 1875, *AJHR*, 1876, D–3, p. 7.

58 *Evening Post*, 24 March 1875.
59 William Heginbotham diary, 33rd· 34th days, 91/68, AIML.
60 Sarah Stephens diary, 16 October 1876, ref no 91-066, ATL.
61 Vogel to agent-general, re. *Isles of the South*, 12 March 1874, *AJHR*, 1874, D–2, pp. 28-9; Commissioners' report on the Apelles, 7 May 1874, *AJHR*, 1874, D–2, pp. 53-6; Surgeon's report on the *Warwick*, 9 February 1873, *AJHR*, 1873, D–1, p. 63; Emma Rose, matron, report on conduct of the *Dallam Tower's* doctor, 24 March 1875, IM 5/4/16 No. 164, NA–W; *Evening Post*, 24 March 1875.
62 John Bigwood diary, 31 May 1874, in M. Noeline Shaw, ed., *The History of the Bigwood Family*, Waikanae, 1994.
63 Christen Christensen diary, 10 August 1872, 92–049, Hocken Library.
64 Letts diary, 12 October 1883.
65 Pirie diary, passim.

Chapter 3

1 Ellen Piezzi to Victer Piezzi, 8 October 1881, courtesy of Teresa O'Connor.
2 Ellen Piezzi to Mrs Victer Piezzi, 12 August 1878.
3 Ellen Piezzi to Victer Piezzi, undated.
4 Donald Harman Akenson, *Half the World from Home: Perspectives on the Irish in New Zealand, 1860–1950*, Wellington, 1990, p. 197. This resounding silence may be juxtaposed with important developments in the broader historiography of Irish migration. See, for example, Patrick O'Sullivan, ed., *Irish Women and Irish Migration*, vol. 4, *The Irish Worldwide: History, Heritage, Identity*, Leicester, 1995. For earlier studies on aspects of Irish women's migration history, see especially Carol Groneman, 'Working Class Immigrant Women in Mid-Nineteenth-Century New York: The Irish Women's Experience', *Journal of Urban History*, 4 1978, pp. 255-73; Hasia Diner, *Erin's Daughters in America: Irish Immigrant Women in the Nineteenth Century*, Baltimore, 1983; David Fitzpatrick, '"A Share of the Honeycomb": Education, Emigration and Irishwomen', *Continuity and Change*, 1 (1986), pp. 217-34; Janet A. Nolan, *Ourselves Alone: Women's Emigration from Ireland, 1885–1920*, Lexington, 1989. The most useful introduction to the topic is Donald Harman Akenson, *The Irish Diaspora: A Primer*, Toronto, 1993, pp. 157-87. Recent studies include Deborah Oxley, *Convict Maids: The Forced Migration of Women to Australia*, Cambridge, 1996; Trevor McClaughlin, ed., *Irish Women in Colonial Australia*, St Leonards, 1998; Breda Gray, 'Gendering the Irish Diaspora: Questions of Enrichment, Hybridization and Return', *Women's Studies International Forum*, 23, 2000, pp. 167-85; Bronwyn Walter, *Outsiders Inside: Whiteness, Place and Irish Women*, London and New York, 2001.
5 See Angela McCarthy's path-breaking study, '"In Prospect of a Happier Future": Private Letters and Irish Women's Migration to New Zealand, 1840–1925', in Fraser, ed., pp. 105-16.
6 This chapter uses the term 'West Coast' to denote the entire region that stretches northwards from Awarua to Kahurangi Point and incorporates both 'Westland' and 'Nelson South-West Goldfield'. See the discussion of nomenclature in Philip Ross May, *The West Coast Gold Rushes*, Christchurch, 1962, pp. 14-16. The most substantial study of the region is Murray McCaskill, 'The Historical Geography of Westland before 1914', PhD thesis, University of Canterbury, 1960. On the West

Coast Irish, see Neil Patrick Vaney, 'The Dual Tradition: Irish Catholics and French Priests in New Zealand – the West Coast Experience, 1865-1910', MA thesis, University of Canterbury, 1976; Patrick O'Farrell, *Vanished Kingdoms: Irish in Australia and New Zealand: A Personal Excursion*, Kensington, 1990; Lyndon Fraser, 'Irish Migration to the West Coast, 1864–1900', in Fraser, ed., pp. 86-104.
7   Bernard Bailyn, *Voyagers to the West: A Passage in the Peopling of America on the Eve of the Revolution*, New York, 1987, p. 239.
8   Philip Ross May, *Hokitika: Goldfields Capital*, Christchurch, 1964, p. 35.
9   Denis O'Hallahan to Bishop John Joseph Grimes, 3 May 1897, Christchurch Diocesan Archives (CDA).
10 Lyndon Fraser, 'Irish Migration to the West Coast, 1864-1900', *NZJH*, 34, 2000, p. 200.
11 *Census of New Zealand*, 1886.
12 Ellen Piezzi to Victer Piezzi, 3 June 1879.
13 Bailyn, *Voyagers to the West*, p. 83.
14 May, 1962, p. 480.
15 *Commission on Emigration and Other Population Problems*, 1948–1954, Dublin, 1954.
16 Terry Hearn, 'The Irish on the Otago Goldfields', in Fraser, ed., p. 82.
17 *Ibid.*, p. 82.
18 *Ibid.*, p. 77.
19 Akenson, *The Irish Diaspora*, p. 169.
20 The denominational percentages for the West Coast sample were as follows: Roman Catholic (79.6%), Anglican (10.6%), Presbyterian (6.0%) and Wesleyan (0.8%). Data on religious affiliations were unavailable for 3.0 per cent of female migrants.
21 Hearn, in Fraser, ed., p. 83.
22 May, 1962, p. 285.
23 David Fitzpatrick, *Oceans of Consolation: Personal Accounts of Irish Migration to Australia*, Melbourne, 1995, pp. 10-11. Yet the Victorian returns for 1852–54 show that only one-ninth of all Irish female arrivals were unassisted, compared with one-half of their male counterparts. Fitzpatrick also identifies a 'gross Anglo-Irish disparity' that is illustrated by 'the contrast between the Irish component of unassisted migration (5%) and of assisted immigration (29%)'. p. 11, fn. 19. On Irish women's government-assisted migration, see Robin Haines, '"The priest made a bother about it": The travails of that "unhappy sisterhood" bound for colonial Australia', in McClaughlin, ed., pp. 43-63.
24 John Macdonald and Ralph Shlomowitz, 'Passenger Fares on Sailing Vessels to Australia in the Nineteenth Century', *Explorations in Economic History*, 28, 1991, pp. 192-207.
25 Descendant information, Teresa O'Connor and Ted Matthews.
26 Joanna Bourke has convincingly argued that many unmarried rural women in Irish society enhanced their status during the late nineteenth and early twentieth centuries by choosing to perform housework for widowed or unmarried male relatives. See '"The Best of All Home Rulers": The Economic Power of Women in Ireland, 1880–1914', *Irish Historical Studies*, 18, 1991, pp. 34-41; *Husbandry to Housewifery: Women, Economic Change, and Housework in Ireland, 1890–1914*, Oxford, 1993.
27 David Noel Doyle, 'Review Article: Cohesion and Diversity in the Irish Diaspora', *Irish Historical Studies*, 31, 1999, p. 419.

28 Descendant information, Ron Patterson and Brian Nolan.
29 For published biographies of the lives of Rankin and Goodwin, see Ted Matthews, 'Sugar Annie (Bell Hill)', in Yvonne Davison and Frankie Mills, eds, *Women of Westland and Their Families*, omnibus edition, Greymouth, 1998, p. 194; Kathleen W. Orr, 'Bridget Goodwin', *A People's History: Illustrated Biographies from the Dictionary of New Zealand Biography, Volume I, 1769–1869*, Wellington, 1992, pp. 88-90.
30 Descendant information, Ted Matthews.
31 Gale Davidson Gibb, 'Memories of Red Jacks: Johanna Shanahan Weir', in Davison and Mills, eds, pp. 185-86.
32 *Ibid.*, p. 186.
33 Descendant information, Mary O'Connor.
34 A substantial body of scholarship in international migration studies emphasises the importance of personal networks in explaining the origins, composition and dynamics of migrant flows. For a useful introduction to the literature, see Monica Boyd, 'Family and Personal Networks in International Migration: Recent Developments and New Agendas', *International Migration Review*, 23, 1989, pp. 638-70; Stephen Castles and Mark Miller, *The Age of Migration: International Population Movements in the Modern World*, London, 1998.
35 Gibb, p. 187; descendant information, Ted Matthews.
36 Descendant information, Teresa O'Connor; Ellen Piezzi to Victer Piezzi, undated.
37 There are three surviving letters in this sequence, written between 1926 and 1927. I am indebted to Brian Nolan for access to the Phelan correspondence.
38 Fitzpatrick, p. 503 and *passim*.
39 A similar pattern is evident in Irish-Australian correspondence. See David Fitzpatrick, '"An Ocean of Consolation": Letters and Irish Immigration to Australia', in Eric Richards, Richard Reid and David Fitzpatrick, *Visible Immigrants: Neglected Sources for the History of Australian Immigration*, Canberra, 1989, p. 69.
40 Catherine O'Toole to Susan Hogan, 30 July 1890, courtesy of Ted Matthews.
41 This view has been advanced by Fairburn, pp. 165-7.
42 Gibb, p. 187.
43 Fraser, 'Irish Migration', pp. 215. Sixty-six testators (62.9%) transferred the residuary interest in their estates to their spouses absolutely (n = 105); another fifteen bequeathed most of their property to their wives (14.3%); twenty-two wills created life-interests in an estate (21%), and two documents completely excluded the claims of widows (1.9%).
44 Will of Michael Scanlon, WP 1/1894, NA–C.
45 Donald Harman Akenson, 'Reading the Texts of Rural Immigrants: Letters from the Irish in Australia, New Zealand and America', in Donald Harman Akenson, ed., *Canadian Papers in Rural History, Volume VII*, Ontario, 1990, pp. 395-6.
46 Descendant information, Bill Nolan.
47 Descendant information, Ted Matthews.
48 Fitzpatrick, pp. 590-93.
49 Mary O'Connor (County Kerry) to William O'Connor, *c.* 1900, courtesy of Mary O'Connor (Christchurch). Johanna O'Leary acted as an amanuensis for her mother, Mary, in writing this letter. Although the transcript is incomplete, the eight surviving pages take the form of a collective narrative in which the voices of both women can be clearly detected.

50 Gibb, p. 187; descendant information, Ted Matthews.
51 See, for example, 'Decrees Regarding the Sacrament of Marriage', in *Documents for the Use of the Clergy of the Archdiocese of Wellington at the Diocesan Synod of 1893*, Wellington, 1893, pp. 3-6, Marist Archives, Wellington.
52 Mark C. Foley and Timothy W. Guinnane, 'Did Irish Marriage Patterns Survive the Emigrant Voyage? Irish-American Nuptiality, 1880–1920', *Irish Economic and Social History*, 26, 1999, Table 4, p. 31.
53 This view has been advanced in a North American context by Hasia Diner, *Erin's Daughters*. There is a rich historiography on patterns of Irish nuptiality. See, for example, Kenneth H. Connell, 'Peasant Marriage in Ireland After the Great Famine', *Past and Present*, 12, 1957, pp. 76–91, and 'Catholicism and Marriage in the Century After the Famine', in *Irish Peasant Society: Four Historical Essays*, Oxford, 1968; Brendan M. Walsh, 'Marriage Rates and Population Pressure: Ireland, 1871 and 1911', *Economic History Review*, 2nd series, 23, 1970, pp. 148-62; Robert E. Kennedy, Jr., *The Irish: Emigration, Marriage, and Fertility*, Berkeley and Los Angeles, 1973; S.J. Connolly, 'Marriage in Pre-Famine Ireland', in Art Cosgrove, ed., *Marriage in Ireland*, Dublin, 1985, pp. 78-98; David Fitzpatrick, 'Marriage in Post-Famine Ireland', in Cosgrove, ed., pp. 116-31; Timothy M. Guinnane, *The Vanishing Irish: Households, Migration, and the Rural Economy in Ireland, 1850–1914*, Princeton, 1997.
54 Descendant information, Peter Dillon; Register of Marriages, 2494/1886, Registrar General's Office, Lower Hutt.
55 Register of Marriages, 335/1881.
56 *Ibid.*, 432/1888, 458/1888 and 2347/1888.
57 Donald Harman Akenson, 'No Petty People: Pakeha History and the Historiography of the Irish Diaspora', in Fraser, ed., p. 17.
58 Diocesan Return for the Parish of Ahaura, 1 July 1892, Christchurch Diocesan Archives.
59 Denis Carew to Bishop John Joseph Grimes, 9 April 1895, Christchurch Diocesan Archives.
60 Descendant information, Ted Matthews and Anne Bills.
61 Patrick O'Farrell, 'Catholicism on the West Coast: Just How Irish Is It?', *New Zealand Tablet*, 3 May 1973, pp. 53-6.
62 I am indebted to Ted Matthews for this story.
63 Jack Greene employs the term 'charter group' to denote the disproportionate influence exerted by the earliest arrivals in new societies, 'who took possession of the land, devised ways to manipulate local resource materials for their own survival and profit, reordered the physical and social landscape, and worked out the political, legal, and other cultural arrangements appropriate to their situation'. See Jack P. Greene, 'Pluribus or Unum? White Ethnicity in the Formation of Colonial American Culture', *History Now Te Pae Tawhito o Te Wa*, 4, 1998, p. 4
64 See, for example, Fraser, 1997.

CHAPTER 4

1 Megan Cook, 'Domestic Workers' Unions 1890–1942', in Else, ed., 1993, pp 211-13.
2 *AJHR*, 1921, D–1, p. 5.

3 Janice Gothard, '"The Healthy, Wholesome British Domestic Girl": Single Female Migration and the Empire Settlement Act, 1922–1930', in Stephen Constantine, ed., *Emigrants and Empire: British Settlement in the Dominions Between the Wars*, Manchester and New York, pp. 72-95, p. 73. Approximately 5000 women went to Australia. With only a very small number of women emigrating to South Africa at this time, I would suggest that the estimated figure of 100,000 should be 90,000 at the most.
4 Dane Kennedy, 'Empire Migration in Post-War reconstruction: The Role of the Overseas Settlement Committee, 1912–1922', *Albion*, 20, 3, (1988), pp. 403-19, p. 407.
5 *Ibid.*
6 Brian L. Blakeley, 'The Society for the Overseas Settlement of British Women and the Problems of Empire Settlement, 1917–1936', *Albion*, 20, 3 (1988) pp. 421-44, pp. 423-4.
7 Constantine, p. 8.
8 Cecillie Swaisland, 'Servants and Gentlewomen on the Golden Land: The Emigration of Single Women from Britain to Southern Africa, 1820–1939, Pietermaritzburg, 1993, p. 5.
9 A. James Hammerton, *Emigrant Gentlewomen: Genteel Poverty and Female Emigration, 1830–1914*, London, 1979; J. Gothard, 'A Compromise with Conscience: The Reception of Female Immigrant Domestic Servants in Eastern Australia 1860–1890', *Labour History* 62, 1992, pp. 38-51; Una Monk, *New Horizons: a Hundred Years of Women's Migration*, London, 1963.
10 Macdonald, 1990.
11 For explicit critiques of such stereotypes see Dalziel, pp. 112–23; Phillips, *A Man's Country?: The Image of the Pakeha Male: A History*, Auckland, 1987, 1996; Erik Olssen and Andree Levesque, 'Towards a History of the European Family in New Zealand', in Peggy Koopman-Boyden, ed., *Families in New Zealand Society*, Wellington 1978, pp. 1-26; Erik Olssen, 'Families and the Gendering of European New Zealand in the Colonial Period, 1840–80, in Daley and Montgomerie, eds, 1999, pp. 37-62.
12 Charlotte Macdonald, 'Too Many Men and Too Few Women: Gender's "Fatal Impact" in Nineteenth-Century Colonies', in Daley and Montgomerie, pp. 17-35, p. 32.
13 Constantine, p. 4
14 Freda Hawkins, *Critical Years in Immigration: Canada and Australia Compared*, Montreal and Kingston, 1989, p. 26.
15 Constantine, p. 16.
16 See Stephen Constantine and G.F. Plant, *Oversea Settlement: Migration From The United Kingdom to the Dominions*, London, 1951.
17 Blakeley, p. 444.
18 John A. Schultz, '"Leaven for the Lump": Canada and Empire Settlement, 1918–1939', in Constantine, pp. 150-73, p. 150.
    Kennedy, p. 416.
20 Bernard Semmel, *Imperialism and Social Reform: English Social-Imperialist Thought, 1895–1914*, Cambridge MA, 1960.
21 Kennedy, p. 415.
22 Plant, p. 5.

23 Marilyn Barber, 'Introduction', in James S. Woodsworth, *Strangers at Our Gates or Coming Canadians*, Toronto, 1909, 1972.
24 M. Bell, '"The Pestilence that Walketh in Darkness": Imperial Health, Gender and Images of South Africa c. 1880–1910', *Transactions of the Institute of British Geographers*, 18, 1993, pp. 327-241.
25 *New Zealand: The Better Britain*, 1926, p. 4.
26 *Ibid.*, pp. 4-5.
27 *AJHR*, 1919, D–1, p. 1.
28 AJCP, 6744 Dominion Office, p. 4.
29 *NZPD*, 1919, 185, p. 483, 17 October 1919.
30 *NZPD*, 1920, 189, p.1022.
31 Cit. in Sandra Coney, *Every Girl: A Social History of Women and the YWCA in Auckland*, Auckland, 1986, p. 100.
32 *NZPD*, 1919, 184, p. 330.
33 *Ibid*.
34 Kent Fedorowich, 'The Assisted Emigration of British Ex-Servicemen to the Dominions, 1914–1922', in Constantine, pp. 45-71. Also see Kent Fedorowich, *Unfit for Heroes: Reconstruction and Soldier Settlement in the Empire Between the Wars*, Manchester and New York, 1995; Marilyn Lake, *The Limits of Hope: Soldier Settlement in Victoria, 1915–38*, Melbourne, 1987.
35 See Melanie Nolan, , 'Employment Organisations', in Else, ed., pp. 195-207.
36 Katie Pickles, 'Workers and Workplaces: Industry and Modernity', in John Cookson and Graeme Dunstall, eds, *Southern Capital: Christchurch: Towards a City Biography*, Christchurch, 2000, pp. 138-61.
37 See Monk, 1962; and Julia Bush, '"The Right Sort of Woman": Female Emigrators to the British Empire, 1890–1910', *Women's History Review*, 3, 1994, pp. 385-409.
38 Blakeley, p. 420.
39 Marilyn Barber, 'The Women Ontario Welcomed: Immigrant Domestics for Ontario Homes, 1870–1930', in Alison Prentice and Susan Mann Trofimenkoff, eds, *The Neglected Majority: Essays in Canadian Women's History*, 2, Toronto, 1985, pp. 102-21, p. 113.
40 A Miss McLean, 'Superintendent of Immigrant Girls' at the Department of Immigration, appears to have been one such woman.
41 Plant, pp.78-80, and SOSBW 2nd Annual Report, 1921, p. 2, A–1054 MG 28 I336, National Archives of Canada.
42 SOSBW 2nd Annual Report, 1921, p. 5.
43 See Barbara Roberts, '"A Work of Empire": Canadian Reformers and British Female Immigration', in Linda Kealey, ed., *A Not Unreasonable Claim*, Toronto, 1979, pp. 185-202; Julia Bush, *Edwardian Ladies and Imperial Power*, Cassell, 1999; Julia Bush, 'Edwardian Ladies and the 'Race Dimensions of British Imperialism', *Women's Studies International Forum*, 21, 1998, pp. 277-289; and Katie Pickles, *Female Imperialism and National Identity: Imperial Order Daughters of the Empire (IODE)*, Manchester, 2002
44 Memo relating to the inquiry now being made in New Zealand by the Delegates of the British Government Overseas Settlement Committee, p. 1, YWCA MS Papers 1536 2:10:2D, ATL, Wellington.
45 *Ibid*.
46 *AJCP*, 6744 D, Report of F.M. Girdler and G. Watkin, August, 1920, ANL.

47 Memo relating to the inquiry now being made in New Zealand by the Delegates of the British Government Oversea Settlement Committee, p. 1.
48 Confidential Memorandum Supplied By Delegates of Oversea Settlement Mission to New Zealand to YWCA, (ATL), YWCA.
49 Memo relating to inquiry now being made in New Zealand, p. 1.
50 *AJHR*, 1920, D–9, p. 1.
51 MG 28, I 17, 4, 2, 8 September 1926, p. 122, National Archives of Canada.
52 *Ibid*.
53 Gothard, p. 80.
54 SOSBW 12th Annual Report, 1931, p. 11, AJCP, M 2306, ANL.
55 *Ibid*.; SOSBW 10th Annual Report, 1929, p. 10.
56 Monk, p. 20.
57 *Ibid*., p. 52.
58 Cit. in Monk, p. 52.
59 Monk, p. 52.
60 SOSBW 7th Annual Report, 1926, p. 61, AJCP, M2306, ANL.
61 Memorandum from Thomson, Under-Secretary for Immigration to Minister of Immigration, 29 October, 1920. Department of Labour, YWCA aid to Immigrant Girls, L 1 129a, NA–W.
62 *Ibid*., Memorandum from Under-Secretary for Immigration to Minister of Immigration, 17 November 1920.
63 President, NZ Field Committee to Under-Secretary for Immigration, 16 March 1920, YWCA Papers 1536 2:10:2D, ATL.
64 Report from Wellington, November 1927, YWCA aid to Immigrant Girls, L 1 129a, NA.
65 *Ibid*., YWCA Secretary to Under-Secretary for Immigration, 6 November 1926.
66 *Ibid*., YWCA Second Report, November 1927, Wellington.
67 See Coney, *Every Girl*, and clare S. Simpson, 'The Social History of the Christchurch YWCA, 1883–1930', MA thesis, University of Canterbury, 1984, for accounts of the Girl Citizen Movement.
68 Auckland report for year ending 30 June 1927. YWCA Aid to Immigrant Girls, NA.
69 Cit. in Coney, *Every Girl*, p. 101.
70 Auckland Report for year ending 30 June 1927. YWCA Aid to Immigrant Girls, NA.
71 Gothard, p. 89.
72 Marilyn Barber, 'Sunny Ontario for British Girls, 1900–30', in Jean Burnett, ed., *Looking into My Sisiter's Eyes: an Exploration of Women's History*, Toronto, 1986, pp. 55-73, p. 56.
73 Gothard, p. 90.
74 *Ibid*.
75 See Rollo Arnold, *The Farthest Promised Land: English Villagers, New Zealand Immigrants of the 1870s*, Wellington, 1981.
76 *AJHR*, 1921, D–9, p. 1.
77 *AJHR* 1921, D–9, p. 4.
78 Miscellaneous Committees 1920–27, Candidates Interviewed and Papers Considered, July 1921, p.38, AJCP, M 2304, ANL.
79 AJCP 6744 Dom Office. The creation of the Irish Free State in 1921 affected 'British'

recruitment possibilities for the 1920s.
80 Gothard, p. 57.
81 Auckland report for year ending 30 June 1927, YWCA Aid to Immigrant Girls, L 1 129a, NA–W.
82 *Ibid*. Griffin to Thomson, 8 April 1921.
83 Coney, *Every Girl*, p. 102.
84 *Ibid*., p. 101.
85 There was mention of the principle of 'placing girls quietly' in the early 1920s. Girls' Superintendent, Department of Immigration to Miss Griffin, General Secretary YWCA , 4 May 1921. L 1 129a ,YWCA.
86 Dunedin Report 23-10-23, YWCA Papers, MS 1536 2:10:2D.
87 Mary Findlay, *Tooth and Nail: The Story of a Daughter of the Depression*, Auckland, 1974.
88 Jean Stevenson, Acting-General Secretary, Auckland, to Ella Fair, Business Secretary, 8 August, 1924, YWCA Papers, MS 1536 2:10:2D.
89 Memo from the Treasury to the Secretary of Immigration, 31 March 1931, L 1 129a YWCA. Recommendation 2 was 'that the restricted immigration policy be restricted as far as possible in view of the financial position, and that the immigration of domestic servants be discontinued.'
90 *Ibid*., Second Report from Wellington, November 1927.
91 *Ibid*., YWCA National General Secretary Bridgman to Hon J.A. Young, Minister for Immigration, Wellington, 28 October 1931.
92 *Ibid*.
93 Report from Coney, 5 July, 1930.
94 Auckland report year ending 30 June 1927.
95 Report from Coney, 5 July, 1930.
96 See Barbara Roberts, *Whence They Came: Deportation from Canada 1900–1935*, Ottawa, 1988.
97 Elsie Griffin, YWCA General Secretary, Auckland, to Miss McLean, Department of Immigration, 30 April 1921. L 1 129a YWCA. Miss McLean was Superintendent of Immigrant Girls at the Department of Immigration.
98 1 April–30 November 1930, Auckland Report, L 1 129a YWCA. Miss MacLeod worked for the YWCA in Auckland.
99 Barber, 'The Women Ontario Welcomed', p. 120.
100 See Joy Parr, *Labouring Children: British Apprentices to Canada, 1869–1924*, London, 1981; Gillian Wagner, *Children of the Empire*, London, 1982; and Alan Gill, *Orphans of the Empire*, Sydney, New York, Toronto, 1998.
101 Monk, p. 77, and SOSBW annual reports.
102 SOSBW 2nd Annual Report, 1921, p. 7.
103 *Ibid*., p. 8.
104 1927 Report of Annual Meeting of the Women's Division NZ Farmers' Union (WDNZFU), Wellington, 27 July, 1927, p. 26, ATL.
105 *Ibid*., p. 27.
106 Auckland Report for Year Ending 30 June 1927, L1 129a YWCA.
107 WDNZFU, p. 27, ATL.
108 Gothard, p. 84.
109 *Ibid*.
110 SOSBW 11th Annual Report 1930, p. 1.

111 Gothard, p. 86.
112 Memorandum no. 272, 9 June 1925, L1 129a YWCA.
113 *Ibid.*, 26 May 1925 Memo for the Under Secretary from Girls' Superintendent A. McLean, 26 May 1925.
114 Coney, *Every Girl*, p. 103.
115 *Ibid.*
116 Report in Coney, 5 July, 1930, L 1 129a YWCA.
117 Swaisland, p. 96. There was still demand for single British middle-class women as teachers and nurses.
118 Coney, ed, p. 198.
119 *Ibid.*, p. 225. There is great need for further research on the history of Maori women as servants for Pakeha, and in the agency of Maori women in avoiding domestic service. Certainly, the practice existed at least from missionary times, but the specifics remain hidden.
120 Robin Hyde, *Nor the Years Condemn*, Auckland, 1938, p. 118, cited in Coney, *Every Girl*, pp. 104-5.
121 Personal communication with the son of a migrant, May 1997.
122 Ethel Law, YWCA to Under-Secretary for Immigration, 1 December 1930, L 1 129a YWCA.
123 Kennedy, p. 410.
124 Maureen Birchfield, *She Dared to Speak: Connie Birchfield's Story*, Dunedin, 1998, p. 53.

Chapter 5

1 This chapter is based on Beaglehole,1988.
2 *Ibid.*, pp. 8-34.
3 According to one estimate, 50,000 refugees applied for permits to enter New Zealand (R.A. Lochore, *From Europe to New Zealand: An Account of Our Continental European Settlers*, Wellington, 1951, p. 81). According to another, 1731 applications were declined and 727 were granted in the period 1936 to 1938 (F.A. Ponton, 'Immigration Restriction in New Zealand: A Study of Policy from 1908 to 1939', MA thesis, University of New Zealand, 1946, p. 114, quoting from C33/253, memo of Comptroller to Minister, 30 November 1938). There are gaps in the evidence relating to pressure applied on New Zealand to accept refugees. The Customs Department files dealing with this matter have not survived.
4 Nash 1311/0593, F.A. de la Mare, 'The Refugee Problem', IC 20/86 part 1, memo for New Zealand Trade and Tourist Commissioner, Brussels, on the admission to New Zealand of foreign European nationals, from E.D. Good, Comptroller of Customs, 3 March 1939, NA–W.
5 IC 20/86 part 1, memo for New Zealand Trade and Tourist Commissioner from Good, NA–W.
6 *Ibid.*
7 Nash's views are expressed in a number of letters. See, for example, Nash 1311/0607, letter from Nash to Mrs J. Hall, 21 March 1939.
8 There are some problems with stating exactly how many refugees from Central and Eastern Europe came to New Zealand. In part this is because accurate figures that distinguished between refugee migrants and ordinary migrants were not kept.

Additionally, a number of difficulties arose when officials attempted to classify according to nationality those people left stateless by Hitler's persecution, some of whom had fled from one temporary home to another. Their passports and travel documents revealed escape routes from Europe rather than nationality. For further discussion of these issues, see Beaglehole, 1988, pp. 14-16.
9 Lochore, pp. 73, 96-7.
10 *Ibid.*, p. 73.
11 *Ibid.*, p. 75.
12 For details, see the discussion in Beaglehole, 1988, pp. 1-7 and 134-40. The names of refugees referred to in this chapter and other identifying details have been changed.
13 *New Zealand Jewish Review*, February 1938, p. 2.
14 Interview with Ann Meltzer, 1 December 1984.
15 George Steiner, 'The Hollow Miracle', in *Language and Silence: Essays on Language, Literature and the Inhuman*, New York, 1967, pp. 100-1.
16 John Mansfield Thomson, *Into a New Key: The Origins and History of the Music Federation Inc., 1950–1982*, Wellington, 1985, p. 29.
17 John Mansfield Thomson, *New Zealand Drama, 1930–1980: An Illustrated History*, Auckland, 1984. Chapter 1 is concerned with the years 1930–45 during which time amateur theatre and play group readings flourished.
18 Lochore, pp. 77-80.
19 *Kai Tiaki, The New Zealand Nursing Journal*, 32 (1939), p. 310.
20 Ponton, p. 114.
21 AD MO 16/15, 'Control of Aliens during World War II', Vol. 1 and 2, NA–W. Some details concerning the restrictions on enemy aliens may be found in a report in the *Evening Post*, 10 April 1947.
22 IA 116/3/1, memo for Minister of Internal Affairs from J.N. Heenan, Under Secretary, Internal Affairs, NA–W, 14 September 1945.
23 PM 89/2/4, part 2, deputation on the future status of refugees in New Zealand, statement by Mrs O.E. Heymann.
24 *Evening Post*, 10 April 1947.

CHAPTER 6

1 Irihapeti Ramsden, 'He Poroporoaki', in Amy Brown, ed., *Mana Wahine: Women Who Show the Way*, Auckland, 1994, p. 202.
2 See, for example, Ranginui Walker, *Ka Whawhai Tonu Matou, Struggle Without End*, Auckland, 1990, pp. 197-247, and the collection of essays in Erik Schwimmer, ed., *The Maori People in the 1960s*, Auckland, 1968.
3 I wish to thank Letty for privileging me by saying 'yes' to this contribution to the book. Her agreement was given in the typical Letty-style of wanting to be supportive of other Maori women. I also thank her daughter, Carolyn Morgan who, with sister Ngaire and daughter Reikura, tolerated my eleventh-hour rush to have the draft read.
4 Interviews with Letty Brown, 25–27 May 1998. Unless otherwise indicated, all direct quotes are taken from this series of interviews.
5 Although some individuals are named throughout this chapter, and identified as leaders, I have deliberately avoided settling on a list of 'Maori leaders in West Auckland'. No such list could be definitive, and I would be courting trouble if I presumed to suggest one.

6. Linda Smith, *Decolonizing Methodologies: Research and Indigenous Peoples,* Dunedin, 1999, p. 39.
7. Walker, 1990, pp. 198-9.
8. Interview with Margaret Harris, Auckland, 28 May 1998.
9. Connie Hanna, 'Evidence for Te Whanau o Waipareira Trust in Wai 414, a claim against the Community Funding Agency', unpublished briefs of evidence, c. 1994.
10. *AJHR,* 1954, G–9, p. 8.
11. Policy paper, 'Social Welfare Work', c. 1954, MA1 Accn W2490, 36/1/1, NA–W.
12. Speech notes, Minister of Maori Affairs, 'Presentation of Young Maori Man and Woman of the Year Awards' Display Centre, Wellington, 24 August, 1968, MA 1, 1/1/64 pt 2, NA–W.
13. June Mariu, 'Evidence for Te Whanau o Waipareira Trust in Wai 414, a claim against the Community Funding Agency', unpublished briefs of evidence, c. 1994.
14. Mavis Tuoro, 'Evidence for Te Whanau o Waipareira Trust in Wai 414, a claim against the Community Funding Agency', unpublished briefs of evidence, c. 1994.
15. Naida Pou, 'Evidence for Te Whanau o Waipareira Trust in Wai 414, a claim against the Community Funding Agency', unpublished briefs of evidence, c. 1994.
16. Ranginui Walker, 'Maori People since 1950', in G.W. Rice, ed., *The Oxford History of New Zealand,* 2nd ed., Auckland, 1992, pp. 505-6.

CHAPTER 7

1. Ann L. Stoler, 'Sexual Affronts and Racial Frontiers: European Identities and the Cultural Politics of Exclusion in Colonial Southeast Asia', *Comparative Studies in Society and History,* 34, 1992, pp. 514-51, p. 516.
2. David Pearson, *A Dream Deferred: The Origins of Ethnic Conflict in New Zealand,* Wellington, 1990, p. 111.
3. Ian Pool, *Te Iwi Maori: A New Zealand Population, Past, Present and Projected,* Auckland, 1991, p. 154.
4. Mary Louise Pratt, *Imperial Eyes: Travel Writing and Transculturation,* London, 1992.
5. See for example: G.V. Butterworth, *The Maori in the New Zealand Economy,* Wellington, 1967; G.V. Butterworth, 'A Rural Maori Renaissance? Maori Society and Politics, 1920–1951', *The Journal of the Polynesian Society,* 81, 1972, pp. 160-95; I.H. Kawharu. 'Introduction', in R.H. Brookes and I.H. Kawharu, eds, *Administration in New Zealand's Multi-Racial Society*, Wellington, 1967, pp. 7-14; I.H. Kawharu, 'Urban Immigrants and Tangata Whenua', in Schwimmer, ed., 1968; Roger C.A. Maaka, 'The New Tribe: Conflicts and Continuities in the Social Organisation of Urban Maori', *The Contemporary Pacific,* 6, 1994, pp. 311-336; J.R. McCreary. 'Population Growth and Urbanisation', in Schwimmer, ed., pp. 187-204; J.M. McEwen, 'Urbanisation and the Multi-Racial Society', in Brookes and Kawharu, eds, pp. 75-84; Joan Metge, *A New Maori Migration: Rural and Urban Relations in Northern New Zealand,* London, 1964; Joan Metge, 'Alternative Policy Patterns in Multi-Racial Societies', in Brookes and Kawharu, eds, pp. 41-56; Robert Miles, 'Summoned by Capital', in Paul Spoonley ed., *Tauiwi: Racism and Ethnicity in New Zealand*, Palmerston North, 1984, pp. 223-43; Bryan Pay, '"a Racist Medium?": The Attitudes Expressed in the Auckland Printed Media Towards Aspects of Maori Urbanisation in Auckland (1960–1975)', MA thesis, University of Canterbury, 1992; M.F Poulson and R.J. Johnston, 'Patterns of Maori Migration',

in R.J. Johnston, ed., *Urbanisation in New Zealand*, Wellington, 1973; M.F. Poulson, D.T. Rowland, R.J. Johnston, 'Patterns of Maori Migration in New Zealand', in Leszek A. Kosinski, R. Mansell Prothero, eds, *People on the Move: Studies on Internal Migration*, London, 1975, pp. 309-24; D.T. Rowland, 'Processes of Maori Urbanisation', *The New Zealand Geographer*, 28, 1972, pp. 1-22; Eric Schwimmer, *The World of the Maori,* Wellington, 1966; Schwimmer, 'The Maori and the Government', in Schwimmer, ed., pp. 328-50; M.P.K. Sorrenson. 'Modern Maori: The Young Maori Party to Mana Motuhake', in Keith Sinclair, ed., *The Oxford Illustrated History of New Zealand*, Auckland, 1997, pp. 323-51; Walker, in Rice, ed.; Walker, 1990, pp. 498-519.

6   See, for example, Barbara Brookes, 'Nostalgia for "Innocent Homely Pleasures": The 1964 New Zealand Controversy over Washday at the Pa', in Barbara Brookes, ed., *At Home in New Zealand: History, Houses, People*, Wellington, 2000, pp. 210-225; Anne Else, 'Recording the History of the Maori Women's Welfare League – Interview with Mira Szaszy', *New Zealand Women's Studies Journal,* 6, 1990, pp. 17-21; Tania Rei, 'Te Ropu Wahine Maori Toko I Te Ora: Maori Women's Welfare League 1951–', in Anne Else, ed., pp. 34-8; Tania Rei, Geraldine McDonald, and Ngahuia Te Awekotuku, 'Nga Ropu Wahine Maori: Maori Women's Organisations', in Else, ed., pp. 3-17; Anna Rogers and Mira Simpson, eds, *Te Timatanga Tatau Tatau: Early Stories from Founding Members of the Maori Women's Welfare League*, Wellington, 1993.

7   Michael King, 'Between Two Worlds', in Rice, ed., pp. 285-307, p. 285.
8   Erik Olssen, 'Towards a New Society', in Rice, ed. pp. 254-84, p. 254.
9   Butterworth, 'A Rural Maori Renaissance?', pp. 160-95, p. 161.
10 Walker, in Rice, ed, p. 500.
11 File note on newspaper article, 2 July 1962, AAMK 869, 30/20, vol. 3, box 1101f, ANZ–W.
12 Butterworth, 'A Rural Maori Renaissance?', pp. 160-95; Maureen Molloy, 'Citizenship, Property and Bodies: Discourses on Gender and the Inter-War Labour Government in New Zealand', *Gender and History,* 4, 1992, pp. 293-304; Claudia Orange, 'A Kind of Equality: Labour and the Maori People 1935–1949', MA thesis, University of Auckland, 1977.
13 Paper, 14 November 1947, L1, 30/1/28, part 4, ANZ–W.
14 'The Changing Pattern of Maori Population', *Labour and Employment Gazette*, vol. 2, no. 2, February 1952, p. 16.
15 Metge, 1964, p. 128.
16 National Film Unit, *To Live in the City*, Wellington, 1967, ANZ–W.
17 *New Zealand Official Year Book*, Wellington, 1953, p. 951.
18 *AJHR*, 1949, G–9, p. 9.
19 See J.M. Booth, J.K. Hunn, *Integration of Maori and Pakeha,* Wellington, Department of Maori Affairs, 1962, No.1 in a Series of Special Studies and Report on Department of Maori Affairs with Statistical Supplement, *AJHR*, 1961, G–10, pp. 14-16.
20 Address by J.R. Hanan to the Maori Women's Welfare League Conference 1965, MS Papers 1396–009, ATL.
21 Coney, ed., 1993, pp. 198-99.
22 Barbara Brookes and Margaret Tennant, 'Maori and Pakeha Women: Many Histories, Divergent Pasts?', in Brookes, *et al*., eds, 1992, pp. 25-48, p. 35.

23 Judith Simon, *Nga Kura Maori: The Native School System 1867–1969,* Auckland, 1998, pp. 113-19.
24 Brookes, in Brookes, ed., 2000, p. 210-25.
25 *NZPD,* 1949, 287, p. 2397.
26 *NZPD,* 1945, 268, p. 778.
27 H.C. McQueen, *Vocations for Maori Youth,* Educational Research Series, No. 23, Wellington, 1945, p. 134.
28 See, for example, Noel Hilliard, *Maori Girl,* London, 1960; Noel Hilliard, *Maori Woman,* London, 1974.
29 Montgomerie, p. 97.
30 Simon, pp. 113-19.
31 Charlotte Macdonald, 'Strangers at the Hearth: The Eclipse of Domestic Service in New Zealand Homes *c.*1830s–1940s', in Brookes, ed., 2000, pp. 41-56, pp. 50-52; Katie Pickles, 'Empire Settlement and Single British Women as New Zealand Domestic Servants During the 1920s', *NZJH,* 35, 2001, pp. 22-44, pp. 38-9.
32 Melanie Nolan, *Breadwinning: New Zealand Women and the State,* Christchurch, 2000, p. 217.
33 Coney, ed., 1993, p. 225.
34 McQueen, p. 137.
35 Metge, 1964, pp. 2-4.
36 K. Riwai, Annual Report, 1 January–31 December 1962, AAMK 869, 36/29/8, box 1107c, ANZ–W.
37 See, for example, *Te Ao Hou,* September 1965, No. 52, p. 12; March 1967, No. 58, pp. 12, 22.
38 Pickles, this volume, C4, fn. 125.
39 Coney, ed., p. 225, Macdonald in Brookes, ed., 2000, Pickles, this volume.
40 See Katie Pickles, 'Workers and Workplaces – Industry and Modernity', in Cookson and Dunstall, eds, pp. 138-61.
41 Catherine Frances Gudgeon, 'A History of Te Wai Pounamu Maori Girls College: He Pounamu Kakano Rua', MA thesis, University of Auckland, 1998, p. 141.
42 Nolan, p. 227.
43 Coney, ed., 1993, pp. 102-3.
44 Nolan, pp. 225-9.
45 The *Press,* 11 June 1952, p. 2.
46 *AJHR,* 1969, G–9, p. 14.
47 *Te Ao Hou,* No. 59, June 1967, pp. 53-4.
48 *Ibid.*
49 *AJHR,* 1959, G–9, p. 37.
50 *AJHR,* 1958, G–9, p. 26.
51 K. Riwai, Annual report, 1 January–31 December 1959 and Annual report, 1 January–31 December 1962, AAMK 869, 36/29/8, box 1107c, ANZ–W.
52 For a discussion of this in the Christchurch context, see Pickles, in Cookson and Dunstall, pp. 145-50.
53 The *Press,* 28 July 1959, p. 18; and 8 August 1959, p. 15.
54 The *Press,* 19 August 1967, p. 3.
55 Katie Pickles, 'Exhibiting Canada: Empire, Migration and the 1928 English Schoolgirl Tour', *Gender, Place and Culture,* 7, 2000, pp. 81-96.
56 The *Press,* 8 August 1959, p. 15.

57 *Ibid.*, p. 15.
58 'Maori Girls Come to the City', *Labour and Employment Gazette*, vol. 10, No. 4, November 1960, p. 16; 'Girls Come to the City', *Te Ao Hou*, No. 36, September 1961, pp. 28-31.
59 The *Press*, 19 April 1961, p. 13.
60 Mrs E.J. Chesswas to Peter Fraser, 18 June 1947, Maori Affairs, Hostels and Hostelries – Policy, AAMK 869, 37/1, vol. 1, ANZ–W; National Council of Women Minutes of Conference, 1947, Dominion Executive and Dominion Conference minutes, agendas and remits 1947–60, MB 126, 5/3, Macmillan Brown Library.
61 Under-secretary of the Native Department to Mrs Chesswas, Dominion Secretary of the National Council of Women, 27 June 1947, AAMK 869, 37/1, box 1115f, vol.1, ANZ–W.
62 Sullivan to Corbett, 8 September 1950, AAMK 869, 37/1, box 1115f, vol.1, ANZ–W.
63 Corbett, to all members of cabinet, undated (*c.* 1950), AAMK 869, 37/1, box 1115f, vol. 1, ANZ–W.
64 Rophia to the Commissioner of Works, 18 April 1951, AAMK 869, 37/1, box 1115g, vol. 2, ANZ–W.
65 Corbett, AAMK 869, 37/1, box 1115f, vol. 1, ANZ–W.
66 Heeni Wharemaru with Mary Katherine Duffie, *Heeni: A Tainui Elder Remembers*, Auckland, 1997, pp. 120-22.
67 Notes of Interview, 11 June 1951, MA 2, W2490, 37/41, box 167, vol. 1, ANZ–W.
68 Kia Riwai, Annual reports, AAMK 869, 36/29/8, box 1107c, ANZ–W.
69 Maori Youth Hostels, undated, Relocation of Underemployed Maoris 1960–61, SS7, Acc W2756, 9/9/15, ANZ–W.
70 J.K. Hunn, Draft report for the Minister of Maori Affairs, undated (*c.* 1961), AAMK 869, 37/1, box 1116b, vol. 4, ANZ–W.
71 *AJHR*, G–9, 1960, p.19.
72 Maori Youth Hostels, undated, Relocation of Underemployed Maoris 1960–61, SS7, Acc W2756, 9/9/15, ANZ–W.
73 Hanan to all members of cabinet, undated (*c.* 1961), AAMK 869, 36/20, box 1101e, vol. 2, ANZ–W.
74 Hunn to Hanan, 3 August 1961, MA 1, W2490, 37/48, box 170, vol. 5, ANZ–W.

Chapter 8

1 Malua Theological College was started in 1844 by the London Missionary Society as the centre for Christian scholarship and for the training of local pastors to spread the gospel message. Early missionaries documented the Samoan language and translated the Bible and religious texts into the vernacular. These materials were printed for distribution on the Malua printing presses.
2 T. Tuvale, *A History of Old Samoa*. Papers held at Nelson Memorial Library, Apia, and Mitchell Collection, Sydney, *c.* 1890s.
3 Malama Meleisea.
4 Papauta Girls' School was set up in the early 1890s by the LMS to provide higher education for girls. The opening of Papauta was considered an important step in the development of women's education in the Pacific: students from the Ellice Islands (now Tuvalu), Niue and Tokelau were educated here, and Papauta girls

travelled through the region as wives of Samoan missionaries. In the early days the Papauta curriculum was very traditional (hence Papauta became affectionately known as the school for pastors' wives), but more academic subjects have been introduced in the recent times. See E.A. Downs, *Daughters of the Islands,* Wellington and Surrey, 1944.

5   The 'flu pandemic of 1918. In the final year of the First Word War an influenza virus swept across the United States, then crossed the Atlantic with American troops infecting both sides of the European battlefield. In 1918 it struck Spain and was named the Spanish influenza or Spanish Lady. The epidemic spread to New Zealand on the SS *Niagara*, and on to Samoa by the SS *Talune*, which had docked alongside the SS *Niagara* in Auckland. Estimates are that at least 22 per cent of the Samoan population died in the epidemic. Other accounts list the death toll at 7542 people: 3265 adult males, 2704 females and 1572 children. In addition to this, others were totally or partially incapacitated by the disease. See M. Field, *Mau: Samoan Struggles against New Zealand Oppression*, Wellington, 1984.

6   P. Dunlop, 'How many people live in your house', in A. Patterson, ed., *Some New Zealand Short Stories,* Auckland, 1988.

Chapter 9

1   Maxine Hong Kingston, *Woman Warrior*, London, 1981.
2   The phenomenon of Chinese females being left in host countries has been examined by R. Peu-Pau *et al., Astronaut Families and Parachute Children: The Cycle of Migration between Hong Kong and Australia*, Canberra, 1996.
3   Malcolm McKinnon, *Immigrants and Citizens: New Zealanders and Asian Immigration in Historical Context,* Wellington, 1996. p. 1.
4   George Grey, *AJHR* 1879, D–3, session 1.
5   *Ibid.*
6   McKinnon, p. 1.
7   Nigel Murphy, *The Poll-tax in New Zealand: A Research Paper*, Wellington, 1995.
8   See Anna Rogers, *A Lucky Landing: The Story of the Irish in New Zealand*, Auckland, 1996.
9   *NZPD*, 1880, p. 91.
10 *NZPD*, 1888.
11 James Ng, *Windows on a Chinese Past,* vol. 1, Dunedin, 1993.
12 *AJHR*, 1871 H. 5B, 'Final Report of the Chinese Immigration Committee', p. 4.
13 Ip, 1990, p. 16.
14 William Skinner, 'Mobility Strategies in Late Imperial China: a regional systems analysis', in Carl Smith, ed., *Regional Analysis,* vol. 1, New York, 1976.
15 Marlon K. Hom, *Songs of Gold Mountain*, Berkeley, 1987.
16 The 1881 act also imposed a tonnage ratio of one Chinese per 100 tons of cargo on ships carrying Chinese immigrants.
17 The 1896 act raised the tonnage ratio to one Chinese per 200 tons of cargo.
18 Murphy, 1995, Appendix 'Poll-tax listings, Chinese arrivals to Wellington, 1888–1930'.
19 *NZPD*, 1907, vol. 142, pp. 839-40.
20 The total Chinese population declined sharply from 5004 in 1881 to 2570 in 1906. It was to reach a nadir of 2147 in 1916.

21 *Statutes of New Zealand,* 1907, no.79, 'Chinese Immigrants Amendment Act'.
22 See Manying Ip, 'Kue Sum Ah-Chan' pp. 3-6, and 'Ken Chunyu', pp. 135-7, in Charlotte Macdonald *et al.*, eds, 1991.
23 Ng, p. 100.
24 Ip, p. 51.
25 Charles A. Price, *The Great White Walls Are Built.* Canberra, 1974, p. 96; see also Sean Brawley, 'No "White Policy" in New Zealand: Fact and Fiction in New Zealand's Asian Immigration Record', *NZJH*, 27, 1993.
26 Labour Department, L1, 22/1/81. Customs Department memo C33/253/M. 'Asian Immigration'. 29 September, 1950, p. 2, NA–W.
27 'GIS.22/10', Series 22, NA–A.
28 Labour Department, p. 3.
29 Decision of Minister, 5 May 1939, C 33/24, quoted in F.A. Ponton, 'Immigration Restrictions in New Zealand: A Study of Policy from 1908 to 1939', MA thesis, Victoria University, Wellington, 1946, pp. 119-20.
30 *Ibid.*
31 Customs Department, Gisborne C–GS 1 22/1–3, box 16, NA–W.
32 James Ng, 'Chinese Settlement in New Zealand Past and Present', October, 2001, p. 13.
33 Ip, 1990, p. 116.
34 The Chinese were subjected to requirements not imposed on other 'race alien' applicants. They had to renounce their Chinese nationality, and had to prove that they were 'closer to the New Zealand way of life than to the Chinese'. Only 'the most highly assimilated types' would succeed. The details were given in an internal memo for the Minister of Internal Affairs, 22 June 1950. IA/116/7, 83/B, NA–W.
35 See Ip, 1996, ch. 3.
36 *Ibid.*, p. 73.
37 *Ibid.*, p. 124.
38 The 2001 census found that the 'Asians' (numbering just below 240,000) have become the fourth largest ethnic group in the country, just edging ahead of 'Pacific Islanders' who numbered 231,801. About half of all 'Asians' are ethnic Chinese.
39 See Manying Ip 'New Zealand' in Lyn Pan, ed., *Encyclopedia of Chinese Overseas*, Singapore, 1998, pp. 286-91.
40 Statistics New Zealand, *2001 Census*, National Summary, Ethnic Group.
41 See Elsie Ho, 'Maintaining Links in Transnational Communities: Chinese "Astronaut" Families in New Zealand', Briefing paper No 1, New Directions: New Settlers Conference 11–12 April 2001, Wellington.
42 Ward Friesen and Manying Ip, 'New Chinese New Zealanders: Profile of a Transnational Community in Auckland', and Elsie Ho, Richard Bedford and Goodwin, 'Astronaut Families: A Contemporary Migration Phenomenon' in *East Asian New Zealanders: Research on New Migrants*, Asia-Pacific Migration Research Network, 1997, Albany, 1997.
43 Ronald Skeldon, *Reluctant Exiles? Migration from Hong Kong and the Overseas Chinese*, Hong King, 1994, p. 6.
44 Manying Ip, 'From Gold Mountain Women to Astronauts' Wives', in Paul Macgregor, ed., *Histories of the Chinese in Australasia and the South Pacific, Museum of Chinese Australian History,* Melbourne, 1995. pp. 274-86.
45 One such research project was carried out by Manying Ip and Ward Friesen in

1996–97. Entitled 'New Chinese New Zealanders in Auckland', the project yielded data on over a thousand ethnic Chinese migrants who arrived between 1986 and 1996 from the three major origin regions: People's Republic of China, Taiwan and Hong Kong.
46 Friesen and Ip, 1997.
47 See *ibid.*, and Tania Boyer, 'Problems in Paradise: Taiwanese Immigrants to Auckland, New Zealand.' *Asia Pacific Viewpoint,* 37, pp. 59-79.
48 See Owen Martell, 'Chinese Associations in New Zealand 1860s-Present: Their Nature, History and Social Significance', MA thesis, University of Auckland, 1998.
49 Elsie Ho, Richard Bedford and Charlotte Bedford, 'Migrants in their Family Contexts: Application of a Methodology', *Population Studies Discussion Paper No. 34,* University of Waikato, Hamilton, 2000.
50 Ann Henderson, 'New Settlers Programme: Encounters, Responses, Policies' Longitudinal Study Summary, Massey University, 2001.
51 See Barbara Thomson, ed., *Ethnic Diversity in New Zealand: A Statistical Profile*, Wellington, 1999, p. 56, for the rationale.
52 Manying Ip, ' Successful settlement of migrants and relevant factors for setting immigration targets', unpublished conference paper delivered to the Population Conference, Wellington, 1999.
53 Thomson, p. 74.
54 *Ibid.*, pp. 75-7.
55 *Ibid.*, pp. 138-41.
56 Manying Ip and Wardlow Friesen, 'The New Chinese Community in New Zealand: Local Outcomes of Transnationalism', *Asian and Pacific Migration Journal,* 10, 2001, pp. 213-40.
57 Christine Inglis, ed., *Asians in Australia: The Dynamics of Migration and Settlement,* St Leonards, 1992; Chung Wing Ng, 'Canada', in Pan, ed., *Encyclopedia of Chinese Overseas,* pp. 234-47.
58 Jacqueline Lidgard, 'East Asian Migration to Aotearoa/New Zealand: Perspectives of Some New Arrivals', *Population Studies Centre Discussion Paper No. 12,* University of Waikato, Hamilton, 1996, p. 33; Boyer, 1996, pp. 73-4.
59 Friesen and Ip, 1997.
60 Elsie Ho *et al.*, 'Identity maintenance, acculturation and mental health: a longitudinal study of Chinese immigrant youths in New Zealand', *Social Science Monograph Series: Population Studies,* University of Waikato, Hamilton, 2001.
61 See 'Introduction' in Manying Ip, ed., *Re-examining Chinese Transnationalism in Australia-New Zealand,* Canberra, 2001.
62 Pan, ed., p. 40.

CHAPTER 10

1 K.W. Thomson and A.D. Trilin, eds, *Immigrants in New Zealand*, Palmerston North, 1970; A.D. Trilin and P. Spoonley, eds, *New Zealand and International Migration: A Digest and Bibliography*, vol 1, Palmerston North, 1986, vol. 2, Palmerston North, 1992, vol. 3, Palmerston North and Albany, 1997. Refer also to Alexander Trapeznik, 'Recent European Migration to New Zealand', in Stuart Greif, ed., *Immigration and National Identity in New Zealand: One People – Two Peoples – Many Peoples?*, Palmerston North, 1995, pp. 77-96.

2   As examples of fieldwork studies in immigration to New Zealand I would like to mention the books of Beaglehole, 1988; 1990; Hutching, 1999; and for special studies on immigrant women see Wood, 1991, and Ip, 1990.
3   For recent attempts to address the problem, see Floya Anthias, Metaphors of Home: 'Gendering New Migrations to Southern Europe', in Floya Anthias and Gabriella Lazardis, eds, *Gender and Migration in Southern Europe: Women on the Move*, Oxford, New York, 2000, 15–47; and Jacqueline Leckie, 'Silent Immigrants? Gender, Immigration and Ethnicity in New Zealand', in Greif, ed., pp. 50-76.
4   The interviews were conducted in an informal, open style using a guideline of questions (if necessary), always starting with the question 'Why New Zealand?' All persons quoted in this article gave permission to use their interviews for publication; some of them have been given pseudonyms at their own request.
5   The full results of the project is to be published by Victoria University Press as *Keeping A Low Profile: An Oral History of German Immigration to New Zealand*.
6   German immigrants of the last twenty years can be loosely described as ecological refugees and lifestyle migrants, fleeing perceived ecological disaster in Europe. The more recent immigrants consider New Zealand a good place to bring up children, and to enjoy an outdoor lifestyle, and do not necessarily want to spend all of their lives here. The immigrant subjects are divided between those in the cities leading a 'normal' working life, and those engaged in alternative lifestyles in rural areas such as Golden Bay, the Coromandel and the Bay of Islands.
7   For specifically female issues on the everyday culture of New Zealand life, refer to Julie Park, ed., *Ladies a Plate: Changes and Continuity in the Lives of New Zealand Women*, Auckland, 1991, especially the introduction.
8   For a discussion of gender-specific patterns of narration and storytelling refer to S.D. Stahl, *Literary Folkloristics and the Personal Narrative*, Bloomington, 1987, Magdalena J. Zaborowska, *How We Found America: Reading Gender Through East-European Immigrant Narratives*, Chapel Hill, 1995, and Deborah Tennen, *You Just Don't Understand: Women and Men in Conversation*, New York, 1990.
9   Several men talked about suffering from the 'tall-poppy syndrome' and had problems making friends at work. But they talked more in passing rather than emphasising the point.
10 Interview with a women's group in Hutt Valley, Wellington. See Brigitte Bönisch-Brednich, 'Being German in Wellington: Female Perspectives', in *Oral History New Zealand*, 1999, pp. 23-9.

Index

A History of Old Samoa 136
Aana Faleasiu 135, 140
Aana Vaialua 136
Adamant 40, 43
Addison's Flat 46, 60
Afamasaga Maua 147
Afele Atoa 147
Aiga 142

Alaoa 142, 143
alcohol 40; beer 94; drinking habits of New Zealand men 94; drunkenness 13, 61, 94, 113; Irish Whiskey 30
Amery, Leo 63
Aotea 24, 26
Apelles 42
Apia 137, 142
Apia Protestant Church 142
Araiteuru 21
Arawa 22
Arawhata 58
Ashmore 39
Asia 38
assimilation, 10, 119, 133
Atoa Soonanofo 138, 140, 142
Atoa Teo Tuvale 138, 141, 147
Auckland 47, 72, 86, 103, 122, 132, 141, *see also* Letty Brown
Auckland Hospital Board 126
Auckland Star 73, 111
Auckland Teachers' Training College 106
Auelua 147
Auschwitz 83, 93
Australia 151, 159, 163; and Irish migration 46, 47-8, 49, 50-51, 54-5, 55-7, 60, 61-2; and single women's migration 63, 65, 67, 70, 73, 80; goldfields 11
Austria 82, 98
Avao, Matautu, Savii 135
Avele College 140, 141
Awarua 47
Ayres, D.V. 131

Ballance, John 151
Ballarat 11, 52, 56
Barrytown 60, 61
Bayes, Joseph 34
Beaglehole, Ann 9, 12, 179

Belich, James 19
Bell, Claudia 25
Berar 32
Best, Elsdon 16, 17, 18
Betham, Lydia 145
Bethlehem School, Tauranga 128
Birchfield, Connie 80
Bönisch-Brednich, Brigitte 13, 179
Bourke, Catherine 55
Brighton 46, 47
British Army 100
British Empire, the 12, 14, 60, 63-80, 150
British Government Oversea Committee 69
British War Brides 78
British Women's Auxiliary Services 69
British Women's Emigration Association 68
Brooking, Tom 9
Brown, Letty 12, 13, 103-16
Buck, Sir Peter, (Te Rangi Hiroa) 17
Byrnes, Giselle 25

Caduceus 32, 34
Cakobau, Ratu 136
Canada 60, 151, 155, 163; migration to 63, 65, 67, 73, 80
Canterbury 62
Canterbury Agricultural College 128
Canterbury Museum 128
Canterbury Public Relations Office 128
Cape Town 32
Cardigan Castle 42
Carew, Father Denis 60
Cartvale 31
Central and Eastern Europe 81, 82
Charleston 46, 47
Chesswas, E.J. 130
childbirth 33, 102, 175 *see also* women's health and well-being
children 65, 97, 116, 175; education of, 146-8, 158, *see also* Chinese women's migration, Ellen Piezzi, German women's migration, Jewish refugees, Plunket
children's literature 17, 23, 24, 30
Chile 33, 38, 43
Chinese Immigrants Act 1881 153
Chinese laundry 88
Chinese women's migration; attitudes towards, 150-51, 153, 154-6, 157-8, 160, 165;

diasporic networks 164-5; domestic work 159; employment 161-3; gender ratios 149, 156; marriage 152, 153-4; model minority 158-9; numbers, 149, 153, 154, 155, 160, 162; new migrants 149, 159-60, 161-5; repatriation, 155; Sino-Japanese War 156-8; sojourning 152; socio-economic background 160, 162-3; sources 159-61; timing and direction 152-3, 159-60; transnationalism 163-5
Christchurch 62, 100, 122, 128, 129, 131-2
Christchurch Rehua Maori Girls' Hostel 131
Christmas 76, 94
Clare, Co. 11, 52, 56, 62
class 36, 40, 77, 92, 93, *see also* migrants and shipboard life, steerage
climate and Empire 66-7
Clohessy, Catherine 60
Clohessy, Jane 60
Cold War 158
Colonial Intelligence League 68
Colonial Office 63
Colonial Office, Women's Branch of the Oversea Settlement 68
colonialism 10, 14
Commission on Emigration and Other Population Problems 51
Coney, Sandra 79
Connaught 53
Corbett, Ernest 131
Cospatrick 32
Coughtrey, Millen 33, 36, 37, 38
cultural history 10
Czech Club 91, 92
Czechoslovakia 83, 85, 86, 87, 99

Dachau 84
Dallam Tower 41
dances 107
Davidson, Janet 18
dentists 97
Department of Health 124, 126
Department of Labour 119, 129
Department of Maori Affairs 107, 112, 113, 119, 122, 126, 128, 129, 131, 132, 133
Department of Samoan Affairs 136
Deportation of Canadian Migrants 76
Depression, the Great 66, 75, 78
Diamond, Ann 55, 56-7, 60
Diamond, Patrick 55
diaspora 10, 12, 62, 165, *see also* Chinese women's migration
Dobie sisters 36
Domestic Immigration Society, Sydney 78
domestic labour 34, 40, 63, 87, 88, *see also* Maori women's migration, West Coast
domestic service 29, 63, 79, 95, *see also* West Coast
domesticity 65, 80, *see also* Maori women's migration, West Coast
Dominion Office, Britain 67
Dominions Royal Commission on Population (1917) 63
Donegal, Co. 53
Doo, Lily 155
Doyle, David 55
dual citizenship 11
Dunedin 52, 55
Dunn, Patrick 56

East Coast 129
Eastminster 41
Empire Settlement Act (1922) 11, 65, 66
England 32
England 48, 52
English 89, 145, 176, *see also* Jewish refugees
Evening Post 148
Evening Star 97

Faavevela 138, 140, 142, 147, 148
Fairbairn, Alfred 143
Fairbairn, Barbara 145-6
Fairbairn, Elizabeth 39
Fairbairn, Emele-Moa Teo 13, 14, 135-48
Fairbairn, Ian 143, 144, 147
Fairbairn, Jim (Jock) 142-4, 145, 146, 147-8
Fairbairn, Jimmy 143, 144
Fairbairn, Mabel 143, 144, 145, 146-7
Fairbairn, Margaret 143
Fairbairn, Peggy 13, 145-6, 148, 179
Fairbairn, Rex 143, 144
Fairburn, Miles 25
Faleasiu Asofana 140
Falkingham, Reverend 131
Famenoth 34
families 33, 34, 35, 65, 98, *see also* Chinese women's migration, West Coast
Fasitoo 135, 142
Fearnley, George 35
Fene 138
Feneliko 138
Fiji 136, 143
Findlayson, Jane 32, 37, 43
First Wave Feminism 68
First World War, the 69, 72
Fono o Matai 142
food and diet 34, 89, 108, 146, 172; apple strudel 99; boil-up, pork-bones, dough-boys, puha and watercress 108; cakes, scones, pies 95; Christmas cake 89;

kumara 21, 22; meat 89; roast 88; seafood 108; vegetable garden 97, 144; weet-bix 89, 146; wiener schnitzel 95; chocolate biscuits 146; ovaltine 146
Fraser, Lyndon 9, 11
Fraser, Peter 130
Friedeberg, 42
Furniss, Samuel 59

Galway, Co. 53, 62
Garlick, Jennifer 23
Gaunt, Lieutenant Guy 137
Geelong 52
gender relations 10
German women's migration, 1980s-1990s; children, 169, 172, 175, 176; decision-making, 168-71; gender roles, 174-5; homesickness, 172, 174-6; comparison with male narratives, 168, 171, 172-4, 177-8; personal development, 176-8; research questions, 168
Germany 82, 85, 87, 98, 136, 138
Gillin, Sarah 58
Girdler, F.M. 69, 70
Girl Guides 73
Girls' Friendly Society 68
globalisation 14, 51, 60, 163-5, 178
Godinet, Alice 145
Goldie, Charles F. and L.J. Steele 19
Goldsborough 45
Good Friday 94
Goodwin, Bridget 55
Grattan, John 56
Great Britain 48, 63, 150
Great Circle Route 31
Great Fleet 15, 16, 17
Grey Lynn 108, 109
Grey, Sir George 16, 17, 23, 150
Greymouth 46, 47, 48, 61

Hanan, J. Ralph 113
Hanmer Hospital 100-1
Harriet Morison 74
Harris, Aroha 10, 12, 180
Hastings, David 11, 180
Hawaiki 16, 22, 25
Hearn, Terry 51
Helvetia Hotel 45, *see also* Ellen Piezzi
Hermoine 29, 31, 32, 34, 35, 38, 42
High Commissioner in London, NZ 78
Hilliard, Noel 120
Hindostan 42
Hitler 81
Hitler's Europe 100
Hoani Waititi Marae, West Auckland 103, 115, 116
Hogan, Susan 57
Hokitika 46, 47, 49
homesickness 13, 107, 108, 172, 174, *see also* German women's migration
Hong Kong 159, 160-61, 164
Horan, Cecilia 57
Horouta 23
Hosking, William 41
household appliances 88
housework 34, 89, *see also* domestic labour, domestic service, German women's migration, West Coast
Humphreys, Mrs 38, 40, 41
Hunn, Jack 132-3
Hyde, Robin 79

Immigration and Restriction Amendment Act (1920) 81
Immigration quotas 83, *see also* Jewish refugees, Chinese women's migration
Imperial Conference in London (1921) 65
Imperial Order Daughters of the Empire (IODE) 69
indigenous voices, discussion of 105
industrial capitalism 14
Ip, Manying 9, 11, 180
Ireland 40, 150
Irish Catholics 39, *see also* West Coast
Irish Home Rule 40
Irish Protestants 39, 61 *see also* West Coast
Irish women 11, 45-62, 76, *see* West Coast
Isles of the South 42

Jenkins, Kuini 20
Jewish refugees 81-102; anti-Semitism 85; arts, the theatre, ballet, symphony orchestras 90- 91; as enemy aliens 82, 98; concentration camps 82, 84; culture shock 86; English classes 89; Holocaust 101, surveillance 100; suspicious neighbours, 99; *see also* Czech Club, homesickness, Wellington Refugee Committee
Jewish Welfare Society 86, 89

Kahurangi Point 47
Kanawa 23
Kane, Patrick 60
Kaniere 46
Kereroa 22
Khaki University of Canada, London 78
Kiernan, Margaret 60
Kikohura, Marama 23
Kilbirnie, Wellington 144-5

Kilcredan, Co. Clare 56
Kilkenny, Co. 52, 62
Killarney, Co. Kerry 58
King's, Co. 52, 62
Knowles, Theresa 58
Kohanga reo 115
Kumara 47

Labour and Employment Gazette 129
Lambi, Mary 97
Lane Walker Rudkin 128
Langton, Hermione and Lavinia, 145
Le Mamea Faletoese 135, 136, 140
Le'auanae of Iva 135
Leaky Liz 55
Lefifi Government School 144
Leinster 62
Leitufa 142, 145
Letts, Emilie 29, 30, 31, 32, 34, 35, 38, 40, 41, 42, 43
Leong, Violet 159
Leufisa 135, 147
life stories and oral testimony 9, 10, 81-102, 103-16, 135-48, 167-78
Limerick, Co. 52, 55, 62
London Missionary Society 135, 136, 142, 145
Luafatasaga Kalapu 141
Lysnar, W.D. 67
Lyttelton 120

McCarthy, Angela 9
McCarthyism 158
McClean, Rosalind 9
McCombs, Terence 120
Macdonald, Charlotte 9, 64-5
Macdonald, Christina 32
McGirr, Margaret 55
McIntosh, Mina 145
McKinnon, Malcolm 150
McLean, Gavin 17
McMahon, Ellen 60
Madden, Rosemary 24
Mafuie 138
Mahoney, Annie 59
Malietoa and Mataafa, kingship battles 137-8
Malietoa Laupepe 136
Malifa 141
Malifa Government School 139
Maloney, Mary 55
Malua 140
Malua Theological College 135, 136
Mamari 21
Manutaki 114
Maori 20, 21, 22, 93; ancestry 93; churches 107; culture, sports and family groups 107; origins 16, 17, 23; *see also* Letty Brown, Maori women's migration, Maori Women's Welfare League
Maori Community Centre, Auckland 108, 109
Maori Creek 58
Maori Education Foundation 110
Maori Land Court 16
Maori Social and Economic Advancement Act 112
Maori War Effort Organisation 112
Maori wardens 107
Maori women's migration, young single; and citizenship 119; demand for labour 119; domesticity, 119-20, 134; domestic service, 121-2, 126; domestic work 119, 124, 122-3, 121; factories 128, 129; hostels 122, 130-33; manufacturing 128, 129; numbers 117; nursing 124-8; office work 129; teaching 124, 126; timing and direction 118-19, 120-22, *see also* Letty Brown
Maori Women's Movement, the 104
Maori women's sexuality 23
Maori Women's Welfare League 103, 107, 117, 113-16; Arahina Branch 111; Te Atatu Branch 111, 113; Waipareira Branch 114
Market Harborough domestic training centre, UK 78
Marotini, Kura 24
marriage 76, 102, 99; *see also* Chinese women's migration, German women's migration, Jewish refugees, West Coast
Massey, William 67
Mataafa Faumuina 145
Mataatua 20, 22, 24
Matamoana 140
Matatumua, Fetaui, Suia, Eni and Moana 145
Matipo Road School 114
matrons (conductresses, chaperones) 36, 71, *see also* protection
Mautuli 142
May Queen 31, 35
Mead, Aroha 24
medical examinations 30, 31, 33, 63, 76
medical practitioners 97, 141, 158
Melbourne 46, 50, 51, 52, 55, 56, 62
Meleisea, Malama 137
Metge, Joan 122
migrants, nominated 71, 74; assisted 33, 71; assisted domestics 63; third class passage 63, *see also* Jewish refugees, German women's migration, Maori women's migration, single women, shipboard life, West Coast

Mili Afamasaga 147
Minehan, Catherine 56
missionaries 30, 31, *see also* London Missionary Society
Mitchell Library, Sydney 136, 137
Moenoa 142
Molloy, Maureen 9
Mongol 33
Montgomerie, Deborah 121
Montieth, Stewart 59
Moss, Joe 131
Mulinuu 135, 136, 137, 138, 139
Mulivai 137
Munster 53
Muriwai 22
Murray McIntosh, Rosalind 18
Myers, A.M. 67

Naitua 136, 138, 140, 142, 143, 145
Nash, Sir Walter 81
National Council of Women 130
naturalisation 101, 102
Nazi Europe 81, 98
Nazism 12
neighbours 101
Nelson Creek 11, 56
New South Wales 52, 53, 55, 56
New Zealand Council for Educational Research 122
New Zealand Maori Council 112
Department of Immigration, New Zealand 67, 69, 72, 74
New Zealand Herald 67, 91, 180
New Zealand High Commission in London 71, 74
New Zealand Hospital Boards Association 124
New Zealand Post Office 107, 108, 129
New Zealand School Journal 15, 17
Ng, Bickleen Fong 158
Ng, James 158
Ngai Tahu 26, 131
Ngata, Sir Apirana 105
Ngati Porou 105, 106
Niu Sila 139
Nolan, Mary 58
Notown 55, 58
nurses 79, 96, 98, *see also* Maori women's migration

O' Regan, Sir Tipene, 26
O'Connor, Mary 58
O'Hallahan, Denis 47
O'Toole, Catherine 57
Oa 142
Oamaru 32, 39, 43

ocean, the; as a concept 19, 25, 15-28, 29-43
Okarito 49
Okuru 58
Orbell, Margaret 16, 20, 21, 24
Otago goldfields 50-51, 52, 151
Otago Provincial Government 151
Overland, Kate 55
Oversea League, 69

Pacific Island Congregational Church 145
Palmerston 42
Palmerston North 96
Pan, Lyn 165
Papauta 138, 139
Papautu Girls' School 138
Parnell, Catherine 32, 34
People's Republic of China, 161, 160, 164
Phelan, Kate 56-7
Phelan, Maria 55
Philipp, Alfonso 143
Phillips, Jock 19
physiotherapists 97, 100
Pickles, Katie, 11, 126, 180
Piezzi, Ellen 14, 45, 46, 49, 55, 56
Pirie, Minna 34, 36, 43
Playcentre 110, 115, 116; Te Atatu Playcentre 109, 110, 111; Waipareira Playcentre 110, 111, 113, 115
playgroups 102
Plunket 92, 102
Police, New Zealand 99
population growth 64
Port Chalmers 52
Pound, Francis 25
Poutasi 144
Poutini Ngai Tahu 47
Press, Christchurch 128-9
protection, of women 35-7, 71, 130-33

Queen Victoria Maori Girls' School 79, 106, 128
Queen's, Co. 58
Queensland 53

racism 10, 13, 146 *see also* Chinese women's migration
Rankin, 'Sugar Annie' 55
Red Jacks 55, 57, 58
Reefton 47, 59
refugees, *see* Jewish refugees
religion 40, *see also* Jewish refugees, West Coast
Rerekohu Maori District High School 105, 106
Returned Servicemen Scheme 67

Rimu 45, 56
Riske, Max 147
Riwai, Kia 122, 128
Rogers, Anna 9
Rongorongo 24
Ross 48, 56
Rutherford High School 114
Ryall, Mrs Jane 61

Saisalui Ieriko 145
Saleimoa 142, 143
Salvation Army 69, 144-5
Samoa College 148
Sang, Mabel 158
Saniie Vinepa 135
Savaii 141
Scanlon, Bridget 58
Scanlon, Michael 58
School Certificate 106
Schuster, Elsie 145
Schuster, George 145
Schuster, Sonny 146
Scimitar 33
Scotland 48, 74, 76
Seamer House 107
Second World War 81, 92
sex imbalance 11, 64-5, 149
Sharp, Andrew 16
shipboard life, in the nineteenth-century; infectious diseases 30, 33, 41; married couples 34; matrons 36, 37, 41; medical doctors/ surgeons 33, 37, 39; quarrels 38; religious and ethnic tensions 39; saloon 30, 35, 41; sexual assaults 37; sexual liaisons 42; single men 34, 37; steerage 29, 30, 31, 33, 35, 36, *see also* alcohol, medical examinations, single women
Simmons, D.R. 16
Simpson, Tony 9
Sina 138, 141, 142, 145, 147
Sinclair, Keith 25
Singapore 159, 164
single agricultural labourers 65
single women 14, 30, 34, 36, 37, 38, 41, 102, *see also* German women's migration, Maori women's migration, shipboard life, West Coast
Siumu 138
Smith, Linda Tuhiwai 105
Smith, Robert 147
Social Security Act (1938) 124
Society for the Oversea Settlement of British Women (SOSBW) 68, 69, 70, 71, 77
Somersetshire 24 34
Soo Teo 146

Sorrenson, M.P.K 16
South Africa 159; migration to 65, 67
South Africa Colonization Society 68
South Australia 52
space 10, 68; for urban Maori 14
Spoonley, Paul 167
Stevenson, Robert Louis 142
St Joseph's Maori Girls' College 105, 106
St Mary's Convent (Wellington) 49
Stockridge, C.H. 129
Strathmore 32
Sullivan, Frances 60
surveillance, 100, *see also* protection and Jewish refugees
Sydney 56

Taimua and Faipule 136
Tainui 131
Tainui 23
Taiwan 159, 161, 164
Takitimu 21
Talisala 138, 139
Tanugamanono 138, 140-3, 147-8
Taonui, Rawiri 15
Tapasu 138
Tapu 22, 23
Tasmania 52
Tauese 142
Taulalo 138, 140, 141
Taupo 141
Te Amorangi 104

Te Ao Hou 122, 124, 126, 129
Te Araroa 103, 104, 105
Te Atatu Maori Committee 103, 112
Te Awakotuku, Ngahuia 23
Te Puea Herangi, Princess 131
Te Puea Trophy 114
Te Rahui Wahine, Hamilton 131
Teo Ieni 147
Teo Tuvale 135-8, 139-40
The Encyclopaedia of the Chinese Overseas 165
Theresienstadt 93
Thomson, K.W. 167
Tikitiki 105
Timaru 32
Timaru 62
Tipperary Mary 55
Tipperary, Co. 52, 62
Tivoli Hotel 137
Tofaeono Aiga 138
transnationalism 10, 14, 163-5 *see also* Chinese women's migration
Tregear, Edward 17, 18

Trlin, A.D. 167
Tuliomanu 143
Tupuola Sepelini 138, 141, 145
Tusi Faalupega 136
Tweed 30

Ulster 53
United Council of Churches 130
United States 150, 151
United States 52, 59, 60
urbanisation 103-16, 117-34

Vaaelua Petaia 135
Vailima 139, 143, 144
Ventnor 151
Vesey, Anne 38, 39, 43
Victoria 11, 51, 52, 53, 54-5, 62, 70
Victoria League 69, 70
Victorian values 33, 34, 71
Vogel, Julius 29, 38
voyage out, the (nineteenth century), *see* shipboard life

Waipareira Maori Committee 112, 113
Wairaka 20, 22, 24, 26
Wairakewa 22, 26
Wairoa 129
Waitakere City 106
waka traditions 12, 15-17, 20, *see also* Great Fleet
Walker, Ranginui 106, 112
Wall, Catherine 39
Walsh, Mary 60
Wanhalla, Angela 12, 180
Warren, Mrs Catherine 60
Wartime suspension of naturalisation 101
Watkin, G. 69, 70
Weddings 80, 149, 153
Weir, Johanna (nee Shanahan) 55, 56-7, 58
Wellington 62, 86, 96, 97, 99, 102, 122, 129, 136, 141, 144
Wellington Polytechnic 126
Wellington Refugee Committee 95, 96
Wellington Technical College 146

West Auckland 14, 103
West Coast, and Irish women's migration 45-6, 61-2; domestic work 57-8; domesticity 61; gender ratios 48-9; geographical origins 52-3; age and marital status 51-52; marriage patterns 49, 58-60; migrant networks 55-7, 60, 62; numbers 47-8; religion 49, 52, 60-61; socio-economic background 54-5; timing and direction, 50-51; widowhood 57-8
West, Pearl 141
Western Monarch 39
Westport 46, 48
Whakaotirangi 22, 23 26
White, Honora 56
women's auxiliary services 64
Women's Branch of Canada's Department of Immigration 80
Women's Division of the New Zealand Farmers' Union (WDNZFU) 77, 78
women's health and well-being 41, 171, 176 *see also* childbirth
Women's Institute 88
Women's suffrage 9
women's voluntary work 68
women's work, 79; in factories, commerce, nursing, offices, department stores 68, 96; needlework 37, 71; professional qualifications 82, 96, 97; sewing, cleaning, cooking, childcare, shop work 94-5; underemployment 96; *see also* Chinese women's migration, domestic service, domestic labour, Jewish refugees, Maori women's migration, West Coast
Wong, Kirsten 159
Wood, Val 9
Woods, Megan 10, 12, 180
Woodlark 38
Workers' Educational Association (WEA) 89

Young Maori Woman of the Year 113
Young Women's Christian Association (YWCA) 69, 72, 74, 75, 76, 77, 78, 79, 80; Girl Citizen Movement 73

OTAGO HISTORY SERIES

God & Government: The New Zealand Experience
Edited by Rex Ahdar & John Stenhouse
ISBN 1 877133 80 9, $39.95

Rewarding Service: A History of the Government Superannuation Fund
Neill Atkinson
ISBN 1 877276 22 7, $39.95

'Unfortunate Folk': Essays on Mental Health Treatment, 1863–1992
Edited by Barbara Brookes & Jane Thomson
ISBN 1 877276 09 X, $39.95

Communities of Women: Historical Perspectives
Edited by Barbara Brookes & Dorothy Page
ISBN 1 877276 31 6, $39.95

The Heather & the Fern: Scottish Migration and New Zealand Settlement
Edited by Tom Brooking & Jenny Coleman
ISBN 1 877276 33 2, $39.95

A Distant Shore: Irish Migration and New Zealand Settlement
Edited by Lyndon Fraser
ISBN 1 877133 97 3, $39.95

Shifting Centres: Women and Migration in New Zealand History
Edited by Lyndon Fraser & Katie Pickles
ISBN 1 877276 32 4, $39.95

British Capital, Antipodean Labour: Working the New Zealand Waterfront, 1915–1951
Anna Green
ISBN 1 877133 99 X, $39.95

No Idle Rich: The Wealthy in Canterbury and Otago, 1840–1914
Jim McAloon
ISBN 1 877276 23 5, $39.95

When the Waves Rolled in Upon Us: Essays in 19th Century Maori History
Edited by Michael Reilly & Jane Thomson
ISBN 1 877133 20 5, $39.95

On the Left: Essays on Socialism in New Zealand
Edited by Kerry Taylor & Pat Moloney
ISBN 1 9877276 19 7, $39.95

Common Ground: Heritage and Public Places in New Zealand
Edited by Alexander Trapeznik
ISBN 1 877133 91 4, $39.95

Studying New Zealand: A Guide to Sources
G.A. Wood
ISBN 1 877133 09 4, $29.95

And an essential read

Decolonising Methodologies: Research and Indigenous Peoples
Linda Tuhiwai Smith
ISBN 1 877133 67 1, $39.95

University of Otago Press is expanding this series and is interested in receiving book proposals from NZ/Australian/Pacific/Asian historians. Please send your proposal to:

Managing Editor <university.press@stonebow.otago.ac.nz>

To order any of the above titles, email the address above, or write or fax to: University of Otago Press, PO Box 56, Dunedin, New Zealand. Fax: 64 3 249 8385.